WARS
OF THE
MIND

VOLUME 2:
(*Beneath a Frozen Lake.*)

By: Jonathan *W.* Haubert

Edited By: Rebekah Almogabar
Additional Editing By: Jonathan W. Haubert

8	X	8

ISBN: 978-1-4669-7841-6 (sc)
ISBN: 978-1-4669-7842-3 (e)

Library of Congress Control Number: 2013901382

Trafford rev. 09/27/2013

 www.trafford.com

North America & international
toll-free: 1 888 232 4444 (USA & Canada)
fax: 812 355 4082

Dreams are now fading away from us once again.
Why can't I seem to hold you?
As we drift away...

(Jonathan W. Haubert)

Wars of the Mind Contents:

CHAPTER 3- *1,000 Miles of Pain*

CHAPTER 7- *Chasing the Darkness*

<u>CHAPTER 12</u>– *Kill Me Already!*

CHAPTER 13- *Beneath a Frozen Lake*

Chapter 1

The 2ⁿᵈ Chapter

Forgotten Memory

On open thrust, side-set and it's dust.
I know now that no one is true, not even you! "I break..."
It was my heart, you ripped from my chest. And it was our love that pushed me to death.
No one to hold, I shiver in ice bent-cold... Everybody is untrue, everyone and you.
I crumble down, with a love so untrue.
Now under the frost of this broken youth, I know now that I was used.
Why won't the mirror stop laughing? Why won't the feeling just pass me?
Now... Here I lie weeping. With this forgotten memory...

Forever Passed Me

Thirteen hidden shadows, of the monster that is behind this face.
Of the forever torment that I gave, now on the whore-bent reason.
Of giving you back what you raped from me, my youth now just a dream.
And on the forever being the monster that I feared in the sleep.
It creeps upon me and I fuck you away. Now all I want is to fade.
I'm so sorry that I spilt that glass and our forever is now passed us.
So sorry that *Always* wasn't as long as we thought. I am sorry that you died and I forgot...
We were the breath of being the now but so faded and away from the truth.
Now you decay and I slip away, into sound-sorrows of the *Madness-Joy.*
Of being the demon I hate but there is nothing I can say but, "wow..."
Oh it could have been the God-Sent and we could have been love-bent.
But you just crumble away. Now here in the hourglass I sleep and sway.
In the twilights of the once broken teeth on white bone.
Of the once torn meat... Salt-sweet as candy-lust on the tip of my tongue.
"Just hit me in the throat." Please laugh while I wish to unwind.
But I can never let it fade to the bottom of the lake.
Here is the last given truth of the forever pass me.
I was just a man and fell to hell. I am but just a child.
Buried deep at the bottom of a dead oak "but we are still okay."
Maybe I could open the door and my soul could escape.
God, I want to just drop to the ground and stay.
Forever passed me... The thought that I could have love again.
"Now here I go, saying the same old things of yesterday."
"I need to awake." Just tell me that I'll be okay.
Just tell me that today holds more than my fate.
Forever passed me... the *Now* is my reason to breathe.
I inhale and drift away, where I wish to stay.
Lying next to my love as she decays and I wake up alone again today.
But the burn in the back of my mouth is still the same.
The confusion is forever passed me. And the tool still lies beneath the frozen lake.
"Welcome home..."

The Last Step

On the only thing I knew, I was broken and so were you.
Now on the last step, into the forever of our only way.
Now only I can speak, the numb-sound of the bloody-grave.
On the only thing that I knew, that I am dead and so are you.

We fall tumbling into a wonderment of the forever we were.
Now in the last thing I know, is that we will forever be the story untold.
How hard was it to scream under water?
Why is it that you sink to the bottom?

Here on the last step, I fall and gaze deep into what you did.
I can never forgive you for what you've done.
I am sorry but this is all I have left.
Here I lay weeping, over the leaves of my forever-truth.
Over so many years weeping and your love stole my youth.

I fall bleeding and no one is there to see.
I scream bleeding, and no one cares to help me!
Please look into my eyes and know that I'm okay.

On the last step, I wonder if I was right.
I sit here in question... *"Dark day - bright night."*
Should I care anymore, here in this haze that I made?

I stand on the last step, just one breath away.
I weep on the last step, just one heartbeat away.
Just one last step, and all will be set straight.
Now on the last step, into the forever of our only way.
"Finally I can open my eyes."

Spitting / Choking

And I was broken, now spitting / choking.
I fall down hitting, now bleeding and wishing.
No one here to care if I die. No one here to watch me fry.
Have I been beaten? Have I been bleeding? Will none of you ever care..?
And I was broken, now smashing / choking.
I fall deep again into despair, did you never care?
No one here to see me scream. No one here to watch me bleed.
Could you ever just help me up? Could you ever just lend a hand?
Will no one care? Why God, have I done something wrong?
Was I not meant to have a heart? Was I not meant to stay together...?
"Just fall apart?"
I lie here bleeding, over my lost nerves.
I lay here screaming, over my wounds that hurt.
I roll over spitting and choking. I die now wondering if I could be free.
It was just because I questioned, it was all because I cared.
I hurt now everyday, drowning in despair.

Golden Sands

Now over her wrist I lick the hate, in drowning wishes of the never-sane.
I was falling but now I stand. I bite the torment and watch her sin.
Over the nothing, that I was once a forgotten man.
Here I lay in a wonderment of the golden sands.
Now I can only remember that face, here I rip the pleasure from her brain.
Digging deep into my chest, you cut and rip until nothing's left.
Why in such a hurry, will you be late?
Now I am buried, *beneath a frozen lake.*
Was there dripping... With sin forming hate.
Now I lick it wishing, that it wasn't fate.
But she just takes it and smiles with a scream.
I can't take it! The monster haunting me.
Of no more love, now I run on empty.
Of the no one on my side, I lie here and whine.
With no one watching, now I poison the wine.
No more watching, as they drink and die.
Now over her wrist I lick the hate, *in drowning wishes of the never-sane.*
I was alone once but now in hell. I bite the torment and seep the nails.
Over nothing... I was once a forgotten man.
But here I lay feasting, upon the golden sands.
Now I can only remember that face. As I throw the dirt onto her grave.

It Was a Happy Dream

Yes, as I seem to wallow around and scream.
Indeed it was a happy dream.
I once held the world in my hands but now I snap and bawl within.
In the once was the forever of just her and me.
But now I sit in question... Dark days and lonely screams.

But indeed it was to be and yes... It was a happy dream.
And you just sit there wondering deep as I bleed.
Enjoying the torment that you and the world seep.
But true as can be, it was my happy dream.
Of once holding it all in my hands.
But now I am broken and weep within.

Darkened clouds loom over head. Now in the dire wishes of her hand.
It was wall to head and blood to floor. It was no rocks and **18** deep shots.
It was the dark tease of *Amore* but now I face the facts...
Faceless beating and ripping the knife from my back.
Now in the remembering of that damn day.
What more could I do but seep back into my happy dream?
Now all I can do is scrub, yet never be clean.
What if I were to choose the fire and except the blame?
But you don't care, laughing while throwing rocks at me.

As now I am tied down and you rub my eyes with your tongue.
As now you hold me and squeeze until life is gone.
But it will never last and the feeling does pass.
As I fade back into my dream, and it was a happy one indeed.
Of holding my love in my arms. Laughing together and loving deep.
But then I awake to see you stabbing me and I scream.
But it was a happy dream, of you being alive.
It was a happy dream, but now I die.

Together we scream, her body on top of mine.
Connected and she screams, fingernails grinding in me.
You once again tear in deep, to see what's inside.
You reach in deep and take away my life.
And the haze lingers over as I weep of my clouded-doom.
And it was a happy dream... Of once again holding you.

A Zombie's Whisper

And the little child balls up in the corner of his room.
Alone he weeps and dreams of being free.
The little child wanders away from his room.
"In the dark of the night should he find me?"
As now he strolls through the house of the *respected-dead*.
The ground shakes open and I lift my head.

And now the child is frozen, in the presence of the *walking-dead*.
And now I do hunger for the flesh of the sane.
And now I do stumble, out of the ground and I stare into his face.
And I do question, his motives and ways.
He does not scream, just wishes to bleed. So now I *smile* and proceed...

On I stumble and the child is crying within.
Now he hungers for the spill of sin.
And I do wonder, what drove him to this.
And I do wonder, of his death-wish.
And now he is crying, and falls to the floor.
Beating his head and weeping some more.
But no one is looking, "*and I must feast.*"
Now onward dragging of this rotted beast.

He looked me in the eyes and told me to kill.
I smiled in surprise and turned back to my hill.
But then he ran to me and grabbed my throat.
He squeezed real tight, thinking I would choke.
The child, he wishes for love but as he had said.
"She was untrue - now he wishes for death."
I whispered a notion into his ear and he stood there for a day on-end.
So once again I slumber, and another mind is set on revenge.

"To be a man is to walk away.
To make your own path upon the road of leaves.
And no one cares, about you and me.
But we are there for each-other and hold true each fallen leaf."
"Love on my children, and truth shall set you free..."

Of This Fate

It must be and I set it free - the notion of being a man.
Does it not feed, will it not bleed?
Why in God's name am I still human?!
Does it not need, will it not bleed?
Somebody set me free.

Of this fate, I find on the shelf in the back room.
Of this hate, that eats at my soul and heart too.
Of nothing that I do not know, and never will.
It was my youth I lost and this pain will never heal.
Now over the bridge I walk, with another drive.
So I close my eyes and remember that surprise.
Then I leap and kiss it goodbye.
Now I fall and untie.

We unwind, and the angels dance in my head.
As I crank the music-box and seep the sweet melody.
Of this fate, I hold in my grave.
And I will never forget her name.
Why won't the years of then just pass and go?
Why won't the heartbreak be covered by the snow?

It was a *one-night miracle*, but now it subsides.
Now I bite my cheek and chew the meat.
No, you do not like the thought but it will never change.
As I drift back to the thought of being sane.

Does it not need, will it never feed?
Does it not bleed, will it never be free?
Does it not give, but only take?
Does it not desire, a war to set things straight?
Now I'm a liar, because I am human too.
Does it not desire, a taste of youth?

Now I break off the tip, and cook it in the sun.
It was all just a tempt of the forever-none.
And it just breaks me.
Of this fate that I must endure.
Now you hate me because I have shut the door.

We Break

And now we break and fall away into the ash of your wretched remorse.
And in the trees I hide the shame... of the *never will I tell.*
And now we break away, into the ash and dirt.
We once danced and played but we are older and less at the game.
Because I had a heart, you were jealous. Must you envy me and sulk..?
Now the rust turns to lime and the blood to wine.
We all must taste the decay but it is finer and much more at my liking.
But we were once inseparable, and now we battle everyday.
You were my shadow, and I - your reflection.
Over the nothing that I throw, and bury softly into the snow.
I was once alive, but now just remember.
It was very cold, our last December.
But now it's set free, just ash and nothing more.
So we fall away, and in the memory we danced and played.
Now we fall from grace... as you begin, pulling off my face.

Grim Nature

Grim is the thought, and dust is the now.
We skip along the blank walkway, "to where" I don't know.
So grim was the feeling, as now it is filling this pit inside.
Grim was the anger, as now it turns inside.
But you were nothing, just a feeling I did not need.
It was the something, of the river that I did bleed.
Now blood is flowing, onto the ground and it seeps.
Now winter is growing and I count one more sheep.
It was the frost of the forever but now it is bleak.
And no one is watching, as I pull on the thread.
So now I unravel, each thought that I've said.
No one to listen yet each wants to know. Grim is the name in which I hold.
Now nothing can stop me, I am on a roll.
Now no one will stop me, they just throw their stones.
And no one wants me, I'm just growing old.
No one wants me as I now turn to stone.
They can't hear me, I am frozen in time.
No one hears me, I just pull and unwind.
"What a breaking nature, of this paper-lust."
What a taking hatred, of the ever-must.
Now we turn to the north and fade in the dust.
It was my human nature, to care and die.
It's my given nature, to grow and die.
What a twisted nature, of living a lie.

Hours is Ours

The hour is ours and no one is on your side. Just give me release then set me aside.

And ours is just hours away, to show it the fact that this is my grave.

And time is spinning, as each bottle is dripping dry.

And no more shots, cold withered spice.

Just give me a second, to think things through.

To stop my head from spinning and give forth truth.

What a game you play, toying with my heart.

Just shut the box and tell it straight, give me truth!

Of the spinning clock and so many hours we gave.

Holding each other so close and true. Now we fade and it's no bother.

It's not like we ever held that truth - and never will.

So take me home and beneath the hill, rock me to sleep and kiss me goodnight.

If only I could dream sweet, yet I toss and turn all night.

And awake by the moon's gravity love, cradling me in her arms.

If only you could fall from above, then maybe you could fix my heart.

Of the hour in our night-wish, of being the knight that I am.

It's just my wish, to seek once again the darkness of light.

And in the hour I just need a second... To set all my thoughts straight.

Stop spinning the bottle in the back of my brain. As now it is dry and bleeds on me.

Of the no more spice, just another long drag of rotted meat.

Of sweet is the salt covered death.

Now in the ice-torment I can rest, knowing that this sting will never pass.

It's all just boxed-torment, of the hour in which we all fall back.

So on I regress to the state of the never-more and the ever-none.

Spine-tangled spider-webs swing over my ear, time sets a jingle and we are near.

In the skull-drip of the feeling, the melt of my brain and I am spinning in deeper the blade.

Just needles shoved into my neck, pushing and jerking me numb.

Now I am yours and ours is done. Just hours and hours till the rise of *The Black Sun.*

In the time's horrid hand, we hold the handle of the whore-bent hate.

Hand me a hand and lift me to heaven.

In the game of playing with my nerves, I always seem to lose.

Now it's just one toss away and I fall deeper into my grave.

So take me home and lay me to rest. Show me release and hold my chest.

As the hours run pass and the monsters seem to skip and play.

Further I fall and kiss her grave, "Because I know she hates that."

Just one last stop and maybe I can lean back.

Because ours is hours away, from being at the right state of fact.

We did not hold true that making, of another grain of sand.

So now I am fading, further into my head.

Just hours of spitting out these pills. Ours is waiting just under the hill.

But you can't hear me, you just throw your stones and I am wishing...

Wishing I could go home, so take me home - take me home - take me home.

Take me home! Somebody hold me...

Broken Dreams

Seven little stitches and now you can relax.
Nine little itches and no one will let it pass.
One last thought, before I lay to sleep.
Why was I not good enough? Why did you hate me?

And I am just a sad little kid. I am what you push aside day to day.
I am only a human, ash and dust of the grave.
Please - no more bitching. I've had enough for one day.
And now you are itching, for one last taste.
Of the mother-given... The candy coating on the tip of your nerves.
Another given and still I am waiting, still I lie here and burn.
Because I am nothing, just a child watching you hurt.

I am waiting, for something to give me release.
I am a troubled nonsense, wanting to be something more.
I am a load of nothing, so just wipe me on the curb.
It was our love that fueled me but now I lay dead on the floor.
I could feel it pulling and such a tug-of-war.
Now I am spewing, "_it spreads across the floor._"

I can't stop the chewing, of the dead rotted meat.
I can't get you out, my head just won't give up.
So now I am falling, out of my bed and out of luck.
No one there to catch me, should I awake and be forever lost?

My dreams are broken and I want to be alone.
Forever you haunt me. Your eyes and kisses have scarred me.
Just seven little stitches and now I can relax.
It was my youth that was raped and stolen.
And you just threw me back...

Now What?

I stand in place, screaming all day. Nobody to hear me, so I slip away.
I run in place screaming all day. No one cares, *as I drift away.*
I beat myself screaming all day, no one wants me.
"Throw me back - into my grave."
Now what could I do to please the world?
Just roll over dead and except my fate and curse.
Now what am I to do?
I see you standing in front of me. But now you're gone and I am too.

Now what was I supposed to do?
Just remember all the facts, or make some too.
"Now what?"
Was there some kind of bigger meaning to all of this?
I swear I can't be this worthless - I never meant to say those things.
But now I'm gone and you're away.
Now what did I do wrong to end up like this?
What did I say to be thrown away?

I stand here in place all day, screaming and cutting off my face.
I run here in place all day, no one wants me.
"Throw me back - into my grave!"
I beat myself screaming all day.
But nobody is there now and you're away.
Now what am I to do and where should I go?
Just sit here in loneliness, or find me some hope?
Now what is coming for me?
The rise of the *Never* and the frost blankets me forever.
Somebody save me and take me back to that day.

Now what was I supposed to do?
Just remember all the facts or make some too?
"Now what?"
Was there some sort of a better purpose?
I know I can't be this worthless!
I never meant to say those things but now you're gone and in your grave.
So what did I say to drive you all away?
What did I say to be thrown away?
There was a meaning, but now it's passed me.
There was a reason, but now it's leaving.
There was a purpose, but now I'm worthless.
I see you standing in front of me.
I see you smile, as you walk away and leave... *"Now what?"*

Dead Night

Draw it closer than you ever have.
Shove it deeper into the sands.
Call me a monster and leave me to die.
Call me once more and watch me fry!

I live a lie and all is mine!
I'm growing to, and show no new!
We live the break and break the limbs!
As all now crumbles and I fall within!

Draw it closer to the angel's side.
Have I a reason or should I die?
Call me to the never and watch me fall.
Call me a demon if you have the gall.

I live life on a higher level.
I find neither God nor Devil - Only this thorn in my side.
We live onward and break the trend.
I move onward and find no reason for your limbs.

Now take me closer to the river of life.
Pull me deeper into the water and away from light.
"Now Death has spoken and all is dead."
No more living... Off with your head.

If you have the answer, you had better tell it now.
If you have the motives, then you are found out.
In deep I found it, flesh had grown over and it was but a scar.
But I pulled and jerked it and found your dagger.
How hard it was to heal the shatter.

In the dead of night I find your reasons.
Now all is bleak and forever leaving.
But you were once my source of life.
Now I can only tremble, in this _Dead Night._

Frost Lust

Would you hold me, if I were clean?
Would you have told me, if I was not so deaf?
Would you love me, if I were dead?

Would I have held you, if you were alive?
Will I still love you, after we die?
Would you just kill me, if I asked real nice?
"Please just kill me, and cover me in ice."

You would have never found hell, if I didn't bring you.
You would have never been held, by that unworthy demon.
I know I'm the devil, but you loved me with that aside.
I know I'm an angel, but you still cast me aside.

We hold over the memory, and venture deep into my mind.
You have found my reality, and burned it alive.
I have nothing to give you, but my heart and soul.
It was already taken, and dropped deep in the snow.

Would you hold me, if I were clean?
Will you still love me, when I am stabbed and bled?
Would you hold my heart and head?
Would you love me if I were dead?

God once told me, to keep my head held high.
But you just hung me, and left me to die.
God once told me, to live and be free.
But now I'm in torment, and under the ice I scream!

Sin was my name, and the death was a joke.
So I sit here in hatred, and on my tongue I choke.
Because I was a demon, and I'm still an angel.
I know I'm the devil, but you left me unable.
You told me to hold you, and to never let go.
I held on *forever* but, "you just left me in the snow."

Cheap Twist

In the bone-dust of the old, I tilt back and swallow down another shot.

Hard hitting and on my skull, it's beating and no one is home.

Because it was her wish, to tear me apart. And in the choice of "*Her Majesty*" I dance.

Over the steppingstones of my daughter's grave.

I wallow and bite down until the death of this day.

Now a spinal-twist as all crashes down and I flake away.

In the hour of the lost and lonely beating of my head...

"And his tongue was gray." I swing above the stairs and what a fun game.

To dance for "*Her Majesty*" upon my grave.

You take me deeper into sound-sorrow.

In the hoping wish of some release in tomorrow.

Could it all just be a bad twist or is one's mind just that far out in the abyss?

We're breathing softly and no one could hear.

"What a lovely monster I heed in my ears."

Now shove me back to my human ways.

And I sit in the wonderment of my happy haze.

Upon the whore's twisted nature. You truly thought that you were right.

It was truly predicable and so am I.

To dance and twirl beneath a "*Black-Sun Sky.*"

And upon the faded thought of eating broken glass.

I crawl on my chest and find the thought passed.

So what a forgiving nature our father truly has. To give us that crutch, forever-blind.

Now it fades me a reason to enjoy the "*Peppermint Spice.*"

And I drown all your hatred with the nonsense of a forgotten mind.

What a cheap twist, of the smoke lingering in the back of my throat.

So did you truly think I would not remember? "As here in her blood I soak."

I do not want forgiveness. I only want to be heard.

I do not want to hold her, only to watch her burn.

Question not my actions and ways. Just bleed on and get out of my way!

And again the sheep stroll to their slaughter. It's only a mind tease of rotted meat.

Now fresh is her death and I want it all to me.

So I drown back the hatred "*all her shameless neglect.*"

I feast upon the fire and smoke back until all is a miss.

Tossing back the shots I take in every day. In the amber-wishes of my yesterday.

The smell of mushroom-freedom rings deep in my teeth.

The sway of the rotted demon shows within the "*Neon Lights.*"

It swings so carelessly in the rainbow-smiles.

Down deep in the skull-drip of a bastard's luck. It's in the spinning of my skull-fuck.

So bring me the hand that holds the answers to the rights.

In the cheap twist of lime, and again into salt I fade.

Melted screams roll over my tongue and all can't be that dire.

In the soul concealing of the Death. The death that's leaking deep into my brain.

Small angels dance on my stone. Reminding me again that I am alone;

So I drink back the hatred and fade away in the smoke.
I never wanted to hurt you, "*but it is you I choke.*"
And such a cheap twist, the lime mustn't have been clean.
Now all is dripping and my tongue is green.
As far as I could throw it, the bottle is now dead.
What a spice of my torment and I smash it against my head.
It's in the worry that you lose your head.
"And only for Her Majesty, shall I dance until death."

Shut It Dead

I can't tell you what to do, but I sure can see the fear in your eyes.
I can't take it all from you, but I sure can see your despise.
I never wanted it to end that way but now it's done and forever set to stay.
I never wanted you to grow that way, but now it's done and I'm away.
Because you hate, it drives me far into the dirt.
Because you hate, I run in far and feel the burn.
I never meant to hurt you, but now that was yesterday.
I never meant to hurt her, "*so she is laid softly in her grave.*"
Now I just wish to end the screams... so late at night!
I want to forget the fright, I want her to see but she'll never open her eyes.
I can't take it away from her. I just can't tell her what to do.
I never meant to hurt her, but she lies buried and confused.
We wished to live, but now I die. I want to scream, but only cry.
I want to love but lost my heart. I want to breathe but you tear me apart.
I wish to live, but feel so dead. I want to bleed and beat my head.
Just rotted meat, falls from the bone. Just tear it sweet and take me home...
Shut it dead - my soul wishing to be set free.
Shut it dead - now my tongue cracks open and bleeds.
Shut it dead - the torment of her bloody grave.
Shut it dead - and throw dirt onto my grave.
I could scream hollow, weeping for an eternity.
I could beat it dead and watch all fall before me.
Someday it shall come to pass but for now I scream and cut my wrist.
It bleeds the truth of the nothing I fear.
That I am a dead man, shut in the darkness of the past year.
Shut it dead - and I want to be no more. Shut it dead - the grave of that whore.
Shut it dead - the box of my comfort. Shut it dead - and tell me no comfort.
I wish I could tell you more, but I'm out of air.
I wish to scream some more, but fear the despair.
I want to be no more, it's just not fair.
Shut it dead, the knowledge of what I've done.
Shut it dead - and all will be calm...

Corpse-Finger

What you call a hole, I call a door. What I called love, you called a bore.
What he called nonsense, I call Amore.
What you think is broken, I hide behind the door.
It was thrown and into dust it broke.
The shatter of the raindrops, beating on my skull.
Now with nothing, she lies weeping within herself.
Now with nothing, I scream bleeding in hell.
The one thing I never meant to tell you, now I will never be rid of.
The fester of the one thing I thought was true, in the smile of the monster.
Jagged rotten breath, the teeth sink deep into my sanity and take me to hell.
With the night of the never forgotten memory I drift further into hell.
Deep where my eyes should stay, I lean back and burn away.
What you call a hole, I call a door. What I called love, you called a bore.
What he thinks is something... I can do nothing but scream.
What she did was whisper, those needles softly into me.
It was thrown and into salt I broke.
The shatter of the raindrops beating on my skull.
Now with nothing to look forward to, I can only weep.
Now with no heart to hold you, I burn away and weep.
She gave me the hope and brought me to life.
Where is she now, in the snow she hides?
No one there to hear my screams.
No one cares as this man lies rotten and weeps.
Cased around me, in armor of the heart.
All breaks around me, as it holds in each part.
The no more of the memory that we now decay.
Cased around me is the memory that shall never fade.
And it takes me deeper into the river of the dead.
Now the monster is blushing and soon he'll be dead.
As I lay cased in velvet, of the Ever-Last of the dead.
And now at the summit, of the passing away our last breath.
What you call a hole, I call a door. What I called love, you called a bore.
What we called nonsense, I now miss so dear.
What you called just a trinket, now incased in fear.
What he thought was nonsense, was his biggest lie.
What she called just a kiss will now hold her till we die.
What he called an art work, was nothing more than my soul.
What you call a corpse-finger. I had buried deep in this hole...

Silent Screaming

The one thing rushing back to my being.
The screaming of the last wish I hold.
Now the monster rises above the old.
Why was I not the one for the moment?
Somehow I will find a way out of this hell.

Now in the reflection of the last thing I thought.
Creeping over the flesh of my being, I feel it tearing and I'm screaming.
Now no one is caring, and I hear her dreaming.
Now no where is clear, I'm blind and screaming.
You just sit there and stare, I know you don't care.

When was I not good enough?
Why was the air so cold?
When was I not man enough?
Why did you leave me in the cold?

Over the last thought of my being.
I felt it stirring, and now I'm screaming.
Can you hear me bleeding?
Now on the top of my being.
It shatters across my head in the dreaming.
The echoes of the silent screaming.

I wonder if I felt it leaving.
Now here I lay, gone and bleeding.
Creeping over the hell-bent thought of me leaving.
I feel it tearing and I'm screaming.
Now where am I going to stay?

I remember the taste of that thought.
Now it rushes back and just won't shut up.
No one was there to hear the screaming.
Now I wait, gone and bleeding.
In the thought of it leaving, here I stay - just bleeding.

When was I not good enough?
Why was the air so cold?
When was I not man enough?
"Why did you leave me out in the cold?"

The Mirror Stain

Now this is something I didn't want to tell you.
But here we are, and you look so confused.
It truly was a disgrace but there it is, such a haunting face.
All facts put onto the slab, and now here we are.
You're at such a loss of facts.

Seven little swinging swans hung out in the sun.
And the torment of your bone-lusts...
It was something I didn't want to tell you.
But here we are and so confused.
There was no honor that day.
And now you shiver endless in your sways.

And no one could change your ways, "so over the edge."
I didn't want to bring it up today, but I fear you already did.
The words were leaning over the ledge, and you just turned your head.
There was no meaning to what you said.
Now here it's beating on my head.

I didn't want to bring it up, the facts of what you did.
But now you're gone and what am I to do..?
There was no honor that day. Now you drift further into your haze.
Damn, what a maze you made - gone and deep in your daze.

I fell upon it, the mirror stain. Of so much time it did not take.
I fell upon your lustful disgrace.
As forever it haunts me, your faded face.
I didn't want to say it, but now it's too late.
Of the fact that you are dead now, gazing deep into my face.
Oh what a disgrace, of the mirror now stained with shame.
I didn't want to bring it up today, the truth of your bone-lust.
Driven deep into the *"Bone-Dust."* I look deep into your eyes.
So red and faded-dead, the blood on the floor.
And the thought in your head.

I fell upon it, the mirror stained with your shame.
But now you're gone, covered in dread.
You can't hang on any longer... Now the mirror stained red.

The Teeth of Shame

Down it's dragging, and I feel it stabbing.
Onward shoving as the trees pull me deeper into the wood.
The howling of the crimson-beast, in deep it sinks.
Rough teeth and fire nails fusing to my brain.
Harder is the shove-in, of the teeth of shame. Can no one hear my pain?
Onward crying, now my soul is frying and nowhere can I hide it.
The left twist of the wrong word said.
In it breaks and my skin flakes off, so I beat my head.
As coming sooner, I feel the monster calling.
Over the notions of the stone that knew my name.
I am nothing more than a number with a face. And I know you can see my disgrace.
Onward it sinks, "I scream" *burning in me...* The teeth of shame.
And it swings above me in the dream, of the now once said.
I can run forever and still be in my bed. I can cut all day and still be in my head.
I can love her always, but still she is dead.
I could ask forgiveness, but God turns his head.
Now onward tearing and my bones become dust.
I fear the crimson feeling, right behind my neck.
And now I know you're stealing, because nothing is left.

Gazing Into The Last Hour

Call it what you will and throw me away.
Draw me under a hill and burn that day.
Fade me in the smoke and find me no hope.
Leave me in the dark, broken child screams...
Call me what you will and cut me again.
Leave me under the hill and think of me no more.
Gaze into the last hour and see what you fear.
Nothing more than a demon with a heart.
I'm nothing more than an insect with skin.
We're nothing more than dead and waiting to end.
I am nothing more than an angel with a fear.
We are nothing more than that last grain of sand.
Falling endlessly through our hands...
So drive it closer and what can you say?
Leave it to that whore and what can you say?
I am nothing but a bore and you wish me away.
We were nothing more than in love.
Now gone and rotted at the bottom of the lake.
I call it a nightmare but it was only yesterday.
I called it my own but this heart you took away;

As you gaze into the last hour, what do you see?
As you wander away upon demon wings, now set free...
I call it *Death* & *Decay*. Yet it's only *Truth* & *Shame*.
Now I break away, in the wind I fail. Now I journey back into hell.
Well, what did you want me to say? What do you see, as you gaze upon that day?
Where will you go when "you" have no face?
And what a disgrace, I know you were mine.
Now gazing into the last hour, I see what you fear.
I know how it ends, and you want it clear......

Filtered As I Burn

Hiding behind the bookshelf, he trembles all alone.
Bruised and beaten, he knows not what it's like to choose.
Unaware of the world that lies beyond the window.
He weeps silent, so no one can hear.
Now he bites harder on his cheek. He's only a child and wishes to bleed.
How many monsters must taste his flesh and gnaw at his soul?
How will he escape this hole? No one's there to let him out.
Now he is rocking back and forth, night upon him cold.
I know he wants nothing more than to scream "*to be heard.*"
But that's only a dream, and no one is there to let him free.
"*So why am I filtered as I burn?*"
What is it you want to hide behind the scars and blood?
Why do you want to hurt me, what have I done?!
In the dark and lonely I wait but I know you won't find me.
Why can't you hear me scream, so far under the earth?
Why do you filter me as I burn?
I'm just a child, and no one cares to hear what I have to say.
Would I have to cut and break myself to set the point straight?
Where did you go when I needed your hand?
Why won't the clouds subside? I just want to see the light.
Is it worth dying for, to be free in body and mind?
Why was I left behind? As no one's here now.
You filter me as I burn, what are you trying to get out?
You wash away my flesh, the blood is my truth.
You peel away my skin, and the demons begin to chew.
You filter me as I burn, what the hell is wrong with you!
You try to get something out, I still wish to choose.
Why won't you let me out? Master as I - now holding the key.
I'm just a child weeping forever alone. I am just a man, burning away his soul.

Slammed

Un-open as I ever have been. I know now my life was a sin.
And un-connected to anything I had ever known.
Now throwing myself over the ledge, heart forever stone.
Un-passing the once and now forever gray.
It slams across my head, skull bleeding but I'm okay.

Overconfident but the sky is growing dark.
Unaware, now all is so very dark.
It screams pass me, rushing deep into the unknown.
It streams pass me, my forehead slammed against the stone.
Now all is faded, the smoke just won't clear.
Now all is fading, and I feel my soul disappear.

Gone without a trace, just empty and in dirt I am cased.
Just over the torment, but then I see their face.
Now screaming-storming, it's gone now without a trace.
But it slams against me, the thought of what she said.
I know all is against me, "I wish I were dead."

Un-open to anything and no one guides me out.
Unaware of the monster behind me but you don't care.
Un-knowing of the doom that lingers in the air.
And no one tries to help me. They but laugh and cry as I dream.
Un-loving the once but forgotten, the memory that still haunts me.

Now it rushes deeper in me, and nowhere can I hide.
It slams against me, and I feel my life subside.
It just can't be that worthless, but I know it is trash.
I know now, I am worthless - just faded ash.
But now all is so very clear, it's gone now. To where - to where?
Then it slams against me, stuck in my head deep in fear.

She asked me the question, without opening her mouth.
I answered her question, now I'm shoved out.
It was only my heart, now slammed against my head.
It was only a question, but now I am dead.
To the unknowing of the situation, God beats me dead.
I lost at the situation, now grave and left in dread.
It was only the notion, slammed across my head.
My skull bleeding, but it's okay... *I'm only dead.*

<u>Slipping From Care</u>

Watching it all slip away, now rubbing the dirt on my face.
Grinding the bone and cooking my heart on a stone.
I fry the feel of the forgiving nature of the forgotten.
Falling further from forgiveness for what I believe in.
Biting and chewing at the back of my eyes.
Now knowing the never will always be the same.
I run aimlessly through the night, forgotten as I fight.
I can push all day, now rushing myself closer to fate.
I swing freely above your dreams, singing away my time.
Now aged and broken, our love crumbles and dies.
I bite and chew away my face, now far too late.

We wish to clean the slate, but now it's come down to faith.
And no one smiles as I run more through the darkness.
Pushing as they grab at my soul, I dash pass the past.
I feel it leaving... I know it's wrapping me in the tomb.
I rush endlessly from the doom, soon it falls and I laugh.

Now I watch it slip away, blood stained on my face.
Rubbing the ash on my grave, on now that taste – *Oh what a waste.*
Now it screams forever in me, the monsters filling my being.
As I grind down the bones of hate, but I fear you're too late.
I want you to hold me one last time, just before I die.
I want to watch you scream, I want to hear you bleed.
Just don't waste my time, pulling away my mind.
And I feel it chewing at the back of my eyes.
I know I will never be rid of this parasite, it dies with me.
I run onward in the dark, I see you smile as I fall apart.
I know it will never change and it passes me all the same.
Burning on the stone, I shiver and beat myself cold.

As once I was told but you just never cared.
I want to breathe but I find no air.
I want to scream, falling further into despair.
You watch me bleed, you just don't care.
I cut and drift, away from here.
It was my last wish, to touch her face and hair.
It was my last wish, watching it slip.
Now, soul stained and I burn in the darkness of my despair.

"I wish someone would care."

Get Out, Get Out

Cut the limb and watch it bleed. Fight the lord and watch you scream.
Lick the blade and never look. Cut my soul and my heart they took.
Don't let me go, and watch it flow.
Don't feel my wounds, salted and I scream.
The bugs eat at it, my rotten flesh.
Don't let me go *"put it back - into my chest."*
Get out! Get out! And I watch you cry.
Get out! Get out! So you lived such a lie.
Get out! Get out! Fall down to hell.
Get out! Get out! And I seep the nails.
Cut the limbs and watch them bleed.
"I fight your God, and watch him scream. Licking the blade and she never looked.
Cutting my soul, my heart they took."
Don't let me go, to watch the flow.
Don't feel my wounds, dripping salt and I scream.
The ants eat at it, my rotting flesh.
Don't let me go, *"put back my heart - into my chest."*
Get out! Get out! So she cuts and cries.
Get out! Get out! And we lived such a lie.
Get out! Get out! Just go now to hell.
Get out! Get out! And I seep the rusted nails...

Taking Me

So broken, I tumble and scream. So un-held, I tremble and weep.
So nothing will take me back. Now I'm dead and you can relax.
There was a day, when all was fine. But now she's dead and I unwind...
"God save me."
Take me home and put me to bed. Hold my hand and comfort me in death.
Sing me a song and all is fine. Put me in, and I untie.
So broken, I do nothing but weep. So untold, my soul grows weak.
And nothing will ever take me back. Now I'm dead and you can relax.
There was that day, when all was fine. But now it's dark and over the line.
"God save me."
Take me home and put me to bed. Hold me close and swing me till death.
I scream in torment but nothing's left. Hold my hand and put me to death.

Take me back, to where I should be. Put me to rest and leave me be.
Tell me a story and I'm asleep. Swing me till death and away I creep.
There was a day, when all was fine. But now I'm dead and you unwind...
"God take me back."

Put Away

Dark as the winged-death flows above your lips.
Can you feel the kiss? And now it all slips.
Soft was the neck of the angel, weeping above the stone.
Now she burns and no one wants to see.
Dark flowing above the bone. In slime it slips and it is missed.

Now we take our last breath to see what is next to be.
In the last word spoken and the world crumbled to its knees.
Hatred flowing and no one's knowing what I see.
Do you care for what was put away?
Would you hold it, deep in the grave?

No more monsters as I fall further away.
No more nonsense and all has become gray.
No one's there but everyone knows.
No one cares... "I just can't lift this stone."

You put me away, down dark and all is gray.
You put me away, what did I do - what did I say?
It's so out of place and I just can't get a grip.
Nothing looks the same... "Why do I feel so sick?"

Dark as the winged-death flows above your lips.
Can you remember our first kiss? "*Now it slips.*"
As the angel took a stroll into the *Forbidden Lost.*
No one hears her scream "*Oh what a loss, what a loss.*"
In the trip of the no one cared, now she's gone.
Burned in despair.

Why did you put me away, was I that evil to your eyes?
Why did you put me away? Just to watch me cry?
Why did you put me that far, so cold in the dark?
I can't see you, please let me out...
I can't see you... "I don't want to be left out."

That Face...

Leaning against a brick wall, taking in a drag, cold in the fall.

Hearing the birds sing and watching the soft fog.

Holding the inferno deep in my lungs, *just a breath...*

Down in the park, my childhood gone.

I hear the world sing, remembering grace and all that could never be.

Walking alone, cold chills to the bone.

I can remember those days, frantic I try to forget.

Holding her hand and remembering that kiss.

So soon I will not miss but it is there, gone in time's abyss.

I stroll along a dirt road, cool from the fallen leaves.

I remember that face...

Forever those words haunt me and should I even care?

I lean against a tall oak, to find some shade and hide my shame.

I watch the ground move, as the insects begin to cover me.

All of it feels surreal and I can't move from this hill.

Once a man but now only stone. Was once a man but now only a joke.

I see the worms eat at me. I do nothing to stop it...

I feel the ants biting and chewing, should I even care?

I do nothing to stop it, I just no longer care.

As I stand, I take in another drag. The smoke lingering in my soul.

I brush off the dirt – another deep drag. "Intake of the old."

I walk onward alone in pain, pulling myself to the next step.

I want nothing more than to forget.

I wish nothing more than to embrace the pit.

Slam - and I stop dead in my tracks. There she is with smiles and joy...

There she is, playing with her son. There she is, and now I wish to run.

I can't forget that face, the joy of knowing that it was once only us.

I remember that look, the bliss of feeling warmth surround us.

I can't forget that face, she's so happy with her new grace.

Now pointless I walk in shame.

It's all my fault - the pain of this day but she's happy now.

Who am I to get in the way "who am I, with this torn off face?"

What am I to do now? I just walk onward in shame.

Right passed her and she doesn't even look.

Is there a better way to hide this pain?

Cold in the amber chill, I step onward and nothing I feel.

God... that face, will I never be done with it?

I reach into my coat, I light up another cigarette.

Does she even care? Should I even know?

I lean back in despair, drowning in the smoke;

I lean against a brick wall, cold in the fall.
I remember that face, and never will it go away.
I want only to forget but here I stay in time's abyss.
It was once just the two of us.
Now I lean back in the fall, resting against a brick wall.
I just want to forget it all but still I have the road of leaves.
Upon the memory of that face... I move onward into disgrace.

Looking Up

Looking up I see nothing but light. Looking up I feel nothing but strive.
Looking up I do nothing but cry. Looking up, I want nothing but life.
Falling down, I feel so hell-bound.
Falling down, I am nothing but dammed.
Falling down, through the time sands. Falling down and I am away.

Looking up I see nothing but light. Looking up I feel nothing but strive.
Looking up I do nothing but fight. Looking up, I want nothing but life.
Falling down, I feel it begin to crush. Falling down, I feel so out of luck.
Falling down, into the ground. Falling down, to hell I am bound.
Thrown away and I sink. Down I fade, and now cold in sleep.

I drift to the bottom and I see your face.
I sink to the bottom, drowning in hate.
I begin to die, no air where I lie.
I begin to know, faded under the snow.
I begin to remember, but only to forget.
I begin to shiver, frozen and I feel so sick.

I can't reach the top, I want to live.
I can't reach your hand, I want to love.
I can't reach the truth, I drown in all the lies.
I can't reach the surface, now frozen alive.
Looking up I see nothing but light. Looking up I feel nothing but strive.
Looking up I do nothing but fight. Looking up, I want nothing but life.

"Looking up... Losing all but sight."

Chapter 2

Still a Struggle

I Hold Only Me

To tell you the truth, I would have taken the other.
I'm not trying to say that you're not as good, "yet you're not."
I should have taken the other road, "but I'm already dead."
I should have said what I wanted to say, "But now in pain."
You could have told me the truth. "There is no truth, there is only me."

I hold only myself and forever it stays.
In what way would you like me to die?
And where would you like me to hide the lie?
You told me to let go. Now falling down the rabbit-hole.
Face the faces and I see the sights in your death, "smile."
Take a picture of my body. Soon I'll be gone and away.
Hold your love while you can. "I hold only me."
And that's the way it shall always be. "It won't be for me."
I will just weep by myself. "I hold only me."
And further into hell I fall. "What the fuck, God!?"

Over the skin, I peel and pull the flesh off bone.
The blood so sweet, it pours out on the action.
The action of ripping out my own eyes, "I smile."
Smile my *Angel*, "Oh what a holly day in hell."
I scream and bleed, I bleed and bleed.
It would be nice to see a better drive.
There is no better drive... only me - only me.
And neglect is the sight, the insight to the pit.

"If life were a falling atom-bomb."
Like a broken rollercoaster, I would ride it into the ground.
To see a better outcome... "Oh what a hell-trip."

So one and two and eleven more pens into my eye.
Laugh and laugh till the dark day passes.
Me, I hold only myself and weep.
I the child now a demon, *a dream.*
I the lover, I the failure - I leave.
You, with another, I scream.
Forever I scream - "I hold only me..."

Before It's Too Late

Where are you hiding and why can't I see?
When will I find you? Please help me.
When will we run away, and forget it all?
When can we just hold each other, warm in the fall?

Where are you hiding, when will I see?
Where are you hiding, please help me.
I can't seem to find you, alone in this torment I weep.
Why can't I find you?! Now I ball-up and sleep.

Deep in the dream of your hand on my chest.
Why can't I see you? Please give me a sec...
I just can't seem to get out. The pain is too much to take.
Please just wake me, before it's too late.

Rage #1

Here it is and shall stay, the monster inside.
The nails shoved deep into my brain. So here I am and will always be.
The torment inside, the demon consuming me.
I hear all your lies, they do nothing for me.
I know it's no surprise, but still it gets to me.
Echoes beating down on me, years passed. "Was it only a dream?"
It was here, now it's passed. It looks down on me.
There - and it's mine. The screw grinding deep within me.
Years as they pass. The world that destroys me.
Deep within I dwell, hungering for the sheep.
Leave me as you do but how far can you get?
Leave me confused. That's how it has always been.
Just bleed me and you're doomed. "You can't run without your legs."
I scream and I'm fused, metal stuck to my flesh.
I fade and I cry, hoping only to die.
I fall and it's done, now gone and it's gone.
Dream and I'm free, beating on my head.
Bleed and I bleed, still stuck in my head.
I can't get it on my own. I tear away at my chest.
I can't get it on my own, seeing the frost on my breath.
I weep out the stones, each one colder than the next.
Deep to the bone, the monster stays and won't rest.
"Hell - but it's home. God tell me what's next..."

46

Won't Tell You

I can't just tell you, what would happen if I did?
I can't just help you, but what if I did?
It brings me back to that doorway.
The question I don't even ask myself.
I tear another hoping, maybe someday...
For now and awhile, I think I'll take a walk.
Again in this wonderment, of the one thing left to be.
I paint it on a canvas, so it can reflect me.
I hope it on a starlight, knowing it's only a dream.
I can't help but to question this motive within-side me.
I can't just tell you but what if you guessed?
I can't just help you, nothing would be left.
Now it brings me back to that question, "the one thing I dare not ask."
Now I fall back in question, "*what lies ahead?*"
I just want a second, to think things over.
I feel the bones break, soon it will be over.
And no one can stop me but you try - but you try.
I won't leave it till it's over, and I just can't help you out.
Please just leave me and move over; I need to get out.
I won't just tell you, you'll have to try.
I won't just help you, "you must fight your own fights."

Shaking My Sanity

It's shaking, my bones are aching.
I feel it waking and now it's taking me deeper into the snow.
The ground is shaking, reality is quaking.
I feel it taking, me deeper into this hole.
When reality is broken, no one is there to see.
And my wrist shifts open and life spills away from me.
I feel them pulling, down-tug on my dreams.
I see it burning, now the world is away from me.
Grabbing a hammer, placing a nail under my teeth.
Screaming in the wonder, if anyone is there for me.
And I feel it thunder, sanity is gone and weak.
I feel it coming and now it breaks out from under me.
Can you take me further, deep where my soul should be?
Can you take me further? Away from this dream that is haunting me?
I know it's time now. The rain is covering me deep.
I know it's time now, to drift far from sleep.
I feel it shaking, my body aching. "*Lord* – what is happening to me?!"

The Un-Question

Behind my ears screaming, beyond the doors bleeding.
Now I feel it seeping, beyond the thoughts dreaming.
Can you hear us screaming, behind the doors bleeding?

What a fear, and now it's here.
The question why, behind my eyes.
Now she runs in, what a slap in my face.
Here in my arms, the biggest disgrace.
What an awkward moment, God let it pass me.
Such an un-forgivable feeling. Of my heart raped in my chest.

This is the question that I never asked.
This is the feeling that will never pass.
Behind me stealing, my very last breath.
Now I see it filling, cracking the amber glass.

This is the un-question, of what I did on that day.
This is the torment, of my forever haze.
Beyond these days, will I ever find a better youth?
Deep in the un-question, buried under each tooth.

Wow and now it's spilling.
As our Mother Earth takes me away.
Won't you just let me drown?
Singing this song, down in my grave.
I was once let down and now must live with it everyday.
Please God let me out, why can't I forget that day?

This is the question that I never asked.
This is the feeling, which will never pass.
Behind my eyelids and under my tongue.
I live with the torment, till this damned day is done.

This is the un-question, of what I did on that day.
This is the torment, shoved deep into my grave.
Why did I hurt you, I never meant it to end that way.
Why can't I forget you, "please God!" Just throw me away...

Never to Be Let Out

Awake in this field, as these wounds will never heal.
Nauseous as I peel, away my scabs and skin.
Against my skull as I build, on and on in my head.
It falls acid and I'm gone, away with each love-song.
Down and it's mine, lost in this world... Broken over time.

You can't hide it, the words behind your teeth.
You can't fight it, the monster growing in deep.
Awake in this memory, I know the answer to it all.
Coming apart at the seams, losing life in this dream.
Not one thing left to see.

Here in the dragon's mouth I slumber and smolder.
Here in the hour let down... I blanket my wounds, ash and mildew.
I question each noon, breaking under my youth.
Where were you going and where am I now?!
Here in a hurry, I tumble swiftly under the cloud.
And God what a worry but I was found out.
Now in this demon-heart I am buried. "Never to be let out."

"My Name is You."

Down my throat it fell, in her broken heart I dwell.
Clinching to my spine I melt, and now I am whole...
"My name is you."

Beat the... Hold the... I love this mouth.
Voices ringing in my brain. Hold me *Angel,* insane...
So now I'm screaming and no one's there.
Now I'm leaving and no one cares...

And I would cry, I run and I forever weep.
The dust in mouth, I fall down and out...

This world against you, "myself against me."
This world against me, *"you're all against me."*

It Warms Me Nice

It holds my hand, as I break away.
It takes me in, when all is gray.
It warms me nice, when I'm alone.
It takes me in, it takes me home.

Where was I, when you called my name?
Where am I? Now all is gray.
Where am I? Into salt I fade.
Where am I? Please show me.

Blanket me, please cover my wounds.
Blanket me, please cover me soon.
Watch over me, hold me till noon.
Watch over me and my soul they consume.

Where am I and who are you?
Where am I? So dark and used.
Where am I? Beaten and bruised.
Where am I? Alone and confused.

Blanket me, just let me dream.
Blanket me, watch me as I sleep.
Watch over me, as I drift away.
Watch over me, for all is gray.

Please my love, don't walk away.
Please my love, don't drive me to pain.
Please my love, hold me tight.
Please my love, un-blanket me in ice.

It holds my hand, as I break away.
It takes me in, when all is gray.
It warms me nice, when I'm alone.
It takes me in, from the cold.

Blanket me, cover me please.
Blanket me, just hold me please.
Please my love, don't go away.
Please my love, don't leave this way.
Blanket me, cover me please.
"I'm so alone..."

Break Down

Darkened clouds rain the torment on me.
Looming death lingers deep within me.
Consuming death with every dream.
Confusing chest, breaking far inside me.

Gloom of the nature that holds my neck.
Dark of the hatred that festers in death.
Hard as it hits me, across my cheek and face.
Hard and it breaks me, never to be replaced.

I can't keep on standing, but all is fine.
I can't keep on losing, I need my mind!!!
I won't go on hurting, but I'll never be fine.
I won't go on falling, I wish to unwind.

Here it takes me, the voice behind my ear.
Here we go now, falling deep into fear.
So here we are now but it's not fine.
Here we break down, and I unwind...

I Want

I want nothing more than to end this dream.
I wish nothing more than to just cut and bleed.
I want nothing more than to open my eyes.
I wish nothing more than to be alive.

I hold nothing close but this broken heart.
I hold nothing close but fear and doubt.
I want to be free, and stop running around.
Just to stop the pain, and end this war.

"I want to know but hate the lesson. I want to go but fear the road..."
"I want to fly, above the sky. I wish to live, free from sin."
Incased around me, I am now whole.
Incased around me, the thought of the old.
Incased above me and now it's gone.
Held deep within me and I am alive.

I want nothing more than to end this strive.
I want nothing more than to open my eyes.
I need nothing more than a hand to hold.
I wish nothing more than to free my soul...

Holly

Echoing roots, crawling through my head.
Damp mildew and fungus, blanketing my breath.
Warm in the evening and cool in the day.
She holds me tight, never ending this way.
I tremble and shiver but she keeps me safe.
The parasites consume me and enjoy each touch.
Here in her arms soothing, the soft memory of us.
Deep in her soul confusing, breaking at each touch.
I never want to lose her, rooted in trust.

Never to turn to the reason but looking back each day.
Holding in the turmoil, deep within this haze.
So now I am breaking and shaking all day.
Here in the echoing memory, of all my dreams.
But then she embraces me and I never want it to end.
Then she whispers to me and I feel warm within.
Of the monsters consuming, my body each day.
Here in this hole confusing, but she keeps me safe.

I want to tell her but she already knows.
Here in the rooted nature, of the words lost in time.
Here incased in the sands, golden and all mine.
Then she takes my hand, to set free my strive.
Then we dance again, free under the sky.
I just want to tell her but she already knows.
I enjoy her company, I am never alone.

Down dark in this hallow I know I am safe.
She keeps me in her arms as crawling through my brain.
Echoing the torment that we are alive.
Down in this hallow, I enjoy my vice.
Here in this memory of the mid-fall leaves.
No one can hear me, as together we sleep.
And God I know she loves me, holding each-other so tight.
Down in this hallow, keeping me safe at night.

I want to tell her, as the rooted memory begins to decay.
"God, please help me!" I never wanted it to end this way.
But then she kisses me, and I just melt away.
God I love you *my sweet.*
Holding me forever in her grace...

Vortex

Pulling me closer to the core.
Rubbing my spine harder with every thorn.
Sucking me in, deeper to the floor.
Pulling my heart in, till ice is there.
And nothing more...

Shoving me closer to the core.
Taking me faster to the never-more.
Cutting me deeper, next to my heart.
Pulling me in and tearing me apart.

As falling further into the vortex.
Knowing the truth of what lies next.
And feeling the light bend, breaking over time.
Feeling my heart break, losing all but mind.

As I am shoved closer to the core.
I try to escape but stuck to the floor.
I rush to get out, the light is gone.
I fear what stands behind me and I know it's laughing.
Why won't it just pass me?
God, please save me!

And now I am stuck, between dreams and life.
Here being pulled deep into darkness and away for life.
In death is the answer but I fear the question.
In deep it takes me, away from compassion.

Pulling me closer to the core.
Shoving me deeper, stuck to the floor.
In mind of the vortex that screams my name.
Winding deep in spiritual belief of his nature.
It grabs me tight and holds me close.
This endless vortex, consuming my soul.

Moonlit Death

Torture of the small demons dancing on my skull.
Enter the twilight of the owl calling this his home.
And twisted is the torment of the voices deep within.
And Her Majesty commands it, call of her next wish.
Sometimes I just can't stand it, this ringing deep in my ears.
Sometimes I just fake it and conceal these scars with tears.
And damn you all, of this hatred swinging behind my teeth.
I just can't hold on, in an eternal wondering I swing.
Sightless singing to my one true love, that we are alive.
In her hand I place a blue rose and we dance by the moonlight.
Sometimes I just want to leave and take her away from here.
Sometimes I just want to laugh and burn away the past years.
Please tell me what is next. Anticipation is a killer indeed.
In my heart, what is left? And together my love and I swing.
And when no one's looking. I begin to pull on the thread.
I smile with my love swinging... *Dancing-Moonlit-Death.*
And no one feels it looming, and clinching to my chest.
Please answer my question, of it all... What is next.
Here in my love's heart blooming, knowing it will be fine.
In her heart warming, keeping me safe at night.
But then you push me over and my love sheds a tear.
Above the staircase swinging, weeping with moonlit tears.
Sometimes I just want it to be over and stop this game of life.
Sometimes I just want an answer yet you turn your back.
But me and my love embrace this fact and on we dance.
Moonlight guiding our way, for what lies next...
"Sometimes I'm just so glad that she is with me."

To Live

To live you must die, and to die you must live.
From beginning to end, of the same faces that I dread.
It holds me close, the *Mother-Monster* of death.
So take me further into the pit.
Please hold my hand, give me a heart to beat.
I need just one more breath...
So take me home, please don't let me go.
"I need a hand to hold."
Please somebody, take me home.
To live we must die, and to die we must live.
I never asked for this life yet I need just one more breath.

Eyes Of Darkness

The eyes of darkness piercing our skin.
Drinking from the shallow pool, of liquid love and sin.
It brings the tool of that, which holds us within.
It takes us cold and brings us away from trust and skin.
And the thought of hoping, as it begins to bite our neck.
It quivers profoundly in the spill of sins.
And we shiver quaking, breaking under our limbs.
As our souls are taken, away from our mortal flesh and whims.
Now we feel it taking, above our notions of forgotten whims.
Now we fall breaking, body caving within our sins.
Now we feel it raping, our lives taken far away from skin.
Now our lives are waking, growing from the ashes of them.
And we feel it taking, us further into lust and sin.
And now we feel it changing, awake in death and we begin.
Through the eyes of darkness, we see their lies.
As now we must feed "*body aching*" yet still alive.

Your Radiance

Radiance of the early day, growing further into grace.
Here, warm in the arms of her charms - held safe.
Unclouded awareness of the mid-fall leaves.
And over the time spent, I know this to be true.
In your eyes shines the power... Un-touched pure light of truth.
Here in the first hour, time cradling your dreams.
Held tight by Gods angels. Swimming through heaven's streams.
As it grows upon the early day.
Your heart cased in the armor of this early spring.
You are held in a wonder of the world so large.
Here in your heart, the light of pure charms.
Not wasting another moment to grasp this world.
Here held in the arms of safety and charm.
Now you wake in a wonder of this warmth shining clear.
Here held in safety, protected from fear.
As now the stars dance twinkling.
Embracing your wishes and taking you to the clear.
Now in the radiance of the early day. Moving further into faith.
Here held warm in the arms of charm, forever safe.
Un-tainted awareness of the mid-fall leaves.
And over the time spent, I know one thing to be true.
In your eyes shines the power. Un-touched, pure and true.

Embers

Embers of the morning haze, falling onto my tongue.
Swinging on the limbs of faith, taking me into grace.
Upon the thoughts of the past years gone.
Looking back and remembering our songs.

In the armor of the Saints, holding me close in arms.
In the wonder of the words spoken and small child charms.
It takes me further into the thoughts swinging in my head.
Dancing embers of the morning haze, holding onto my chest.

Here upon the road of leaves, holding me close to truth.
Embracing me in the arms of my loves true bind.
Un-broken heart-warmth of the last things said.
Here holding me in the answer to all that I seek.
Now taking me further into the morning ember dreams.

Shivers

Intake of the last thing I never wanted to say.
Heartbreak and now my nerves are wiped away.
The journey lost and time crumbling away.
Shivers here and none of it goes away, so why the wait?
Was it not the blood of the sheep that was sweet?
What a tool and still you think I'm a fool.
You've got the nerve but not the gall.

The moment passed and the thought is still here.
The mourning passed but lingers with fear.
The notions struck but not a dent.
It breaks me cold, hanging on my consent.

Laid under the sea, cold as you stare up and into my eyes.
Now laid upon a dream and no one is left alive.
Here holding me close and cradling my hopes.
"I shiver nonstop, freezing in the cold."
Blanketed here in the snow, holding nothing but me.
Damn, I am that cold and there's nothing else to see.
What a fool, but you touch once more to feel the hurt.
What a tool - and now I shiver as I burn.

I Need Out!

I need a new point of drive, something to set me straight.
I need some sort of logic, better than this pain.
I need to get my head on and out of your shit.
I need to get a move on. I just want to escape this.
I would like to have an outlet, other than this hate.
I sure would like a release, better than this tormenting pain.
I need to see the horizon and hold out my hands.
I need to feel my freedom and leave these thoughts in the sand.
I just need to leave here and forget this pain of you.
I need to get it out and stop feeling so confused.
I sure would like an outlet, something to set me right.
I just need to leave your darkness and then feel the light.
Please God get me out of here and into something new.
I just need to escape here and not feel so used.
I need to get my life back and this world out of my head.
I need to give you your knife back, I just don't feel that dead.
I need you to stop laughing and take this noose off of my neck.
I need to get it all back and see what lies next.
I sure would like a ride back into my head.
"I would stop laughing if I were you. You are the one who is dead."

What I'm Saying

I'm not trying to say that all is that dark.
Nor am I stating that you should go that far.
I'm only telling you what I have come to learn and fear.
Not all is black and white, yet still you wait and stare.
Forcing the emotions deep within our hearts.
Now driving us further and ripping us apart.
But I'm only telling you what I feel and know.
I don't want to control you but you never let it go.
To come across this nightmare twice in a life.
I'm sure it wouldn't be that dark if you gave me some light.
But don't take it lightly nor think it's alright.
Just listen to what you're saying... None of it is right!
I'm not trying to guide you into anything other than truth.
But you scream there whining about this all day.
I'm not trying to think for you but still it's the same.
You push me hoping to get a reaction. Laughing behind your smile.
And now it drips off the edge of the sane.
As looking into the mirror and nothing is the same;

But the scars never lie and I only wish to unwind.
But you just won't let it go. I am truly sorry that you didn't get your say.
But not all is that dark and gray.
Come on now, did you think you were right all along?
Rubbing your eyes and seeping those songs.
I'm only trying to get you to see it my way.
I never meant for it to end this way. I'm not trying to control your life.
What I'm saying is "this is my fight..."

The New Age

Moving on to the next spot of ink, to taste the new age.
Onward tugging of my spine and brain.
Just to understand your shames and unforgivable lies.
Here under the stars, of truth and strive.
Waking at the dawn of her demise. You still gaze at me with spite.
As forever undying is the demon inside my chest.
Now holding me tighter and freezing my breath.
It slimes its way into my thoughts. It holds me decaying as I rot.
I break here forgotten as the world pulls away.
I rush there frantic, undying in shame.
For her love that keeps me, and pulls me to the next page.
I lay here weeping, stepping into a new age.
And it takes me onward into the awesome of her dismay.
It shakes me frantic, breaking away my faith.
And I try to stop it but the sands are more than I can take.
I wish I could forfeit and just step away.
But she takes me onward, stepping into the new age.
I want to forget this and to just go away.
Please someone stop me and place me into my grave.
Please just end me and let me drift away.
I don't want this pain anymore. I only want to dream.
I no longer have the drive, to keep me upright.
I back away from your torment and fall down on your knife.
Then you crack a smile and laugh at my pain.
So I hunger murder and the sweet-release of revenge.
And ongoing into the next page. To bring me away from rage.
But nothing comforts me from this hollow shame.
So onward I move strolling into a new age.
Then it drips the ink onto my eyes, shadowing me in fright.
So it holds my fate and brings me to life.
But then I fall away and awake at her demise.
And I am the one you despise, covered deep in your lies.
I know that I am the one, who was right.
But that never meant that I didn't want you to stay at my side;

So I move on to the next spot of ink, to taste the new age.
Here bleeding frantic and hoping for release.
So say what you will but it doesn't change a thing.
As onward I move, into this new age...

No Other Way

For reasons unknown but yet it is shown and no one backs away.
For the darkness is thrown and here etched in stone.
Because the small angels know the way.
And for the years of despise and the words in her eyes.
And no one wishes for it to stay this way.

So give me the tool and take me to the next page.
Just wipe me down and clean my wounds.
"The monster is coming this way."
But then it is dark and "*the rain*" as red as blood.
Indeed no one knows this fate.
So howl at the moon and awake at noon, so no one can take it away.
Here for the food and not for the room.
The ants are just tearing me away.
So come back real soon and never look away.
For ours is there and drowned fear, then you walk away.

The hunger of the end and swine of men.
And you just don't understand my ways.
As it drops from the sky and then burns alive...
The angels have no other path to take.
So show them your love and please don't look away.

The child now walks and asks for his crown.
And his smile breaks you away.
So grab me real tight and drain me of life. Just to free yourself of hate.
"It is far too late, there is no other way."
"Now you've set it in stone. Forever you shall burn alone."

Then and Now

Avoided yet planned from the start.
Then to now and now and then I jerk the bone out of place.
Grinding my ribs into dust and ashes of the grave.
For the wolf's smile shaking me in fear.
Now and then I still can't awake from the tears.
Then throw me down into the circle.
Pushing the acid into my spine.
Then and now I feel my heart untie.

Shattered and shoved under my teeth.
So you could understand and they won't see.
For the goblin's madness and not for your tools.
It's all just knowledge and not what you think.
So bring me back and watch me sink.

For all those times and so many more.
It brings the thunder and I break-away in lighting-screams.
For the moment and not what you think.
I fall down and hear the angels scream.
Then and now and now and then I watch it bleed.
Time after time I seep the dreams.

It was unavoidable yet I held it dear.
It was nonrefundable, so I kick and scream.
Just to watch it bleed, only to give it time.
Then to now and now and then I ask it so clear.
And the wolf holds me shaking. As the monsters consume my fears.

Here For Misery

Murky walls of the hallway that leads the path.
The hour draws and once again I see what is next.
For the moment paused and now it's lost. As the Gods begin to take my breath.
For now it's lost and what a rush. As her fingernails rip into my chest.
I hand you the tool, looking in deep "I fear what is next."
Please just give it back and let me up.
I do think that I've been stuck for far too long.
Please move away so I can end this song.
I was not ready but here we are. I was not willing but now too far.
You were stealing, my soul and heart.
Now I am chilling "under this ice," torn apart;

It was not the shadow that had followed you home.
It was not the hallow that consumed your soul.
It was not that hard but now it is thrown.
I have no time for this. Place me back under the stone.
I'm not here to make you happy, nor should you be.
I'm not here for you to smile, left alone and you weep.
It has been awhile but not for some time.
I'm not here to help you out, get your own damn spine..!
I just don't have the time, here sent for misery.
I just don't have the time, here stuck with nothing but me.
Stop wasting my time and get out of my head.
I'm here now for misery. Until the sweet release of death.

Faces In The Water

Far out in the middle of the lake.
Quite a way out, laying down in shame.
Rocking back and forth, a small wooden boat.
Quite a way out, far from the shore and deep in the smoke.
Here laying down, looking at the sky.
Just there lying, asking God why.

The smell of the wind on the tip of my lips.
Pushing me along with the waves holding me sick.
Gazing at the clouds, each one is another dream.
Looking but never found.
There is just no more reason for me to be.
And then I lay down, embracing the sunlit sky.
Just there laying down, losing all inside.

Lifting my hand and holding my heart.
Drifting away, further into the lake.
For the sands, golden and under my nails.
In the wind, a lost age speaks its tales.
For not that reason, I look at the sky.
Here in a small boat, drifting away my time.

Time to Go

So here we are and it's time to go.
The release of my last dream and hope.
Now I only want to hold her again.
But that heart has gone and died within.
We're on our way.
And this mind grows gray.
I just wanted to stay.
Yet here we are and there we go.
It's about time you understood.
So now we're gone.
And I can't let it go.
I've died twice over this game.
Still her eyes drive me insane.
We are onward once again into shame.
Please don't let it stay.
I just wanted to get away.
It's time to go and I step away...

In The Mood

Come on tell me, it's feeling alright.
Come on tell me, it's starting to feel nice.
Come on tell me, before it's too late.
Come on hold me, kiss me again that way.

So now you're gone, I'm in the mood.
So now you're gone, it was too soon.
So you're gone, "hold me tight."
So now you're gone, but I'm alright.

Come on hold me, till it's all done.
Come on hold me, just end it all.
Come on love me, I'm right here now.
Come on love me, just let me out.

Come on now, I'm in the mood.
Come on now, the light fell too.
Come on now, just kiss me good.
Come on now, while I'm in the mood.

Shattered Tooth

Bring me back to the hill. The acid-lust taking the feel.
Bring me out, at high noon. I know it's too soon, please hold me.
As the gravity hangs over my breath. For the hour, that never ends.
And all the trees are still the same. My mouth broken on your lies.
Biting down, the blood runs sweet.
I enjoy your screams. I love the fact that you hate me.
Down it's clinching. And the demons are eating my head.
Broken and I'm screaming. The mushroom death within my chest.
Just one breath. Broken and slammed till death.
Shattered torment... Get me out!

This Knight's Pledge

One foot upon another stone. My heart racing, taking me home.
Still the twilight feels the same. Walking onward and embracing my fate.
Yet nothing will ever keep me down. As onward I am bound.
For the answer to all that I seek. Taking me onward into sleep.
I have nothing more than this. "My pledge keeping my wits."
And the battle has yet to change. Steel and armor, rust and pain.

On I move, waist deep in their bodies, sun beating me dead.
Now is the time to keep my pledge, "nothing in my way."
Here in the war, bloody shines of this Knight's sword.
So no more dragons left to slay, or are we just both the same?
How many more demons have yet to lose? "Who is the one to choose?"
"Lord please give me, just another day. Take me back to your faith."

Now her voice starts to fade, then I reach for my blade.
I snap back and remember, all in which I had said.
"I'm coming home my love, alive or dead..."
So nothing can or shall change this pledge "it's my word."
Of all that mattered. She would be the one, my true love.
Although God's hammer beats me down, still to you I am bound.
So take my world and let me decay. Take my road and cast me aside.
I want nothing more than to see her eyes and kiss her lips.
I wish nothing more and her love I will never forget.
The answers to all, in her warm heart.
As I fall bloody down, resting in her soft eyes.
I remember all in which I said.
"I'm coming home my love... Alive or dead."

Chapter 3

1,000 Miles of Pain

1,000 Miles of Pain

Sliding forward into the next tears shed.
Slipping forward into a time I'll never forget.
Feeling caught-up with all that I have said.
Falling in deeper, until I am dead.

Now rushing me, the twilight behind my eyes.
And crushing the bones with the lime.
I'm running onward and fearing the next.
Now breaking the honor, these tears I have shed.

For her smiles, each one snapping my neck.
It was for that honor but now we are dead.
It never really mattered who went first.
Now breaking down the matter...

"Miles walked and nothing learned."

Mommy Save Me

Dancing devils on the tip of my tongue. *Mommy save me.*
Three nails shoved under my tongue. Heart breaking.
Winding down into my lungs. *Mommy save me.*
God forgive me for what I've done. "Save me!"
Now nothing is left but one. *Mommy save me.*
So the dark pain is screaming. Please don't leave me.
Now the time's sand is fleeting. Never leave me.
We were there for the chaos. Don't leave me lost.
It took some time to find the cost. *Mommy I'm lost.*
It never did seem to come to the surface. "Tell me I'm not worthless."

Spinning fast, three inches into my head. Don't leave me dead.
Lifting faster in my veins. Don't leave me in pain.
I want an answer but have no questions. *Mommy help me.*
Here drowning in my confessions. *Mommy save me.*
Lying there without a second. No compassions.
Swift falling into my wrist. Will I be missed?
Rough biting onto my eyelids. I try to fight this.
Down-broken, *I'm a minus.* "Help me fight this!"
Now seeping the frost of my forever... "*Forever?*"
Swinging now, dancing as I scream.
Mommy save me... "*Please.*"

Again, Again, Again

The spider smiles as he eats my eyes.
The torment files deep in mind.
It was forever breaking, my heart torn and raped.
I'm left here forsaken, lost deep in shame.

Now the demon whispers his needle into me.
I feel it tickle, cutting as I scream.
It was all just nonsense but now I descend.
Upon the 5th level of my demise.
I sit here and smolder, forever despised.

Passing the Graveyard

Have I gone too far? I fear I'll never know.
How long has it been, buried under the snow?
Now I swim in sin, her eyes shining sweet.
Now I lean back in question, passing their deceit.

I know the balance has been thrown off just a bit.
Why did you leave me here to drown in your shit?
Just give me some air. The smoke in my lungs.
No more despair. I don't want to care.
But now I'm there and nothing shuts it up.
You just never cared. Passing and I'm shook.

The ghosts of Mississippi, dancing under the moon.
They embrace her gravity, freedom coming soon.
I shake endlessly in presence of the dead.
They embrace me eternally, taking my hand.
Passing the courtyard, a field of headstones so grim.

The tires screeching, coming to a halt.
I begin to feel my soul fleeting, swallowing the sand and salt.
The driver dumb and bleeding. Gone under the soot.
The fire not leaving, my flesh falling off.
My teeth breaking, falling out.
Slam! And I'm awake...
The ghosts embrace my company, as I pass their graves.

The Trees of November

I'm so tired, the hour coming closer with every breath.
Strolling over a long bridge, the water gentle with me.
How much more did it matter to you? *Maybe I'll never see.*
It was very tender, so warm with shades of orange *"the trees of November."*
Oh so calming, her hand on my chest.
She feels my heartbeat and tastes the frost on my breath.
Dancing fall-leaves, blanketing my dreams.
Warm in November, her-love holding me.
So here we are now, stepping passed those days.
What a haze that I wish so dear.
Then taking another step into the awesome.
"So that was the gift that I gave to you." And now forever it shall be true.
So sweet and tender, the beautiful leaves of the trees of November.
Then she quivers, she starts to shiver. I'll never let anybody hurt her.
What more am I to do? Strolling over this bridge, the water calm and passing.
Taking me into a new age, yet it's all the same.
I stand here broken, a whole man for the first time.
"Do you remember what I told you? As we walked upon that line?"
None of it changes, the age growing into me clear.
So she holds me sweet and tender and she shivers...
Nothing will stop me, then she quivers.
So I ask you, do you remember? It was growing cold, our last November.

Sea of Sorrow

The last day of feeling, this hollow.
It took us onward, drowning in sorrow.
While we break and swallow, I feel you follow.
And I know this hallow - such sorrow.
Forever as I dream of tomorrow, down in sorrow.
As watching the leaves consume my soul.
Forever drowning in this hole. Gazing up as you pass me by.
I want nothing more, than to unwind.
As you are swine, wasting my time.
Drowning forever in what I've committed.
As breaking down while I was lifting.
Nothing stops it, the hatred shifting.
I cannot fight this, my arms are tired.
God help me fight this, as I drown in this fire.
Swinging, grabbing - I cannot get a grip.
As I drown in this sorrow, their faces I will never forget.

Upon My Face

The thirteenth hour upon my face.
Swinging me to the left, throwing me into disgrace.
The seconds hammering the minutes into my brain.
The age of a new thought taking me from grace.
Now out of place, as the moments fly by.
Stuck in that memory. Forever lost in time.

Frozen next to that tool. Eternally just a fool.
Dancing forever as I was told to do.
The seconds pushing us in two.
Now and forever just one.
As the thirteenth hour pushes until done.

It is stained upon my face.
And the whispers pull me to faith.
It was the whisper pulling me to fate.
It was a clean slate...
As the angel kissed my cheek.
Swinging me to the left.
Bind, snap! And nothing's left.

Forever rubbing in deep.
The angels embracing me sweet.
And Satan does love this poetic lie.
Upon my face.
The thirteenth hour eating me alive.

In My Eyes

Rub your tongue on my eyes, to taste my fate.
As the purple neon-noose swings me away from faith.
It drips sliding down my throat, burning so cold.
The owl smiles as I decay, embracing my rage.
The torment smolders. I do feel much older.
How bold must I have been to eat your heart?
Three inches of ice covering my eyes.
Now the fingernails rip open my arms.
Pulling on my bones, grinding them on the stone.
It was all for you yet you turned away. It was all for love, now in the grave.
So rub your tongue on my brain. To know where I've been.
Rub your tongue on my feet to taste all of my sins;

I place my lips on the ground "*I know she hates that.*"
The clouded noose brings me back "*God knows I hate that.*"
It's spinning in my eyes, can you taste my fear?
It begins to melt out of each pore, buried under the floor.
Now I know the answers but I've asked no questions.
I break away from all compassions.
Shoving my arm through the door.
Oh never more - never more.
The candy-death, so sour under my teeth.
Now riding the missile, into shattered dreams.
While pushing the blade into my wrist.
Smiling... Knowing I'll never be missed.
It's just a setback. Grinding the stone on my teeth.
You rub your tongue on my eyes to taste what I've seen.
You rub your tongue on my eyes.
So my death can set you free.

Ashes of Then

I guess the truth is that we were only at the end.
I could scream here for hours.
But it's just the same as then.
I held on for hours, losing all.
Nothing changing but them.
You want the answers but they never seem to show.
I held on for hours, I could just never let go.
Breaking-down with no power.
My mind twists and I'm away.
Then set aside all that mattered and we fall away.
Nothing left as I cower in presence of them.
Then screaming louder, breaking-down in the ashes of then.
And what a waste of my knowledge.
Breaking-down, tears and sand.
I can taste nothing now. Except the ashes of then...

Sweet Chosen

I am held sweet chosen, above your dreams.
And nothing's left growing, the acid in the streams.
Laid down on a bed of leaves.
I know I am sweet chosen, above all your dreams.

For the tiny angel singing inside my ears.
Of all the little demons feasting upon my fears.
I lay here and drown in my tears.
Each word shoved under my nails.
As now I kneel with my eyes shut tight.
I know I am sweet chosen.
Laid down in the light.

So then you turn me over.
Anticipating a better fight.
But I know I am sweet chosen.
Here with you at my side.
So dream as you will, your wounds I shall heal.
And nothing will ever push you aside.
Laid here on my heart.
Bleeding profoundly in my whims.
It holds me soundly.
Sweet chosen until the end.

This End

The thought of growing, it's forever flowing.
Dear God leave me growing, forever knowing the end.
For now it's blowing, my fears are showing.
The ground begins to shake and bend.
Please take it back my Lord.
I never wanted it to feel like this.

So for now I swim in this abyss.
Red-ice clinching to my wrist.
Please let me go, stop this helplessness!
I hope you to see a better end.
"*Oh Lord*, give me a better thought than this."

In the Smoke

The faces fading, in the smoke.
Falling freaking, in the smoke.
Faithless fading, as I choke.
Further fading, I'm unknown.

Hours draining, in my mind.
Days just burning, I'm undying.
Lives just breaking, it's my fault.
Faithless drowning, in the salt.

Voices screaming, in my bed.
Faces fading, in my death.
Mouth is broken, under the moon.
The smoke just lingers, bringing on doom.

The faces fading, in the smoke.
The hour rushing, I'm unknown.
This mouth is broken, armor of war.
Still faithless screaming, behind the door.

LockJaw

I'm running up a staircase. Rushing and I dare not look back!
I'm climbing higher. I cannot look back!
Faster rushing, I feel the eyes behind me.
The stairway lit in red, the walls are hot and wet.
Here I am rushing, running out of breath.
I dare not be caught. Faster I am running, dark and lost.
The monster cannot find me. Just let me out!
You will never find me. The steam burning, just no way out!
The faces begin to show, from the dark they grow.
I cannot reach the top. You'll never find me, in the dark-lost.
It was perfect timing, to see what I saw.
It threw me back then, world broken... Locked jaw!
I cannot reach the surface. I feel it right behind me.
It was perfect timing, but it was nothing I could stop.
Of all the things I've seen, running through the steam.
Rushing now forever lost. Red stairway, darkness growing.
Fear behind me, the hate is trying. I cannot stop it, yet faster I run.
My jaw is locked now, until it is done...

99 Screams in the Dark

The shadow of the *East* coming forth to take me home.
The smile of the beast, licking his lips and grinding his teeth.
"Damn it" was the last thing I said.
As kissing her lips and holding her hand.
Now what more could I do?
In the dark we scream and cry.

6, 7, 8, 99 - How many more times?
In the dark I waste away... Falling from faith into fate.
Seeing the slate break away... Shoving the death into my spine.
Watching my heart burn and unwind.

And I never closed my eyes.
As her lips haunt each step of mine.
I never asked for it, now we live in sin.
Greed holding the knife in me.
Laid in the dark, 99 more screams.
So as I bleed and forget her face.
Falling deeper into fate "going home."
99 more screams. As I burn alone.

The Wolf of Me

My heart racing, my soul pacing.
My mind rushing, my soul flushing.
My blood boiling, my body pulsing.
The earth singing, the moon kissing me.
The world moving, my body lifting.
My mind shifting, my heart shifting.
Swiftly leaving mankind - human gone.
The voice of our Mother-Earth holding me sweet.
The love of the moon, embracing me in care.
The dirt now clean, the taste of the air.
Now leaving without a care to "*Nowhere.*"
Running through the trees, loving me.
Seeking the blood of the pure.
Lifting my soul to our Mother-Earth.
True as the woods do say.
Left behind all but the true sense of faith.
Running onward into the haze.
Leaving behind my human nature.
Forsaking the world of man...

Nothing is the Same

I once thought that I had to be right.
I once thought that there was another side to light.
I once thought that I could just walk away.
I once thought that but now nothing is the same.

I had it all once, now left only alone.
I had it all once, now forgotten in the snow.
I had it all once, then it slipped away.
I had it all once but now nothing is the same.

I once held it, her hand holding me tight.
I once held it, the thought of being right.
I once held it, the love deep and true.
I once held it, but it's not the same without you.

I had a dream once, of being alive.
I had a dream once, of leaving it all behind.
I had a dream once, with you at my side.
I had a dream once but it's not the same this time.

I once thought that we would be together.
I once thought that it would last forever.
I once thought that you would love me true.
But nothing is the same now - "not even you."

Just a Shell

3 years can change a man but the answer is still the same.
Those years could kill a man but nothing will ever change.
These years can destroy this man. For I am but a shell of who I was.

How many times must I fall again?
The eyes of the monster never seem to look away.
Those things I put away, for no one to find.
Please just look away as I unwind.
Nothing but a hollow man, cast away.

3 years can change a man "I never wanted it in the first place."
Those years could kill a man. These thoughts have come again.
They take me far into the gray.
I'm just a shell of a man "here I break away..."

About to Snap

It's about to snap.
The pressure building.
The blood filling my eyes.
It's about to crack.
And the glass is broken.
The tears are dripping red.
The fear is holding me dead.
At last we understand.
The path is not ours to choose.
At last we are not the ones used.
So abused and tormented.
I'm left here to taste your decay.
Placed under the earth to rot.
Please just go away...
It's about to snap.
And the thought won't pass.
Please just turn away.
It's about over now, but I have more to say.
It's almost done.
But none of it feels the same.
It's about to go.
Please don't let us end this way.
For now it's done and all is gray.
The path was not mine to choose.
But I took it anyway.

Hello Again:

Well, look at you now...
It's been a while and you've grown.
It sure does seem like a lifetime but then again, it shows.
Please smile on this day and leave those thoughts behind.
I just wanted to stop and say hello and you sure have grown.
So stand tall here and now. Be strong here on out.

I know that fate threw us a curveball.
But here we are now, standing strong and tall.
Well, I think I should go now "I just wanted to say hi."
Well, here I go now and - well...

"Good-bye."

Bleed Me Dry

Here on the edge of all that mattered.
Standing on the tip of my faith and hopes.
Giving up all that was once held close.
Laying here now, deep in the cold.

For hours I tried to fight. Now I'm bleeding dry.
My heart no longer has a pulse.
My thoughts no longer have a mind.
But it was good time spent. On our childish games.
Now here I stand frozen and still the same.

And what a waste of my strength. Holding onto those devils.
And all the angels laugh as I bleed here dry.
It did take me some time. Standing on the tip of my fate.
And all that truly mattered. It's no longer the same.

So I swing here on the edge of all my thoughts.
Looking back and feeling so lost.
I try to remember something sweet. But that face is all that I see.

I'll Be Nice

So, you want my opinion? "*Okay, I'll try to be nice...*"
It was that vice that drove you to that. You're asking what I think.
I'll try to hold back... The worry of losing again.
It's written on your face. The thought of regaining...
It will never be the same.

So you want my true views? Okay but I'll try to be nice...
It was that child that started this strive.
And not much changes over the years. You and I are still the same.
Stuck forever in our own fears but you asked me and I'll say.
There's more to think about now, "*It's not the same.*"

I can't begin to put myself in your shoes but my hope is.
That you can be happy in truth but I'm holding back now.
"You know I am." You're better off, but then again...
It's only my opinion, just think about it a bit.
You should worry about your "*true love.*"
Before you end up like this...
"Just think about it."

Rage #2

Here ripping the flesh off my bones.
Tearing the salt, sand and stones.
Heart dripping, the blood running cold.
The bones are twisting and death now unfolds.

And I do hold it all on top of you.
The headstone speaking my name.
I hold it all just that close and love my rage...
Here in my hole, seeping the coal.
Knowing that I'll never be free.

What more could I do, nailing this hate into you?
Knowing that we are forever alone.
Left here to lift my own stone.
Enjoying the breaking of my bones.
And I pull on that rib, until it snaps.
I pull and pull and laugh and laugh.
Never looking back, never knowing why.
Left here in the dark, buried alive.

Finding the Answers

Holding my head under the water.
Watching my breath fade away.
Open eyes and all is over... Left now in the gray.
I lay back and try to remember.
The past is so far, I cannot see.
I lay back looking for an answer.
But the blood in the water begins to consume me.

Holding my head under the water.
Watching my breath fade and leave.
I keep open my eyes, trying to see.
I just want an answer but darkness is all I see.
I lay back and hope an outcome.
Something better than what I have.
Holding my head under that water *"welcoming my death."*
I lay back looking for an answer.
But I can no-longer hear a thing.
I lay back hoping an outcome, yet fire is all I see.

So Naïve

How many demons have tasted my soul?
How many angels left me in the cold?
Why do I fight with you my Lord? Forgive me for being naïve.
I never wanted to have this thing between us.
So I kneel here on broken glass. Gazing up at your burning sun.
And I will stay here for days on end.
I just want you to hear me my Lord. I wish to be forgiven.

I truly am sorry my father.
I know that I can be so naïve at times.
I was just a child then, forgive me for being swine.
I never wanted this thing between us my Lord.
But you already know what I'm trying to say.
Please forgive me my father.
For being lost in you. For living in shame.
"Forgive me."

Unchangeable

The hour of growing the death in my heart.
Now taking you with me and tearing us apart.
I know that truth is not all black and white.
But the answers are and shall be the same.
"The pride in my heart will always be this way."

All Alone

The red stone, dripping life into my heart.
The destruction coming forth. *"Lost in despair."*
Leaning back in a rocking chair. Losing it all but I don't care.
Developing a new disorder. Lying, bleeding - a heaven-soldier.
And I am bolder and very much older.
But come to think of it, you don't care.
I'm leaning back and I surely am at a lack of reach.
I have nothing anymore but what does it matter?
All alone I tremble and weep.
I did care once but now I know that you are weak.
All alone I hope for hope but nothing I see.
Lain down in fire. Leaning back in my chair. Trying to fall asleep.
I asked for your help once but you were too weak.

Relapse

I'm waking, I can see nothing. I'm reaching, I can feel nothing.
I'm searching but nothing I can find.
I'm hurting and it's just the same as last time.
The cloud is growing, rolling over my grave.
My head confusing, the pain tastes the same.
The answers are darker, the lies never change.
I want some release but you will never change.
I try to fade away and grow into my death.
I try to consume my grave and empty out my chest.
It comes back twice as hard. Reminding me what I've done.
I try to escape the memory and become just *one.*
I'm waking at the beginning, I see no sun.
I'm reminded of your sinning, these emotions overdone.
I'm searching for reason but it all comes back again.
I'm hurting all day now, feeling those pains once again.

Forget It

That picture never seems to go away.
God knows I hate that, so it just stays.
I try to let it fall back, I want it no more.
I want to just forget it, behind the broken door.
Then it all comes back, the facts that I despise.
Then it all comes back and inside I weep and die.
I just want my life back, is that too much for me?
Oh just forget it - you don't even care.
When is this ride over, who even cares?
I want to step back and watch the world clear.
The water is dirty and the blood's full of fear.
Oh just forget it - all of what I said.
That picture is stuck now, forever till death.
But I just want my life back and to be alright.
Please take this fight back. It was never mine to have.
When can I turn back and unwind?
Please pull this picture out of its frame.
Please put my eyes back, glued to my brain.
Oh just forget it - you don't care anyway.
God knows it's true, right? That's why I'm still in pain.
Label me insane if you wish. I know I won't be missed.
"So give me my last kiss..." Oh - just forget it.

Something

Why does it hurt when I breathe? Why am I alone and deceased?
Why don't you care for me? Please answer something... something.
Well, to tell you the truth, I never did ask for this life.
And to tell you the truth, I really do live with strive.
And I did hold on far too long.
Now I bleed here forever, wishing it all gone.
Why does it hurt when I speak to you? Why did it hurt when we died?
Why don't you care anymore? Please open your eyes...
Something has gone wrong here, nothing seems right.
The water is much colder. My heart is torn and raped.
Okay, so it's all the same... But you don't truly care.
Why am I alone here? Why can no one hear?
Why won't you answer me?
Please say something... something.

Raped Inside

Pushed down in the dark.
Innocence taken and torn apart.
Held down by those that I trusted.
Tied down bleeding and flushed.
Broken and crying all night.
Lying there soaking, deep in fright.

And all was taken, just raped away.
In the darkness waiting, cutting these feelings away.
My soul is breaking, my heart raped away.
It was all taken, now nothing is the same.
Tied down in the darkness, watching my soul drift away.
Lying down beaten, cutting the pain away.
Everything was taken, just raped away.

Held down in the darkness, my soul raped away.
Pushed down into nothing, bleeding forever sound.
Torn inside and broken in lies.
None of it will ever go away.
In the darkness waiting, raped by those I loved.
Held down for forever, never getting up.
Heart stolen in youth and I'm never to regain.
Raped inside - my heart and mind.
Now cutting these pains away...

Chapter 4

Alone In Hell

Get Away

Finding new ways.
To say those old things.
Losing everything.
All – over – again.
But I don't care.
You are not here.
Who really cares?
Oh - just get away.

For all those old fears.
Lost in the clear.
But who was there the whole time?
When will you - give me back my mind?
You are not here.
Lost deep in despair.
But who truly cares?
Oh - just get away.

I held on too long.
Singing those old songs.
Remembering that taste.
Forgetting that face.
Trying to just let it go.
But it's all the same.
I've never changed.

But you are not here.
Standing in the clear.
Wiping away the fears.
Holding in the tears.
Knowing it will always be.
Oh - just get away.
So now I see...

I Don't Care

Eating at its flesh, reaching in and feeling blessed.
Knowing the answers to all of this world.
No longer worrying about what you think.
Feeling my heart and soul sink.
Away with all those hopes and dreams.

Eating at its remains, the carcass stiff and mine.
Knowing that it's all sweet this time.
Not caring whose face this is, even if it's mine.
Tearing at the corpse, bloody and decayed.
Enjoying the fester of its cheek and face.

Try to tell me it matters but I won't think twice.
Eating at this vice, humble is this thing in my hands.
Why is it you look away, as I lust upon the grave?
What does it matter to you if I love the taste of death?
So away with all this nonsense, gone and all mine.
Do you think I care, as you weep and whine?
Human as swine and all mine - all mine.

Breaking away each tooth, swimming in the spilt youth.
Loving the festering body, laid under our earth
From death to birth, loving what I can do.
Breaking each rib one by one. Eating the sins - two by two.
"Why must you look away?"
And you act like I should care, what a joke...

Oh - to watch them choke, their pain I soak.
Loving the feel of death between my fingers.
Laughing as life fades dim, swimming in sin.
Lusting the grave and all its glories.
Knowing each step of what I've done.
And you start to scream, knowing I'll never be done.
Oh, so much fun and you think I should care?
Eating away the death and decay.
And loving each second that it takes.

Something I Lost

There was that place, I can't wipe away.
Trying to forget it all and leave it in the fog.
But I seem to return, back to that hallway.
Something I must have forgot, something that I lost.
So again I come back, wondering why.
Lost and forgotten, something left behind.

What was it that you were trying to say?
The message mustn't have been clear.
Again in the hallway, remembering those fears.
Lost in the clear, left there all alone.
Why does my mind turn back?
Why can't I just let it go?

I can't seem to escape, the torment of my brain.
Those lingering memories which just won't leave me be.
Left in the clear - something lost in fear.
So what was it that you were trying to say?
I couldn't hear you over the screams.
Now drowned in the fog, left in the past.
But never it was forgot.

Please wipe away these thoughts and let me just go.
I no longer need to stay in this hole.
Darkness of the brightest days, fading in my brain
The cells forever burst and bring back that curse.
Reminding me, of the thing that I lost.
Returning to that hall, consumed by the fog.
The memory that I hate, lost but never late.

Please tell me what you were trying to say...
Your kisses I could just never wipe away.
Please lift me above this hell and push in place that nail.
Hold me up to the light, look through me and end the strive.
What was it that I forgot? Something that I lost.
And I know I am never to regain.
End this torment of my brain. Take me back to the womb.
Leave me forever in my tomb, just so I can dream you away.
What were you trying to say??? What were you trying to say???

Let Me Out

Let me fall down and spit on my wounds.
Let me break-down and pull out my tooth.
Let me scream loud and watch the world melt away.
Let me out now! It's time to end this pain.
The hour of growing back my flesh. The knowledge of rebirth and death.
Take this knife out of my chest. Let me come back, to end this test.
So I want my life back, "Is that too much to ask?"
So I want to fight back and to see the torment overlap.
Let me run away and find a heart to beat.
Let me fade away and never surface again.
Let me fall down and rub the salt in my wounds.
Let me out now! For my name is "You."

No Matter What

Remembering those days and beating myself as I try to forget.
Knowing that I loved you, now left with only pain and shit.
But I think it was all worth it, the selling of my soul.
Only to watch you walk away and leave me in this hole.
"What hope did I have, knowing it was over before it began?"
So looking in the mirror at my scars, seeping the smoke.
Watching the breaking of my heart, it's all apart.
Now what hope do I have, of ever waking from this hell?
It was you that took me to hell but it was all I ever wanted.
I held you close, only to watch you walk away.
I sold my soul only to end up alone in my grave.
Those nights of lustful heart-warmth and dread.
Oh - those thoughts that I'll hold till death.
You with your hand in my chest, grinding my heart away.
But do you remember what I said?
Now lifting me in the hour of dread "consuming death."
Now a hollow chest and nothing is left *"only pain."*
You were my world, now I'm stuck in space.
Just a hollow man thrown out of place.
And I beat myself as I try to forget your face.
What a waste of my heart and mind, soul and time.
But in the end I think it was worth it, the breaking of my heart.
It was dead from the start and I should have acted faster.
But I am as much at fault as the devil himself.
I tried to keep you and wound up in hell.
I said I loved you but where did you go;

So now I'm left alone here, stuck in this hole.
And the armor never seemed to work.
Now I feel my heart race and burst for nothing's worse.
As I try to forget you, something seems to return.
I think it was worth it, watching my soul burn.
But in the end, I said I'd love you no matter what.
But somehow it's over now, thrown in hell and stuck.
So that's my luck and forever shook.
But I think it was worth it - the killing of my heart.
"I think it was worth it." And no matter what - I'm torn apart.

I'm Ready to Go

I only need one for where I'm going.
The gun is loaded, the tears are flowing.
I don't need your consent for what I'm doing.
The gun is cocked, now I'm ready.

As I hold it steady and peer down the barrel.
So now I'm ready, straight pointed arrow.
Pushed against my forehead and I smile.
I only need one for where I'm going, down the spiral.

So you swim in your denial, it's been a while.
But the answers are and will always be the same.
I'm ready to go now. Gun loaded - tears of shame.
I only need one for what I'm doing. I don't need your consent.
The gun is cocked now - it's time to end this...

Drowning in the blood of my sins and knowing what I did.
I'm ready to go now, drift into the abyss.
The hours are longer and the pain does insist.
So the fine hair trigger, I squeeze tighter and tighter.
My head gets lighter and lighter.
And I see the flash of fire - glowing before my eyes.
I'm ready to go now, deep into the light.

I only need one, for where I'm going.
The gun is loaded, the tears are flowing.
I don't need your consent for what I'm doing.
The gun is cocked... now I'm ready.

On the Playground

On the playground, I ran for the swings.
I tripped over a rock and screamed. No one was there to help me up.
I fell down crying - bleeding on the ground.
No one helped me up. So out of luck and my heart was shook.
There was nothing for me to say. My bone exposed, bleeding like rain.

On the playground, I ran to the swings.
I tripped over a rock and screamed.
My body laid on the ground - no one around.
And so cold I could do nothing but weep.
Freezing rain, left in pain. "No one helped me."

On the play ground, I ran for the merry-go-round.
Spinning, spinning and thrown to the ground.
No one was there to watch me fall.
Left there alone, bleeding alone and lost.
I wanted someone to help me up.
But that's my luck, now my childhood shook.

On the play ground, I walked slowly to the swings.
I pushed off and no one was there to see.
I sway back and forth and no one seems to care.
On the playground - running out of air...

Was It?

Was it not time or am I too late? Was it not mine or is it fate?
Was it not love but a true form of hate? Was I not the one laid under the slate?
I think I was too late, far out with no help.
I know now, I have no means to come back.
So I tilt my head back and you laugh.
Was there some kind of bigger purpose?
Please tell me I'm not worthless.
But still you throw me away like trash. But I'm not coming back.
I've spent too long trying to help you.
Only to lose my mind in the end.
I only wanted to love you but ended up in sin.
Was it not mine to have but yours to keep?
Was it not a lamb but a dead rotted sheep?
Was it not the blood that was sweet?
Was I too late because you were too weak;

Please tell me it's all going to be okay.
Please take me far, so very far away.
Leave me at the bottom of the lake.
Was it not time or am I too late?
Was it not time to live but just die?
Was it not time to scream but to cry?
Was it not you that I loved so dear?
Was it not our love that had ended in fear?
I've spent too long trying to regain my heart.
I've had enough already. I'm so torn apart.
Just get it over with for God's sake!
Was I right on time or am I too late?
"Was it not mine, that was left beneath the frozen lake?"

Spitting Out the Pills

Endless hours of spitting out those pills.
Nonstop screaming, under the hill.
And mother tries to wipe away that feel.
As I lay upon the broken cradle, lost deep in your fable.
Why must you try to take it all away?
Not done till it's over. Not over till it's done.
Hours of this torment. "Now I'm just one."
As so it was sung. Not gone till I'm done.
Spitting out these pills. Screaming under the hill.
Mother wipes away the feel...
Endless needles, shoved under my eyelids.
Endless hours, I tried to fight this. And what a miss and no last kiss.
Upon the doom of the soon ending pain. Wiped clean and torn away.
So many times I wanted to tell you but you turned a deaf ear.
So many hours of burning in the clear.
Mother tries to wipe away the fears. And God holds each tear.
Upon the endless hours of spitting out those pills.
Cradled under the hill. And you try to wipe away the feel.
Now and forever I wish a better knowing.
As so it was showing. And the tears are flowing.
The hatred growing within this abyss.
So I sit here for hours, spitting out those pills.
Consuming this world of shit.

Will You Remember?

So, please tell me what this all means.
What is the means for all of what you see?
I would like an answer, if you please.
But in the end, I only want you to care.
But again, I'm left in the dark - "no one cares."
And the pain begins to tear, away at my soul and heart.
What does this mean? Why am I so far apart?
Why should I go out of my way?
Just so you can enter my world of pains...
But this war is far from over.
In fact, "It has only just begun."
So, what was the purpose to what I have done?
Please - an answer is all I need.
To the question I've been asking all along.
What does it matter, if you don't sing along?
But I won't be gone for long.
Only eternity and still the worm is in me.
Tearing caverns into my soul.
So, please look into this hole and tell me what you see.
Would you care if it weren't me?
Again in the state of mind, in which I live.
I come to know only one simple truth.
Smashed against my knowing.
That it was all worth losing my youth.
So, again I only want an answer to one little question.
I sure do hope it's not too much to ask...

In the end, will you look back?
And remember all the steps you took?
In the end, will any of this ring true?
This is my question, that I ask so dear.
In the end, when all is done.
Will you maybe stop?
And remember all, in which I have done?
Please tell me, I need to know.
Why have I done this, why am I so cold?
I only want an answer, to this little question of mine.
When all is said-done and over.
Will you remember, *The Wars of the Mind..?*

When I'm Gone

I place my feet firmly on the ground.
I set my eyes on the goal, to which I am bound.
Wide aware of the troubles ahead of me.
I hold my heart steady and I think I'm ready.

What was the meaning to all of your tears?
Rolling down your face and throwing me out of place.
And into my nightmares I fell.
What was the purpose, to setting my standards so low?
As now my heart is lost in the snow.
Deep down below and Oh what a fate.
But I think I'm ready, I hope I won't be late.

I place my hands on the headstone.
Aged and the text I can just barely see.
I keep my sights on my goal, to that which I need.
Truly aware of the grim fate that awaits me.
I hold my heart steady and I think I'm ready.

For what purpose did I need to give?
And my eternal damnation you did insist.
And the road seems a bit longer than it ever has.
The headstone has aged "*soon*" only sand.
But that's the fate for you and I.
Smile and cry, weep and die.

To live and be free, to set it right.
To feel the light and end the strive.
For what meaning did I give?
And now to just wash away.
I placed my hands on the gravestone.
Shivers ran to the bone.
I knew the answer and then I turned away.
I dare not look back.
Nothing would be left.

I placed my feet, firmly on the ground.
I set my eyes, to that which I am bound.
So wide aware of the fate that awaits me.
I hold these words firm and steady, now I'm ready.
"When I am gone, will you remember me?"

This Place Within

What is this taste, where is this place?
What an awesome race, who is this face?
Looking me in the soul, what a taste I behold.

What is this place, drawn in lace?
What is this taste, pulling me out of place?
Who is this face, looking up at me?
There he lies under the sea...
"What do you want from me?"

What is this place, racing into my eyes?
Where is this place, from deep within my mind?
Who is left, other than the swine?
Please let me out now, let me untie.
And as I unwind, I turn back to that door.
Blood on the knob, tear-drops on the floor.

Why was it so hard to let it all go?
Why can't the sun melt away the snow?
When will you just let me go?
"Just let me go!"

Where is this place, my broken hole called home?
Who is this face, so hollow and alone?
What is this taste, sour biting on my cheek?
Why is this place, stuck so far within me?

But the hunger never seems to subside.
And the needle's forever shoved inside.
And there I lay on a bed of leaves...
What do you want with me?!!
Why won't you just release me?

What is this taste, in the back of my mouth?
Where is this place, stuck within and out?
Who is this face, tearing at my brain?
Why is this lace, holding me insane?
What's with this place, within my head?
And numb goes the screaming - under my bed...

Infection

It all started with that affection.
Drawing me closer to the last section.
Of my heart and being.
Then the years grew to infection.
Now drawing me closer to the end.
What was the meaning to this infectious noise?
I told you not to come back.
"If you turn that corner then we're over."
But again I welcomed you with open arms...

It all started with that affection.
Drawing me closer to the lesson.
But as I burn I know nothing.
And it sure is funny.
That I can do nothing but speak of this.
What's left now, other than this pain?
I want to get out of this madhouse.
But again the infection stays.

Out from my brain.
The marrow is pulled down.
My body caves in and I tumble away.
I should just fade to gray.
And let the horror stay.
Yet again I fight this infection.
Trying to learn a new lesson.
And hoping that there's something more than this.
I want to end this torment.
And wipe away that last kiss.

Yet there's nothing I can do.
Other than live in sickness...
Forever twisted away from reality and those dreams.
Of maybe rising above the cloud.
But someway and somehow I'll get through the day.
Left here with this infection.
Eating away at my brain...

Three Stones

Slow – steady – cool – "I'm ready."
As the morning dew begins to lay a sheet over our earth.
The screaming-birth, shutdown in the sunrise of her.
And all the monsters run back to their holes.
Finding darkness beneath the leaves.
Away and the winds begin to warm.
As the dew strolls in and kisses your cheek.
Cradling you in her arms, embracing each-other so tight.
Slow and steady heart-beating and I'm ready.
And the sun now stands on top looking down.
And your son dances upon the ash and ground, sand and stone.
Rubbing your heart on a bone, leaving it all alone.
For that reason, I only want you to know.
The morning dew, so soft and cold.
And the dirt and coal - dust and soot.
It screams a story, forever untold as it should.
Forever in the ear of my lover, leaving that child behind.
As so it begins to linger in my mind and I only wish to let it out.
Here I welcome you to my break-down, down so far and out.
For what reason is your lover stabbing me?
And by what means do you have the right to breathe?
But that's just throwing stones and calling names.
What a childish act and you never called me back.
I thank God for each day that I have.
Of holding revenge in my blood-stained hands "It's sweet."
And again with the hours of skipping stones upon the ice.
Lost in the fields of rice, misplaced and gone.
And I could scream this song, yet no one understands.
Again I find myself at a loss of grip...
Yet I will fight for what I believe and you let those pictures go.
The sun begins to melt the film away.
The morning dew gone, evaporated stains.
So I weep a river of tears, now drowning in my fear.
Slow – steady – well... "Are you ready!?"
As your son dances upon the dirt.
I lean back in the memory, screaming-birth.
Years of nothing but hate and love.
Left upon the notion but now it's done.
So I lean back yet again, to enjoy revenge.
I place my hands over my eyes.
As the *Atomic-kiss* brings forth your demise.

In the Back Room

Shakes and shivers, yet it's blazing hot.
You weep and quiver, stuck in shock.
I stood up quietly, hoping you wouldn't see.
I made one noise and you screamed!

You rushed real quickly to find your fix.
Tearing at the mantel and nothing but tears of pain.
You throw around the books on the shelf.
Hoping to escape hell, "Oh what demons have you made?"
There was nothing I could do for you.
I tried to hold you down.

Each touch like a hammer upon your surface.
My porcelain love "what have you done?"
And you stare at me as if we never met.
You push and shove and bite my neck.
No blood drawn but something's wrong.
"What did you do with the woman I love?"

You lie there bleeding from your mouth and nose.
Red eyes and in such a surprise.
Oh what a demise - What utter nonsense before me.
I wanted to help you but you wouldn't let me!
So there I sit, beating my head.
You're lying on the floor, screaming for death.
I wanted nothing more, than to see a smile on your face.
The one that you made when I met you...

Yet you rush to find your fix.
Drowning yourself in the snow.
Left in the dark alone, weeping for hope.
I want nothing more than to hold you tight.
But you shatter so easily, my porcelain-vice.
And you run for the hills, escaping the demons of your past.
I wish I could have saved you.
Yet you flake away, until nothing's left.

Laid in the back room - the memory of her doom...
"Damn I miss you."

A Forgotten Shadow

I feel like the world is against me.
No one seems to be on my side.
There's nothing I can do.
To make the pain subside.
I find no escape, other than this endless page.
Forever stuck in this book.
A story of those loves I lost.
Please God, give me a better thought.

The hand rises out of the darkness.
In dread I begin to shiver.
Yet somehow I find warmth.
Something very tender, holding me in care.
I feel like the world is against me.
"No one seems to care."
In this sea of faces, drowning in despair.
The memory will never leave me alone.
Here with no one at my side.
The forgotten shadow eats me alive.
I feel like a lonely tree in a field of memories.

Everything I seem to know, I never knew.
"Every one has been untrue.
Every one has been untrue."
Even you..!

So what could I do?
Left here with only a forgotten shadow.
Dripping within this hollow mind.
I feel like I should unwind.
And let the torment pass me.
Just a lonely tree, in a field of dreams.
And nothing seems to take it away.
So here I sit, lost in shit. Forever in the gray.

Please God - Remind me.
Please God - Just kill me.
Please God - Help me.
Erase this forgotten shadow.
Take all these memories away.
Please God...
Please.

My Prayer

Lord hear me, please my love, don't fear me...
Lord help me, please my friend, lend a hand...
God save me, it's getting darker with each step...
God wake me, I'm getting colder with each breath...

Hear my prayer, and please show me grace...
Please forgive me for being naïve and growing disgraced...
Oh my lord, hold me close to your heart...
Please my lord, keep me from coming apart...
I know you've been there to see each step I take...
I know you are here to watch each sin I make...

Lord hear me, please my love, don't fear me...
Lord help me, please my friend, be a man...
God save me, it's getting darker with each step...
God wake me, I'm growing colder with each breath...

Hear my prayer, Oh please take me home...
Please forgive me my father, for being a child of sin...
Please my lord, hold me tight and my soul you cleanse...
Show me no more fright and take me back to the light...
I know you were there my lord, as I cursed your name...
I know you are here my lord.
Holding me as I weep in shame...

Hear my prayer my lord, I wish to come home...
Take me back to your side and hold me tight...
I truly am sorry, for being a child of sin...
Yet you and I know nothing will change within...
Hear my prayer my lord, forgive my sins...
Hear my prayer my lord, cleanse my soul...
Hold me tight my lord, please take me home...

Texas Roadside

Dragged out, stumbling along the road.
Held out, hot beating on my soul.
Shoes worn down, melting on the road.
Dragged down, myself I can barely hold.

A long walk, to where? "I don't know."
It's been awhile but I'm still the same.
Pulling myself out of hell, along this highway I sing.
It's been some time but nothing has changed.
On the Texas roadside, holding myself as I sway.
Along a wide road, the heat beating on my soul.

I want nothing more, than to find some shade.
I want nothing more, than to be saved.
I kick a rock to find some faith.
Along this highway, 1,000 miles away from sane.
This Texas roadside - Hot blistering sores on my feet.
Along this roadside a better drive I seek.

Dead-meat boiling in the sun.
A maggot feast of the one laid next to me.
Sorry friend but I have places to go.
Festering carcass melting away the old.
Sorry friend but I have places to be.
Along this Texas roadside. I know that I'm free.
Laid out in the sun, heat beating me dumb.
Sorry friend but I need to leave.
Sorry friend but I must pass up the maggot feast.

Dragged out, stumbling along the road.
Held out, hot beating on my soul.
Shoes worn down, melting onto the road.
Dragged down, myself I can barely hold.

"*The lone star*, yeah that's me..."
Along this highway, a better drive I seek.
And yes it's been awhile, but nothing has changed.
It's good to be home. Along the Texas roadside.
I kick a rock, and my faith I now see...

Eye Gripped to the Stone

You know I just can't take away what I did.
You know that it was what had to be done.
I am sorry for laughing as you came undone.
It shined nice but now it lies under the ice.
You know that I'm sorry, laid under the fright.

Deep in the night, can you hear the beast howl?
Away from the light, in darkness it waits.
For little children like you, "stay out of the woods."
There the beast creeps, hungry for human meat.
Little girls so sweet, this pleasure can't be taken away.

You know I can't just take what I did away.
You know that it was what had to be done.
I am sorry for laughing at you as you came undone.
It shined real nice, now it lies frozen in time.
You know that I'm sorry, laid under the ice.

Far away the monster goes, waiting for you to show.
Years of planning, just to take you down.
He licks his lips and waits for you.
"Little girl, stay out of the woods! Far away..."
Eye gripped to the stone, in darkness he waits.
Please little child, I forbid you to go.
And I weep, as away you stroll...

You know that I can't stop it, nor make it go away.
You know that it's a monster, waiting for a taste.
I am sorry for laughing, as you came undone.
It shined real nice, it's the only one.
You know that I'm sorry and it had to be done...

I warned you but you just wouldn't listen.
I told you of the danger, yet still you ventured.
Now you lay on the leaves, skull wide open.
And on your brain I feast "so damn sweet."
Oh little girl, you'll never learn.
Now in pieces, you begin to decay.
Eye gripped to the stone, spilling out your brain...

All Night

Place me deeper, keep me warm at night.
Hold me tighter, yes that feels real nice.
Let me come inside and no longer feel cold at night.
Place me deeper, within-side her love I hide.

Keep me down to earth and take me to the stars.
Love me forever and some, to show me it's alright.
Show the grace and shove me further into this place.
Oh lord I love this taste, give me a little more.

So far out of the picture but nothing really matters.
Take me to the awesome. Show me a better scream.
Hold me tighter, all night she dreams.
Keep me deep inside and look me in the eyes.

Please tell me a story and rock me to sleep.
Hold me tighter, to the stars we swing.
All night in her grace, a look of bliss on her face.
Hold me in deeper, take me from the grave.

Place me deeper, into her lovely dreams.
Never let go, ride out this evil beast.
Let me come inside, it's getting dark out.
All night we dance to our song.
Midnight upon her dreams.

I love this taste and what an awesome gift.
In your hand I lay it down, what a face I adore.
Whisper it in my ear and wipe away those fears.
Keep me in all night, held in darkness and away from fright.

Keep me warm all night, love me the way you already do.
Kiss me good and hold me close. What a ride - What a night.
Look me in the eyes and show me the bliss on your face.
Bite your lip and hold me in - hold on tight, under the starlight.
All night - all night.

My Sworn Enemy

It's drawing closer to the end.
And I want to just let it go.
I now reap that which I have sown.
I wish I could just let it go and leave it on the stone.
No matter what, this ride just won't quit.
Please let me off at the next stop.
The end draws near and I no longer want to fear.
But the truth still stares me in the eyes.
Creeping throughout my mind, behind the lies.
Please just cut my throat and laugh.
Please just push me off and let it pass.
Pull the trigger and I fade away.
Stuck in this boat, all alone with only you.
Please tighten the noose and watch me swing.
You, the only thing I've had in life.
Shake the mirror and wipe away the shame.
Please give me darkness and let me go.
The end draws near. I no longer want to fear.
You are the only thing I've had in life.
Please push in deeper your knife.
I no longer want this strive.
And no matter how much I fight.
The answers are still the same.
You are my sworn enemy "to the grave."
Please just choke me, till life is no longer here.
Please pull the trigger and wipe away the fear.
By God's good name, you were once my love.
I hold this in my heart, as I crumble apart.
I no longer want this life, the end is soon.
Please turn off the lights, in darkness I wait.
You are the only thing I've had all along.
My sworn enemy, with my face in your hands.
Take my youth and wipe it on the curb.
Truly, I don't care anymore. I just want this to stop.
I'm drawing closer to the end now.
The lights flicker and dim.
I'm getting closer to the end now.
Fighting my sworn enemy within...

This Living Death

I can't escape this, all of what has come to pass.
I can't fight this and pull it from my back.
I can't just end it, what would happen to you?
I can't just turn back, truly I've had no youth.

In living death, without a breath.
Finding no home, under the stone.
What a twisted nature, of eating human flesh.
What's with this hatred and this living death?

You can't escape this, all of what we did.
You can't fight this and shove it deeper into my back.
You can't just end it, what would happen to me?
You can't just turn back, then swallowed by the leaves.

In living death, without a breath.
Under the mistake, drowning in your hate.
What a twisted nature, reality torn away.
What's with all this hatred and this living death within me?

So Sick...

I feel I'm coming close to the end.
I know the tide has gone, growing thin.
I watch the clouds drift by and my old loves die.
I have only to see the destruction of your world.

Now your son stands on the horizon.
And there is nothing for us to say.
I sit here with my arms crossed.
So sick... Growing a new form of decay.

I feel I'm coming to a checkpoint.
I know there is nothing for me to say.
Maybe I'll find a way out of here and into the clear.
Please, show me a new drive.
Please give me destruction, bring forth my demise.
The clouds drift by and your son begins to cry.
Standing on the edge, what a monster you have made.
Please end this torment and give me back my brain;

Take my pain and cover it in salt.
Please give me an answer, to all that I've asked.
I feel the blood begin to boil.
So sick... I just can't take it.
I know that there is some sort of meaning.
As the trees speak my name.
I know that there is a bigger meaning.
Please take away this pain.

I feel I'm coming close to the end.
I know the tide has gone, growing thin.
I watch the clouds drift by and my old loves die.
I have only to see the destruction of your world.
Now the sun lays on the horizon.
There is nothing for me to say.
I sit here with my arms crossed.
So sick... Growing a new form of decay.

Behind My Eyes

Darkness... Above all in the room, laying a blanket of shadow.
The hopeless - such a wonder that this is still the same.
So damn pointless, what was the meaning to all of this?
Give me an answer, I'm tired and need to lie down.
Please just go away and end this torment of my brain.
The hour is longer and the blood tastes the same.
Darkness above it all, dust, mold and decay.

A lonely man with no face, a pointless life with no faith.
A hopeless act of my dismay, a rusty ax forever bloodstained.
Behind my eyes, the hidden truth.
Forever in despise and there... Is where you'd find my youth.
Please take my life and give me death.
Please take that knife and shove it into my chest.
I have no breath, the walls are caving in.
It's getting darker, I can just barely see.
I'm fading quicker, colder with each breath.
Truth is behind my eyes - and the answers are in death...

The Dead Empire

Damn! So that's all I have to say after this.
The tower now falls, the dream was a miss.
And nothing could replace this.
Damn you for thinking you could.
Nothing will replace this and nothing should...

I'm fighting it all, beaten and bruised.
Laid on the ground bleeding in pain.
Left alone in the darkness with only shame.
And my kingdom begins to rot.
Fester of the hopes I once held so dear.
And after it all, that's the only thing I could say.
"Damn you all" get out of my face.
I swing as hard as I can, hoping there's something to hit.
Left here all alone, to drown in your shit.
So should I just quit and walk away from that dream?
It's easy for you to say that "just get the hell away from me!"

Nothing could replace it and nothing will.
I've been beaten too much. These wounds will never heal.
So I stand here alone and watch my kingdom fade away.
It was my dream, now just a steaming pile of decay.
There is nothing to take its place.
"Damn you for thinking you could."
Nothing can replace my dead empire "as nothing should."

Hopeless Little Girl

In the end, who will ever stop to remember her name?
In the end, who will care about that hopeless little girl?
In the end, who will care about her wretched face?
In the end, will anyone stop to remember her name?
In the end, who would care about her pointless life?
In the end, who would care about this pointless strive?
In the end, what is the meaning to what we say?
In the end, who would care about this pointless fate?
In the end, will the story make any sense?
In the end, would anyone care about her dreams?
In the end...
Who would care about that hopeless little girl's screams?

Tooth and Bone

My arms shoved through the wall. A torn painting at the end of the hall.
My heart and head in perfect flux. Tooth and bone tearing away at your luck.
Pride broken over the edge of the table. Truth hiding beneath each fable.
All the nightmares come forth to break me down.
My soul broken "just a heartless clown."
My skin flakes off and in the wind it fades.
Torn down in the prime of life. Left at your side with only shame.
Under my tongue goes the pain. Beneath the blade goes the hate.
Metallic warmth bringing me home. *Burnt pencils - a stale lingering smoke.*
Under tooth and bone. No hope - no hope.
Where can I find you and when can I look?
Was there any purpose, to the slaughter in my brain?
Between tooth and bone, eternal insanity and pain.
So thrown to the wolves, is my heart and dreams.
Laid beneath the water, fading in the stream.
So go ahead and rape my dreams, in front of God's eyes.
Go ahead and take my life, I've had quite enough.
Now tooth and bone. Head and heart, in perfect flux.

Unclean / Un-free

Three inches of dust, laid a blanket covering my head.
Deep in the slime and sludge, festering on my breath.
Nine spine tangled webs holding in each piece.
God wipe me down, forever unclean, so un-free.
Give me a shower. Please rub away the stain.
Please take my heart out and clean it in the stream.
Please take the acid and wash away my face.
Light the torch and burn away my faith.
Forever unclean, forever un-free. Left in the darkness with only me.
Laid in the shadow, please wipe away my fears.
Please clean my soul and scrub away the past years.
I only want some freedom and maybe some hope.
I would like an answer and warmth in this cold.
Please wipe away my nightmares and free my head.
Please wipe my soul clean and end the dread.
Three inches of dust, laid a blanket of decay.
Left deep in the slime where my love should stay.
Nine little hopes but then they are all pissed away.
God wipe me down, wash away the stain.
Forever unclean, forever un-free...

For Her Majesty

Flustered - lain down on the leaves of the old.
So frustrated, freezing my soul.
On now and it's my damnation, left forever cold.
Drinking down these demons, watching them drown and die.
Enjoying the torment of my liver and lungs.
Knowing the soon end, wanting it done.
And for her majesty, I shall dance upon my grave.
Only by the moonlight will my soul be saved.
Drinking the dust of the grave.
Only in her eyes can I find a reason to breathe.
It was for her good grace, forever fused to my being.
And nothing will ever take its place.
Consuming the smoke and losing my faith.
Religion of the little voices screaming at night.
Far in the back of my head.
Drinking the smoke, until I am dead.
Left here frozen to the floor, stuck to the ground like a pill.
Knowing that only her warmth can bring me from hell.
So on seeping the nails, knowing this love is mine.
It is for her majesty that I shall rip out my spine.
Only for her good grace will I burn alive.
Here tied to the stake, melting away the hate.
Mind-torn, on the edge of those hopes of this grave.
So grim and it stares me in the eyes.
Choking down another shot, eating the bad lime.
And I stop it on a dime, hoping to unwind.
Only to see my skin burn away.
So I tilt back once more to accept my fate.
And for her majesty, I will dance till death.
Knowing that I have only her love in my chest.
Lungs caving and bones aching.
I cannot stand up straight, I cannot see.
I know that the lime wasn't clean.
I know that those words were the only truth I know.

Please my love shine me hope.
And take this taste and turn it sweet.
Oh what a tang, of human flesh and meat.
So over the stones goes the story.
And only by the moonlight will it be told.
Forever I am left here in tragedy. Forever in love with Her Majesty.

Never Forgiven

It was on that old thought, that I once again took a walk.
Into the twilight of this unforgettable daze.
I hope once more to escape this haze.
Wanting nothing more than to lie down and go to sleep.
I wish nothing more than to erase these thoughts.
I wish nothing more than to cure this disease.

Onward these images haunt me.
Reminding me that all is lost and so am I.
I have nothing more to do than sit here and cry.
Looking back at those faces I will never forget.
Remembering those words and feeling so sick.
So now once again I'm on this road I know "Oh so well."
I wish I could escape this and just go to hell.

Endless needles shoved into my brain.
Reminding me of this eternal pain, "Oh what a haze..."
So with one foot in front of the other.
I stroll onward and hope to end this strive.
Maybe in the darkness, maybe in this light.
I want to search but have nothing to find.
I need to escape and erase this from my mind.
But I can remember those words.
God knows I will never forget.
Eternally I am never forgiven, "*not for what I did.*"

So I jump back two years or so, to see the truth unfold.
So there I am, laid with blood stained hands.
So there she is and just one more kiss.
Nothing could have changed the outcome.
Only a lie I just could not say.
Truth has damned me forever and I scream.
Touching her fingers, she was kissing my neck.
We made love one last time.
Only for me to lose everything and die.

It was cold and I will never forget,
All of those so called brothers / friends.
On top of the world and they all jumped.
Left me all alone, "forever just a broken man."
And I tried my hardest, not to lose them all.
But I have now only heart-ache, awaiting the fall;

I live on with this utter nonsense.
Knowing that this is all I deserve.
Forever never forgiven, just like her.
I'm walking onward, into the darkness of my mind.
Hoping for hope, just wasting my time...
Was there nothing I could have said?
Was there something I could have done?
Why is it that I gave away everything and now I'm just one?

I stood at the doorway. She said she would call me back.
She laid there, weeping behind me. I just could not look back.
"*Always & Forever*," was the last thing I would say.
Now I walk forward into this maze.

So she found comfort and what could I say?
I fought and died, forever in pain.
And all that I said, driving me to death.
Pushed and shoved, to break its neck.
Oh what a nightmare, "I want to awake!"
But here I am, moving onward into my shame.
Never forgiven for a pointless night.
Now left in damnation, forever in strive.

I got a phone call once, it was an old friend.
She wanted some answers "did she really have to call me?"
I gave my views, only to once again lose.
All of everything that I know.
Forever my soul is lost in the snow and where should I go?
Please give me an answer, to all of my youth.
So now this cancer is driving me into my tomb.
For all of you to see, walking forward towards revenge.
Never forgiven for what I did.

I loved you all only to lose. I died in the frost, hoping to save you.
The road of leaves was only the start.
Into the truth of my dismay. I took another walk into the day.
Hoping to find hope, in the darkness or in the light.
I've never forgotten the *truth* of her and me.
"I've never forgiven her - because she has never forgiven me."

Chapter 5

"No Escape"

His Name

A little cricket named Jesus Christ.
Screaming in my ear, pulling me from wrong to right.
These are the things I live by. These are the words I write.
Who is wrong and who is right?
Since when has it been mandatory to push all of those out of the picture?
All of whom are not of their pretty world.
There must be a point where the nonsense stops.
There must be a reason for all of your shames.
And he has so many names, call him what you will.
And forever more these words bring me to the hill.
Place me on the leaves and sing into my ear.
Lord, give me an answer to why I'm still here...
It's not a test, this is no game. Hold me please and let me escape.
I want some downtime, away from this place.
Yet in the end, I am stuck with this fate.

Trying to Run

Awake... The wind howls through my mind.
The dust begins to cover my eyes. There is nothing to do but accept this fate.
To bring forth the metallic warmth and to just run in place.
Miles of nowhere, I just can't leave.
It's hard to get over it, when my enemy is me.
I rush so frantic, just to get nowhere fast.
Trying to run and never looking back.
Waist deep in the sands of my youth.
Nothing being done, just my mind burning you.
The wind howls through my mind.
The dust begins to cover my eyes.
There is nowhere to go, when you're never alone.
There is nowhere to hide, when you're lost inside.
I try to run but I'm stuck in place. Trying to run but can never escape.
Miles of nowhere, I just can't go.
Escaping to nowhere, waist deep in the snow.
I can't complain, when I'm not alone.
I can't escape, when I'm on my own.
There's nowhere to go when you're inside of yourself.
There's no way to win, when you're locked in hell.
Trying to run but getting nowhere fast.
I try to escape and be freed at last.
But there's nothing I can do, when my time has run out;

There is nothing I can do because I'm left out.
There's nowhere to run, when my enemy is myself.
I can't burn you away, when I'm already in hell.
There is no escape, from all of my fears.
There is no other way, to escape those years.
There is nothing, to wipe clean the tears.
The dust covers all and I'm left behind again.
I can't escape myself, not while *I'm* still locked within.

Pointless Screaming

There is no more point to what I do.
Forever left to commence your doom.
So only to be here for pain and demise.
To cut away your flesh and see your surprise.

Filthy humans with your endless suffer. Pathetic creatures stuck in a rut.
Bound and gagged, hogtied and hung out to dry.
Stuck on a limb, beaten upright. Tied up real good, blindfolded in fright.

Guided by the moonlight. I peel off your skin, one layer at a time.
Lust by the moonlight. I eat your flesh before your very eyes.
Taking my time, seeping your pointless screams.
Filthy human pigs, such a disgrace to me.

I am the demon you hate. I am the monster you love.
I was once an angel of pure. Now I stand at your door.
Guided by the ghosts, on my way.
Scraping at your skull, to get to the brain.
Loving your pain, you shake endless, bleeding away your life.
Laughs standing on the tip of my tongue.
Awaiting purification of the sun.

I take this blade and ram it into your chest.
Hearing your lungs fill with blood. Seeing the death on your breath.
It's pointless to run, when your legs are sawed off.
It's pointless to scream. You shall get no pity from me.
Don't take it the wrong way. I hope I did not offend you.
It's just pointless for you to scream. When no one can hear you...

Kissing Death On the Lips

Can you tell me where I am, my friend? The mist is starting to stain the glass.
How long has it been my friend, since the beginning of this joyride?
Can you tell me my friend, where the answers hide?
And so the gravity flows above our flesh.
Smooth friction and skin against skin.
"Here it starts and here it will end."
Until all the questions surface and death becomes my bride.
For all of which may have meaning. For all of which reflects my pride.
Can you tell me my friend, where I am now?
The haze is growing thicker. I hope a better grip.
Please pull over "I think I'm gonna be sick..."
And so here it starts and this is where it'll end.
Thrown down on the hood of our ride.
Kissing death on the lips. *"Kissing our reality good-bye."*

The Glory of Death

Well, I guess there could have been a better way.
But that's all done now, left in the shade.
I hope we can move beyond it now and just leave it be.
So take my hand and place it on your heart.
I can feel your breast begin to sweat. I can taste the glory from off your breath.
Slow and gentle, I begin running my hand up your leg.
To step into the God's place of grace.
I kiss your neck and your heart it does race.
"I think there could have been a better way to say this."
But in the end, who would know the truth?
So I just shove my tongue into the house of the Gods.
I begin to tango with Death and Fate. I leave to sleep away the fear of the grave.
Well, I guess there could have been a better way.
But that's all done now, left in the shade.
I know we are moving beyond it now and only just a step away from grace.
Writhe my love and in the dark I dance.
Place your tongue into my mouth, speak the words of truth for me.
Please sing me that song once more and let it seep through my ears.
Now left with only glory of no more fears.
Stuck with this nightmare, riding me into the ground.
I place the key, just where it should be.
Ramming the nonsense as hard as it ever could.
Regurgitating the emotions upon the stars.
Left now with the glory of death *"well, I guess I went a little far..."*

When the Bones Break

"Hello........" Am I too late?
Where did everyone go?
"Please don't hide from me."
Damn it's getting cold and the monster is still behind me!

To where does the thought go?
When it starts to break the bone.
And now the clock throws the pills back at me...
"Fuck you and your acid-face!" Your dirty hopes and filthy lips!

"God, can you light my cigarette from there."
No... please don't get up.
No, it's all fine - Hell's just around the corner.
"I'll pick you up something to drink."

"Hello....." Is anyone home?
Shit! Tell me that I'm at the right place...
So to where do the feelings go.
When the bones begin to break?

Holy fuck in a handbag.
Tell me that you're still alive!
God, can you tell me a bedtime story.
And give me my stuffed doll...
Her name was very pretty.
But I just can't seem to remember.

"Hello...." Damn it's getting cold.
Are you out there or am I alone?
Shut your damn hole and piss off!
Take that switchblade and place it between your legs!

Hey - I know that song....
My Ex sang it once "but I think she did it wrong."
Well - who gives a shit anyway?
And to where does all the pain go...
When the bones begin to break?

Alone In Bed

It was a little bug.
Just an insignificant little waste of God's time.
It crawled into my mouth and found its home in my lung.
So then I awoke, slam!
I was stunned...

Tossing and turning, left and right.
The mattress smells like old sweat and liquor.
This pillow feels hard and reminds me of back then.
Just years of pointless sin.
Endless bottles shoved down my throat.

I want to reach over and hold her tight.
But no one's there, just another lonely night.
So again I rest in the fright of knowing that I am alone.
It was that horror that opened this hole.

It was a demon.
Just an insignificant little waste of God's time.
It just climbed up into my bed and made its home in my head.
Then I awoke, slam!
I wanted to choke, spitting out the smoke.

I toss and turn.
Until the sun begins to rise.
I dream in fear, until the haze brings on the tears.
I shake and tremble yet I'm burning up.
I lay in bed, still I'm up...
There I am, alone in bed.
I want to reach over and hold her tight.
But no one's there, just endless fright.

So I weep, until the tears drown all my fears.
I begin to drift slowly away.
Only to find... I'm still awake.

A Little Birdy Said

Damn, you wouldn't believe what I just heard.
A little birdy, just so happened to fly my way.
Sang me a song, of things I just didn't want to hear.
A song of a truth, that brings only fear.

Walking along a park sidewalk.
Strolling to see what just might be.
To learn a story of you... not me.

Of all that may be set in stone.
I don't think it true that you're alone.
But in the end, I have nothing to lose.
I know what you're thinking and still you're confused.

A little birdy said, that my love is still alive "*not dead.*"
But is it fact or only a dream?
Please my friend, continue to sing.
And bring me the answer to what I fear.
Take me onward into that haze.

Damn, you wouldn't believe what I just heard.
Whispered into my ear, swinging me into fear.
A little birdy told me a story.
Of the fact that I still love you... "*I just laughed.*"
Now left in dread, of this story of death.

Walking along a park sidewalk.
Strolling to see what just might be.
To learn a truth of me... not you.

Of all that may be set in stone.
I know you're happy while I'm alone.
So now little birdy, please take my life and just fly away.
Just fly away, just fly away, just fly away.
Fly...

Would You Like Some Tea?

Welcome back, was your trip very long?
Please sit back and put your feet up. Relax and tell me how it went.
Would you like some tea? "Please tell me."
Dragging your feet along the road.
It must have brought you to what you sought.
I bet it was hard to see what you saw.
To step into the past and feel so un-free... "Would you like some tea?"
Pulling that load on your back, knowing death is behind each step.
Fearing that fall to the wayside. Knowing that you have nothing but time.
Much like your reflection called me. "Well, would you like some tea?"
Please don't get up, it looks like you've been to hell and back.
So weak, with that load on your back.
Of all those memories you try to hide but you could never lie to me.
So my friend, "*would you like some tea?*"

Howling at the Crosswalk

Summer treats, old rotted meat.
Throw me a bone, now buried under the stone.
Give me affection and I'll be eternally devoted.
Not to let anyone near, only what you say is right.
I'll know nothing other than your demands.
Please give me that honor and I'll die at your command.
Tied to a chain of our eternal love.
Brought to the park so we can stretch our legs.
Now I'm growing old but you're the same.
Taken to the funhouse of where we met.
Howling at the crosswalk, feeling so sick.
I was just a child then and I'd have done anything for a bone.
But you came along and took me home.
Please, give me a treat, "*old rotted meat.*"
Now I want only your affection to hold me tight as I dream.
Command it, anything you want of me. You say it and it shall be.
Just show me warmth and I'll be at your side.
Show me love and on your command I would die.
Summer treats, sweet rotted meat.
Nature dancing in my ears. All the beauty of those years.
Now devoted to my love full and true.
I was howling at the crosswalk and you brought me home with you.
Forever devoted, to my love simple and true.
Just show me love and I will love you too.

Eight Years Ago

On a downward spiral.
Right where my life should be.
Draining away and left un-free.
It was eight years ago and nothing has changed but me.
"Or maybe it's the other way around."

It was long ago, when I felt warm - not cold.
And that face will haunt me till the day I die.
It was all the thought of a child called me.
But now I'm in hell, right where I should be.

I'd dream if I could but I have only this knife.
I'd plan ahead but I'm already dead.
And it was all for her smile, which I tore away.
I know I'm guilty and left in shame.

It was eight years ago.
When I was warm and growing cold.
But in the end, I alone - know the truth...
Eight years ago, destroying my youth.
Taking that blade into her mouth.
Loving the taste of warm blood.
Now draining, like it should.

Eight years ago I had a love.
It was the one called me.
Now on a downward spiral.
Right where my soul should be.
Left in the darkness with only me.
But I am truly sorry, for the life I took.
I am truly sorry but I'm just a forgotten book.

Her smile haunts me forever now.
I am happy I get to see her face.
Yet again I remember that taste.
Of fate growing deep in my lung.
Only to know, I'll always be just one.

Now I can see, the monster called me.
You were right and so was she.
So please, oh please, God please.
"Just kill me..."

Hammering a Screw

There might have been a dream.
There must have been a scream.
To echo in the darkness of where my soul should be.
There could have been a fight.
There must be a source of light.
To echo in the darkness of where my heart should be.

And it just hammers on me.
Pushing when you needed to pull.
Wishing the glass was half full.
Knowing that you can't hammer a screw.
Endlessly labeled as a fool.
And the ice begins to cover.
And the fire of hell could never melt away my soul.
Forever lost in the snow.

There might have been a dream.
There must have been a scream.
To echo in the darkness of where my soul should be.
There could have been love.
She should have stayed above.
And echo the dreams where my heart should be.

And the tears hammer on this paper sheet.
The rain turning to sleet.
You know, you just can't hammer a screw.
Why must you push when you need to pull?
And again I'm just a fool.
Left for the torment I deserve.
You can't hammer a screw.
I do wish this pain not upon you.

There must have been a fight.
There must be darkness in the light.
It could have been a dream.
There must have been a scream.
To echo in the darkness, right where my heart used to be.
To echo in the darkness when my love leaves me.
And these tears hammer on this paper sheet.
You can't hammer a screw.
You just can't do this to me...

Yet Again...

Torn eyelids and broken dreams.
Salt in an open wound... It's nothing new to me.
Why must time play this game with my heart? Yet again, I fall apart.

Moon-lust upon the bone-dust.
Given and all was as it should be.
So give me a verse and send me to hell.
Left in torment, so overwhelmed.

Break me over the headstone.
I would like to go home now.
Rain the blood over her wrist.
So I can lick the hate off the ground.

Side-mind, lost in a lord-trust.
Death is death and this it must.
So turn around and give me a hand.
Break the world in two and I do love you... Yet again, only I lose.

Only One Way!

A fire is hottest when first lit.
A romance is most precious... *But I'm full of shit.*
Behind the paint is a better picture but there's no way to reach it.
My head is pounding. The light is burning my eyes.
Why is it that I never know what to say?
When you're around I hold myself down "and wish for a release."
So by the ax I rest. Frozen in time and left in a lie.
And God, why am I damned for telling the truth?
There is no other way - I cannot save you.
So I drink down the shame, consuming the smoke of yesterday.
There is only one way! To take it all back and erase what we did.
And on this ledge I begin to shake.
The noose growing tighter around my neck.
So this is the only way! To save my soul and forget yesterday.
I wish you were here to see my face.
I wish I were there at your side, "it's too dark now."
I reach and reach but so damn blind...
A fire is hottest when first lit.
"Our love meant everything." *But I'm full of shit.*
Behind the paint lies a better fate. But there's only one way to reach it.

No Exit

Rush, fast, get out!
The monster is still coming.
You need to escape.
Please run while you can.
And the staircase is beginning to decay.
Please leave while you can.
The devil has no sympathy.
And the ash begins to fall.
A death-cloud.
The hate is falling.
Bringing me down.
There is no way.
You can't out run it.
So just pray...
Because death plays no favorites.
And fate is a cruel mistress indeed.
So hold on tight.
The monster draws near.
Close your eyes to accept your fears.
Running deeper beneath a frozen lake.
And all the questions are hidden in death.
All the answers found in life.
Run if you wish.
Head towards the light.
You find a door...
Locked and you see the decay of the roof and floor.
All the walls are breaking.
The pressure is building.
The smoke is filling the halls.
Scream if you will, as all your hopes fail.
At the end of the lobby.
You see a door.
The ceiling is falling.
Soon at the floor.
So you come to a door, hoping an end.
To all of this death and mayhem.
The ground is shaking.
The walls are braking.
You reach for the doorknob.
And read the sign.... "No Exit."

Damn..!

Behind These Bars

Judgmental but all is still a miss.
Sub-mental and those pains I'll not soon miss.
Her tensions, rising to their peek.
Under pressure, that's nothing new to me.

Locked in the darkness, with no one but me.
Left in the corner, with only needles in me.
The room's growing cold, the air so heavy.
Now I have only me, I need now only to see.

So where was it, when the pill rolled down my throat?
Where were you, when I started to choke?
Why was it, that fate took you away?
Why is it, that I'm left with no escape?

Behind these bars, I feel only remorse.
Behind this face, you'll find only disgrace.
Beyond this life, lies only demise.
Behind these words, will they ever find truth?
"Behind these words, with only you..."

A Demon on Her Tongue

It smiles and I begin to grind my teeth.
You cry and I want only to release. In denial, yet no one cares but me.
And it smiles, blowing a kiss to me. The mint on the tip of her lungs.
And the demon dancing on her tongue, spewing its lies right to my face.
Behind a smile, growing away from faith.

It smiles and I begin to clinch my fist.
You're crying and your escape is all I wish.
An ax in fine grip. An answer beneath each slit.
And on her tongue the demon sits.
The moment thrown to the gutter.
And God waits for the bus to arrive but you sit there and try to lie.
Pointless, no more hope I see.

Because I cared, I was thrown to the side.
Because I loved you once. I died for the honor of who loved who more.
And the demon laughs, as we lie there dead on the floor.

Faces!

2 - Dark... It's too dark to see.
The line between - I walk and scream.
So many faces around, I wish to escape. This, to which I am bound.
You the world I crush. Till your skull - Twists - busts.
Family, heartache - "Head-loss!" Running between...
Dark room, closed! All alone - you don't understand.
Scream as I may - scream as I must. It is you, I wish to dust.

A Bullet For Me

Just give it, so I can die and leave.
Just shut it, and get the hell away from me.
Take that bullet, and push it through my brain.
Kiss me on the heart and just tear me apart.
So take this nonsense from me, tear away my soul...
"This bullet is for me."

Don't

Call me.

Kill me.

Hug me.

Burn me.

Love me.

Leave me.

Please don't walk away.

Please don't walk away.

Heal me.

Feel me.

Take me.

Kiss me.

Be me.

Hold me.

Hurt me.

Beat me.

Love me.

Need me.

Please don't walk away.

Please don't walk away. I'm so cold...

In Chains

Fused to the core.
Knowing the face of this whore.
Tied up and the mood's right.
Beaten real good.
Lust by the moonlight.

I can't move.
And no one's here to see.
I can't scream.
Open mouth and all bleeds.
So un-free.
Justice as blind as me.

Hold me tight.
Chain me to the floor.
And kiss me goodnight.
So set it right.
And the notion brings itself forth.
Nothing more.
Just fused to the core.

Chain me to the train track.
Kiss me sweet, then laugh.
Chain me to the bedpost.
Squeeze real tight.
Rip me open, to see the light.

Lust by the right wish.
The gun loaded with their shit.
So chain me to the wall now.
Call me hollow and shake me down.
So give me the answers and free me true.
Chain me to your fate and the love will follow soon.

Where No One Can Find Me

Decades of mold.
Years of stories untold.
But mine's a keeper indeed.
Laid next to the atomic smile.
I now dig deeper to escape this denial.

Under the ice, next to the tool.
Beneath the torment.
Where no one can find me.
I dig faster and no one's behind me.

For all of those faces.
I try to leave them in the dark.
Now all of this racing.
Each word tearing me apart.

Lost in the romance.
Left here for you to beat away.
Loving the taste of comfort.
Where no one can find me.

It's next to the answer.
But the question you'll never acquire.
I left it in the darkness.
To age over time.

So the rust to lime.
The bones begin to grind.
Placed under your teeth.
Rotted natures festering within me.
And years of laughing.
While the miles just pass me.
So I stroll further within me.
I dig deeper inside.
Where no one can find me...

Not Dead Yet

These pens can't help me.
No longer will the papers shelter this mind.
The vibrations confusing.
The 13th hour bringing demise.

You can't out run it.
Only pray for God to give a damn.
We can't just kill it.
Nor could we rip off the limbs.

I won't stop you.
But you're making a mistake.
I can't just love you.
No, it's too late - too late.

Under the acid rainfall.
Millions of pills beating on me.
A rising sun and darkness falls.
These thoughts consume me.

I'm not dead yet.
But hopefully soon.
I'm not dead yet.
Just awaiting noon.
"For the hour-hand to strike upright."
"For all the confusion, to be set aside."
I'm not dead yet.
But really soon.
It's not done yet.
I'm just awaiting noon.

These notions, you just can't wipe away.
So my hands are stained red.
Never to wash away.
I'm not dead yet.
But I'm in my grave.
It's not over yet...
Not over yet.
Not over yet.
Not over yet.
"Just a step away."

Drinking From the Hourglass

Hours away, from the right turn of fact.
It's been hours a day and still at a lack.
Of the emotion that brings me closer to you.
For each teardrop that rains onto me.
I await the ice-storm to set me free.

Every second that passes.
My eyes roll to the back of my head.
Hours of throwing out these thoughts.
And every word pushing me to death.

And for that heartache.
Pouring the sand over my head.
Just hours of watching.
And now I am dead.

Because you loved me.
That's why I'm burned here alive.
Because you loved me.
That is why I die.

Just days of drinking from the hourglass.
Hoping it will bring me to life.
Just days of chewing at the back of my eyelids.
Knowing that I'll go blind.

So I tilt back and swallow down the sands.
Hoping it will bring me closer to you.
Just days of drinking from the hourglass.
Knowing my fate lies with you...

Rage #3

Lost dreams but they're mine.
Lonely screams, wasting time.
Hopeless wants, of a demon inside.
Festering corpse and needles in my mind.

Broken jaw, of what she held dear.
Shattered thoughts, drowning in fear.
Hatred raging and growing inside.
Demons fusing, the nails shoved in mind.

Now it pulsates, the heart is beating on the knife.
Now you're too late and out of time.
Rage of a monster within-side.
Your hopes dying before your very eyes.

Time's a bastard with no remorse.
God gave an answer, for each and every whore.
Yet you will never listen, only fade away.
I could break it and tremble.
As I place it into the grave.

Hatred growing and tearing at my flesh.
The corpse begins to fester, growing sweet.
Ripe as it ever has been.
The monster proceeding, from under my skin.
Purple moons of Saturn, kissing me on the lips.
And I place my hand inside and tug on that broken rib.

Sin of the voice that holds you true to that.
Scream if you wish but nothing will be left.
Biting down and consuming your flesh.
Call me a devil if you will.
But nothing can stop this monster from hell.

Held Down

Held down for all to see.
Beaten down, rocks thrown at me.
A screaming child.
No friends for me.
A lonely child.
Beaten as I screamed.

A scapegoat, for all your regrets.
A sideshow, to get your kicks.
Stones were thrown.
Against my, skull now bleeds.
So they tied the rope.
And now I swing.

Held down for all to see.
Naked on the playground, rocks thrown at me.
A bleeding child.
No hope in sight.
A scared child.
With no lights, just fright.
Beaten down.
Laughing all around.

Just a sideshow, to get your kicks.
Just a freak-show, to take out your shit.
Beaten all day, finding no rest at night.
Left in fear, of their face.
Knowing not how to fight.

Stand tall one day.
The rope tied tight.
I stood tall one day.
And Oh, to my surprise.
I swung there all day.
Just for the birds, to peck out my eyes.

Chopped to The Knee

Rush me the spice.
Throw me the dice.
Hit me in the throat.
Watch me as I choke.
For all the hours free.
And the demons hunting me.

Chop me to the knee.
Watch me as I scream.
Laugh while I bleed.
And puke on top of me.

No escape for the damned.
No rest for the dead.
No hope... Off with my head.
And hours of these lies.
So just laugh as I die.
Scream as I bleed.
And dream as I wander away.

Chop me to the knee.
There can be no escape for me.
And hopeless is my life.
Read me gone and burn away my eyes.

Chop me to the knee.
Lord Jesus help me.
Chop me to the knee.
And I pray to be free.
Hopeless as I wait.
Next to the devilish snake.

So I'm left alone in hate.
Hating your every thought.
So laugh as I bleed and rot.
Scream as I bitch and die.
So I'm chopped to the knee.
And burned alive.

Eating the Ash

Long a day, as so many before it.
Miles away and days before it.
Warm in my lung and cold in my heart.
Dark in the night and black in the sun.

I'm eating the ashes, to taste my fate.
I'm burning my eyelids.
And you're laughing at me.
So turn the page, to find a better hope for me.

I'm eating the ashes, to taste your hate.
I'm consuming the needle, to know the truth.
Stuck in my heart, for every thought you scream.
I'm eating the ashes, to bring you closer to me.

A Broken Frame

Red - that lingering thought in my head.
White is all that's left in the end.
Blood stained on my face.
And love stuck in my hands.

A picture that just won't leave me be.
A word that forever haunts me.
Her lips forever stuck to mine.
Those smiles frozen forever in time.

It's been years and I still beat my own head.
It was a nice thought but now it's dead.
Because we are human and nothing more.
Because I loved her, now I'm a bore.

What a great thought of her and me.
But that frame is broken.
Just like me.

Embrace the Monkey

Clinched to my bone.
A broken thought, a lonely home.
Pages of nonsense, or only my fate.
Years of turmoil, just fused to my brain.

What a load on my back.
Still I'm at a lack of reach.
To the knife in my spine.
And the demon behind me.

Would it be better, if I just took the blame?
Would you like it better, if it were me?
Should I grab that blade and shove it into me?
I should embrace these thoughts, to set them free.

Off my case, so get out of my face!
I'm not in place but I'm starting to feel fine.
This monkey won't leave. I'm forever in a bind.
But it's okay, for me to die inside.
It makes for another page...

So I guess I'm fine.
The pain will cost only my life.
The hurt is only in my mind.
I'll embrace the monkey, to free my mind.
I'll embrace the knowing, I am alone inside.
So I embrace this fate, because it is mine.

Clinched to the bone.
A broken heart, a shattered soul.
Pages of torment but it's only in my head.
Years of this nonsense, groping me till death.

I embrace this demon, to let it free.
I embrace this fate and keep it to me.
I'm left in the back, just out of reach.
I'm left in the dark, with this monkey on me.
I'm frozen cold but it's all fine.
I'll embrace this fate, because it is mine.

Chapter 6

Over the Edge I Go

Hold That Thought

I would say what I want to say.
And I would do what I want to do.
Yet in the end, I know it would only hurt you.

Would you like me to be myself?
Or do *demons* drive you away?
What do you want from me?
What would you like me to say?
Please God, give me a hand to hold.
Give me something. Reason or a drive.
And over the edge I go.
Sorry to all, sorry to you.

A Simple Love

Why won't it stop screaming in my soul?
Loud dripping in my ear.
Winding deeper into my fears.
And no one's here.
Where I would love to be.
Someone please, set me free.

Shut the demons up and let me die.
This angel is in front of me.
But I've ripped out my own eyes.

I lost the time, I had a life.
But now I'm dead.
And waiting to die.
I want to live but still I cry...

On My Way to Nowhere

It's been a long trip. I think I should rest my eyes.
Before I miss the next step and fall away in surprise.
It sure has been a while since I've seen your face.
It sure has been a lifetime, still clouded in shame.
But not to worry, I just need a little rest.
To shut out the voices and empty my chest.

I'm on my way, to find what I seek.
I'm on my way again, into the festering abyss.
So I take my next step, hoping I won't miss.
For dreaming all day and working all night.
I'm on my way again, to find me some light.

Into the *Nothing*. I feel my soul slip away.
Deeper into the darkness. Where my body should stay.
And again I feel the heartbreak. Every time I turn around.
And I wish I had an answer. To what you found out.

On my way to *Nowhere*. To find what I seek.
I'm on my way to *Nowhere*. Hoping you'll meet me.
So I run into *Nowhere*. Hoping I'll find release.
Deeper you dig to *Nowhere*. Just like me.

I had - *once*, the means to destroy the world.
I had - *once*, a love to keep me warm.
I had - *once*, the truth to hold me tight.
I had a dream *once*, but now awake all night.

It's been a long trip. I think I should rest my eyes.
Before I miss the next step and fall away in surprise.
I'm on my way to *Nowhere*. To find what you took away.
I'm on my way to *Nowhere*. Hoping you'll meet me.
I can't stay awake any longer but I keep open my eyes.
I'm on my way to *Nowhere*. To verify all your lies.

The Death of a Dead Man

Kind words will get you nowhere.
"But it's a start."
Those nerves were broken and torn apart.
For what is an answer, truly if you think...
What was the point to my heartbreak?
Why should it have mattered to me?

Sink as I may, away from time and grace.
Fade as I will, under the memories of joy.
And so I take this blade in again, to set it right.
To finish what I started, "to stop this game."

Gone away, from time's sight and life's charms.
Taken down, into the pits of a bastard's fears.
Wiped completely out, away from those cheers.

No longer in the clear and not what I had in mind.
But this is only the start of what I've created.
"This war of yours and mine."

Now I'm under the earth - gone.
Away from those hopes and dreams.
I was taken away from all the rivers and streams.
So never shall I be clean, complete filth of rotten decay.

So I slumber and wait for you to awake.
I've tried to reach, "was short of length."
So this is the death of a dead man.
Was only a boy when it began.

Now darkness is my mistress.
And silences floods the land.

Hopeless Thought

Totally in a bind, forever left here to die.
And no more nauseous ways, only your toxic faith.
"To a God that doesn't give a damn."
What a hopeless thought "That you could win."

Left here to waste away, knowing only revenge and shame.
And no more twisted looks, only your Gods behind the books.
To give facts to all your lies, to give a reason to our eyes.

What a hopeless thought, of maybe holding true that grain.
What an un-luminated whim, that I would be the same.
And what a hopeless thought, "Of regaining your toxic ways."

Between Each Rib

Pounding down...
The hour of the voices telling me to jump.
Taking that last breath, of smoke filling my lungs.

Precious thoughts of what we've done.
Taken to the limit and shaken to its core.
Grinding the bone and burning our souls.
For each heartbeat that I don't hold.

You embrace me warming.
Taking those nails, shoving them into my heart.
We writhe together, under the moon.
You seep the darkness and I do too.
But that was my last wish, now I'm out of time.
I tried my hardest but you left me to die.

Between each rib, you put the needles in place.
Between each rib, hides the truth of shame.
Between my heart and soul, lies this broken man.
Between each rib, hides the death of this land.

Pounding down...
The echoes of the voices screaming in my lungs.
Now taking our last steps and then together we jump.

Toast to a Black Heart

The oceans can't hold it.
So I think I'll drag my feet.
The wood isn't strong enough.
So I'll just go to sleep.
The sun's just right now.
For the honor of this blackened heart.
"My enemies and friends - raise your glass and toast with me."

To this black heart, in which I hold so dear.
A toast to this crumbled soul, in which holds all your fears.
To this bright moon, embracing me at night.
To our broken love, left eternally in fright.

The darkest days, were left only for me.
The longest breath, under the sea.
But no one can match this, as no one should.
A toast to this black heart, filled with tons of soot.

To the bone breaks and child screams.
To the frozen lake, forever encrypting me.
To the acid charms and liquor lusts.
A toast to this black heart. Filled only with dust.

Why Couldn't I Die?

Was there a reason?
When the leaves flowed through my veins.
Was there a reason - for this bane?
I could run through this darkness but never be found.
I could cut it all day and scream out loud.

Why couldn't I die?
When I jumped off the ledge.
Why couldn't I die?
When I shoved this knife into my chest.
Why couldn't I die?
When you took my heart from me.

Why won't I die? – "I just sit here and weep."

God, Hold Me Close.

There's no more reason.
For denying what you see.
God, hold me close.
Please set me free.

Search as I may.
But there's nothing to find.
What is an answer anyway?
God, hold me tight.

You ran from it all day.
Now you're blind.
I cursed his name all day.
"Please forgive me."

God, hold me tight.
Keep me warm when I'm alone.
Please, give me strength.
"God, hold me close."

Dumb Ass

Do you really believe in what you say?
Do you really think I'm the same?
Do you know what you did to me?
Do you understand my pain and grief?
Who was the one who took the first step?
Who was the one that raped my heart in my chest?
Who was I then and who are you now?
Who was the demon behind the clouds?

What a dumb ass, to think you cared.
What a dumb ass, roaming anywhere.
What a dumb ass, the little girl left in shame.
What a dumb ass, losing all over again.
Do you really believe in what you say?
Do you think you could just walk away?
Do you know how hard it was?
Do you know what I've done?
"Dumb ass."

Cheap Words

To all those intentions.
Lost in your dimension.
Un-taught the lies you speak.
Left only for me to weep.

Years of spilling.
Blood, sweat, tears and pain.
Only to age and fade.
Growing mold and ashy decay.

A picture is worth a thousand words.
A thousand words, worth only the ink.
So why must I sink, into this reality for you?
Why are we left to fade, away in truth?

Hours of stabbing, tearing away my faith.
Days of torment, stuck into my brain.
Only to age and fade, words forgotten with time.
A picture growing through the years – alive.

A picture is worth a thousand smiles.
A thousand words, worth only the grief.
To spill a mans heart onto these sheets.
For only the fact of the age.

A poet remembered for his grace.
A picture of a nameless woman's face.
Lost in the intentions.
Stuck in your dimension.
For only a nickel or two.

What cheap words.
Overflowing, at the rim of my soul.
What a pointless nature I have chosen.
To tell this story to you.

Rust

When the meat begins to fester, you seem to come back to me.
When the moon gets closer, you come running to me.
For what a reason you have in mind.
Coming home to me. Just to pass your time.
When the rust begins to flake off, you do nothing but stare.
When the years begin to break off.
You just don't care. So why are you here?
The pain seems to be, the only one on my side.
This thorn never seems to leave my mind.
As the rust turns to lime and the words just pass our time.
God I wish we weren't here.
So take this as a message, you can let go of this monster now.
Take this as my last request. "Just kill me now."

Jagged Screams

Behind the door, dark-red. The decapitated heads.
Rolling through my mind.
Behind the door, the puzzled whims bending in me.
Behind the door, her jagged screams.
So she takes her dress, soaked in blood.
Stunned at the sight, of what she's done.
Behind the smoke, her lustful eyes.
Behind the door, "what a surprise."
Behind her teeth, freshly torn meat.
Behind the door, her jagged screams.
Twirling in the embers, the hazing tweaks of she... Stuck into her cheek.
Chewing on the meat of her own... She wants to go home.
Behind the door, a sight un-seen.
Behind my pride, you might find me.
Behind those truths, just another lost youth.
Jagged teeth, grinding in me. Her rotted smiles, blistering cheeks.
Her last kiss, to a child named *Shit*. What a surprise, for her and him.
Behind the door, dark-red. More thoughts running through my head.
Rolling out of the amber lusts. Just embers and dust.
Behind the door, a puzzled whim without me.
Behind the door, "*her jagged screams.*"

144

Soon to Know

Symbolic to the very end.
And soon to know when.
For every step that is made.
For every breath we intake.

What a head-case.
And what a heartbreak.
Such a symbolic fate.
Of nothing else but rage.

Soon to know, when the grass begins to grow.
Soon to know, when the clouds will unfold.
Soon to know, why I'm even here.
Soon to know, when all will be clear.

I've Never Stopped

I don't think the train goes that far.
I don't hide that pain behind these scars.
I don't want you to picture me like that.
A broken man, a rusty ax.

I've never just stopped and thought of this.
Of how I could have kept it all.
I've never just stopped, to think out loud.
Of what I haven't lost.

I don't think the plane goes that high.
I don't think you'll care after I die.
I don't want you to be that mad.
And you just erase me, when you turn your head.

I've never just stopped, to smell the grass.
I've never just stopped, to look you in the eyes.
I've never stopped loving you.
Even after we died.

Faithless Fate

An arm's reach away.
Was too short of length.
She smiled and I melted away.
Was a broken man.
Left frozen in the rain.

Twice the man then.
But she never flinched.
Was twice the heartache.
Fueled only on sin.

The moon was darker.
The days short of light.
Her smile was bigger.
Now lost in time.

Just a shell of a man.
And twice the fool.
Was left in the darkness.
With un-fated pull.

Faithless wanting.
An answer to these games.
She turned back once.
And pushed me away.

A faithless fate.
Of this hollow man.
Left in the darkness.
Under the sand.

Time was a bitch then.
Now that's all I have.
Just a faithless fate.
Since she turned her head.

Twisted Body

Illuminate my heart with faith.
Clean the slate and rinse the blood.
Off of my wrist, you clean the mud.
What a picture, "our love as a flood."

An essence of her soft lips.
Friction across our smooth flesh.
Writhing over the picture-press.
And I place my hands on her chest.

Twisted out of place.
The light glowing on her face.
Warm as it ever should.
Taking each breath that we could.

A twisted body.
A flower in her hair.
My forgotten nature.
Of eternal despair.

Illuminate my heart with faith.
Rub my eyes with your tongue.
Clean away the blood and empty my lungs.
What a picture, of our twisted love.

Legs over my head.
Her body commencing my death.
Our flesh fusing as one.
We'll never untie.

Our twisted body.
Together for all time.
Thrust against the frame.
Illuminated by the moon.
What a picture, of our twisted doom.

Nails Through My Feet

What will it take, for you to awake?
Why was I late, to wipe clean the slate?
What was the same, other than me?
What's with this, these nails through my feet?
Stepping over the rusted bridge. Looking over, with crimson wrist.
What was a miss, other than me?
So I just scream, with these nails through my feet.
Because you never cared. I stood on the ledge.
Because it was understood. I never slit my wrist.
Because you held him tight. I took my last step in fright.
What will it take, for you to see straight?
Why can't I just clean this slate?
What was the point, to this life of shame?
I opened my eyes... Nothing was the same.
I stood on the edge, with nails through my feet.
I stood in the cold, ice clinching to me.
I walked to the railroad, narrow as could be.
I wait for you to awake, with these nails in my feet.

In My Hands

Brought forth on my instrumental doom.
The words that ring behind each tooth.
In my hands I hold our truth.
Our lost and forgotten youth.
By the years were turning.
And my eyes were burning.
In my hands I hold the truth.
The truth that was forgotten by you.
Left under our skin.
The words of honest truths.
It was left in my hands.
For me to cradle through the years.
For me to hold and purify its tears.

Brought forth for me to realize. For me to hold and close my eyes.
In my hands I hold our child. The true answer to our sick games.
In my hands I hold the ashes, brought forth from its grave.

148

Salted Wounds

I lay on my back, watching the clouds drift by.
I lay on my back, watching the Gods cry.
I lay on my back, just wasting my time.

Up at attention, I see her push me down.
Up with my intentions, then all is shoved out.
I fall away from your dimension, soaring by myself.

I stood at attention, only to be pushed down.
I fall away in frustration, then only let down.
Scraped on my knees, my arms and legs bleed.

You come to me with a bandage of warmth.
You just rub salt in my wounds.
And laugh while I hurt.

I scream down-biting on my tongue.
I lay on the ground, alone as just one.
I scream-down with salted wounds.
And you laugh as I hurt.

Along the Stream

I came to the edge of the stream.
Only hoping she would see.
I stood there at the edge of the stream.
"My heart felt lighter than a dream."

Kind words said, "On a very cool spring day."
What a week to remember, of her beautiful face.

We sat in the little boat.
Drifting with the stream.
My heart felt lighter than a dream.
"A day forever held within me."

We held hands and exchanged names.
It was a day I just won't forget.
It was her face, I'll never let fade.
We drifted along the stream.
"Our hearts lighter than a dream."

The Letter I Found

Digging through some papers.
I found an old page.
Written to me on a Friday.

I read the letter, it rang so true to me.
She said she would always love me.
No matter what would get in our way.
She said she would love me.
She said it throughout the whole page.

I began to remember, only her smile and face.
I began to remember, her lips and grace.
I remembered her words when she held me close.
I remembered her thoughts, so very close to mine.
I read the letter, remembering those times.

The years of when I held a love true and simple.
A love that would always last.
I remember it like a yesterday, that just won't pass.
I read the letter and thought of her name.
I thought of those words "*always and a day.*"

She was right, about one thing.
We would be together, *forever and a day.*
She was right, about one thing.
I would always love her and it wouldn't change.

I read on in the letter, knowing how it would end.
I burned it fast - like our yesterday that just won't pass.
I burned the letter I found before I got to the end.
I burned it on those words, "*always and a day.*"
Just so the memory could stay sweet.
Oh that letter I found...
It reminded me of her grace, so meek.

So I ended the thought on a smile.
The way it should be.
So on I dig again.
Finding more letters addressed to me...

Against the Brick

For some, it's just a way to pass time.
For some, it's just a way to lose your mind.
For some, it's a better way to go.
For some, it's the darker story un-told.

The miles of the ashes dancing in my lungs.
The hours of cutting it until done.
The days of remembering this taste.
The years of the nothings that just won't fade.

I take this brick and smash it across my head.
Just to see, if I'll wake up dead.
I take this brick and smash it across my head.
Just to see the other side of then.
I take this brick and smash it across my head.
Smashing and smashing, until the end.

Against the brick, goes my heart and mind.
Against the brick, goes my soul and time.
Against the brick, goes my loves and dreams.
Against the brick, goes more than you see.

For some, it just a way to pass time.
For some, it's just another way of losing mind.
For some, it's a better way to know.
For some... It's our darker story un-told.

For Only One

Out in the distance, in a field of wheat.
A dancing angel, on the tip of a grain. She dances for only me.
On the one grain, the one and the same. As it was supposed to be.
She was there for only one, she danced with grace.
A look of honesty on her face.
She was there for only one, the one who could see.
The angel danced on the tip of the grain, out in the field of wheat.
With a flowing white dress, her angel-wings.
Getting ready to carry me away.
She was there for only one. She was there for only me.

When I Knew

Stepping onto the face of the Gods.
Standing on my fate in awe.
Of the once but left behind.
Trembling in dread.
Of the horrors ahead.

I knew the answers, before she even asked.
I knew the answers, to these questions on her breath.
I knew the answers but would never tell.
I knew the answers, would bring only hell.

When I held it, the angel of my doom.
When I held it, the hour coming soon.
When I held it, I knew only my fate.
When I held it, I was closer to faith.

When I knew, she just walked away.
When I knew, as I stood on the God's face.
When I knew, the answers that you seek.
Now I know. There is no hope for me.

A Night-less Dream

My self-portrait has no face.
Just a blank canvas, stained only with shame.
And nothing can drive me, further than this rage.
No one will hold me *"I'm left alone in the rain."*
So nothing can wake me.
From this night-less dream.

My self-sacrifice had no gist.
Just a pointless step over the edge.
Falling deeper into my head.
Where no one could find me and no one cares.
No one will wake me *"I'm running out of air."*
So nothing has reason but this point I make.
This night-less dream holds the answers.
Of why I have no faith.

Why Me?

For death to all.
And now I fall.
Away with this.
A knife I hold.
For death to us.
In the frozen cold.

Why me? Was it something I said?
Why me? Is it because she's dead?
Why me? Of all those it could have been.
Why me? Drowning in sin.

For death to all.
And now I fall.
Away with this.
A lifeless chest.
A soulless wish.
For death to us.
And what a fuss.
Left out in the cold.

Why me? Was it what I said?
Why me? Because I'm dead?
Why me? Tearing out my spine?
Why me? Left here to unwind?

Why was I, the one you chose?
Why was I, the one so cold?
Why did you, do this to me?
Why was I, the one burnt alive?
Why was I, the one who cried?

Why did you love me, when I fell dead?
Why did you have to, push it till death?
Why was I, the one you held?
Why was I, the one who failed?
Why me?

A Narrow Road

My name no longer has meaning.
My points no longer have their roots.
This road is getting narrow.
This cliff must be my doom.

It's been a while, since you cared.
I've been walking for years now.
My feet no longer hurt.
The pain is all I know.

This road is getting narrow.
Soon over the edge I'll go.
For all that had a reason.
No longer means a thing to you.
Whatever had a purpose.
Now just worthless.

My face no longer has a reflection.
My words won't echo through time.
My fate no longer has a meaning.
Just pointless strives.

This road is getting narrow. Soon I'll be over the edge.
This road is getting longer. I'm finding no reason in my head.
This road is getting narrow, the cliff is getting close.
This road is getting narrow. Soon over the edge I'll go.

Awaiting Summer

Stumbling along the sidewalk, "a crowded street"
Cold rain, beating down on me.
And her face, in the snow it hides. All those sins, left far behind.
For no one to know but for all to see.
I'm just walking alone, waiting for someone to save me.
Knowing the truth of what I see and just strolling alone.
Knowing the conclusion, for you and me.
Stumbling along the sidewalk – "a crowded street"
Cold hands, held down on me.
And awaiting summer, so all the snow can melt.
I'm awaiting summer, to bring the angels to me.
I'm waiting for summer, to bring my soul back to me.

When Can I Let Go?

Fluttering heartbeats, swaying in my mind.
Frozen compassions, lost under the sand.
Forgotten love-notes, found once again.
Struggles of once a love, now only a thought.
Wars on a whim, of those who believe what you say.
When can I let go? And just fall away.

Unsanctioned notions, bringing me only doubt.
Uncensored emotion, just tearing us apart.
Fluttering heartbeats, swaying in my mind.
Pushing and pulling, so I can unwind.

When can I let go? And just fade away.
When can I let go? And accept my fate.
When can I let go? And awake from this dream
When can I let go? And heal this heartbreak in me?

Miles follow but the tears anchor me to this.
The flame is burning, just under my wrist.
The tires are melting, to my skull and fist.
The untainted love-wish, of once I knew you.
When can I let go? And just fade away.
When can I let go? And awake from this daze...

Chapter 7

Chasing the Darkness

Fire

When the fire had a mind of its own.
It danced and twirled upon the stone.
Then *Satan* came and whispered to me...
"This is nothing more than a dream."

The Candle Drained

Was it my shame, lain out in the rain?
Darkness found just the same.
And the romance gone.
As the candle drained.

Dancing upon the leaves of then.
Burning over the ashes of sin.
Draining over my face, into my eyes.
The candle fading over time.

Was it my shame, for you to blame?
Darkness found just the same.
And sanity forgotten over the years.
Building up like my fears.

Dancing devils upon my lips.
The wax draining over my wrist.
I've lost the notions over the hours gone.
Fading the demons into my heart.

Was it my name, lain out for the blame?
The romance frozen in the rain.
And darkness found just the same...
As the candles begin to drain.

What You Think

I held the blame, I took the shame. I know this face that pushed me out.
I took the rage, onto this page. Of the child slaughtered before your eyes.
You think I'm going to waste my time.
You think I'm going to forget my lines.
You think I have nothing better to say.
You think I'm a freak, expressing my rage.

What really mattered? Now gone and shattered.
What really mattered? Now beaten and battered.
What really helped me? Now burnt and bleeding.
What really helped me? Now taken and screaming.

I held the blame, I took the blade. I know this face that pushed me down.
I took my rage, onto this page. Just before my eyes were ripped out.
I'm going to rape this soul, that's what you think.
I'm going to dig this hole, so I can go to sleep.
I'm going to take this blame and release my rage.
I'm going to slit this open and accept the shame.
I don't care what you think... I'll never change.

The Monster Behind Me

Like a feather in my throat, I feel it begin to choke.
And I can't escape the smoke, not while this monster's behind me.
Not while she's still screaming. Rushing as I may, to the true side of decay.
Falling from my place, burning off my face.
I rush to the door, the monster's behind me!
I see his teeth shine in the dark. I can smell his breath in my heart.
I can taste his horror behind my eyes. I fight the darkness but just can't win.
This monster behind me, he's trying and trying. Soon I'll be just a corpse.
I'm trying to escape this but can't find the door.
Like a whisper in my heartache. I just can't get to her in time.
Like a devil to remind me, always bad timing.
So take this as a last request. Grab the blade, rip open my chest.
Find the answer, to what you need. Kill the monster, like he killed me.
I've run the furthest but feel him glaring.
I know he's out there, I feel him staring.
He's right behind me, licking his lips.
Like a bastard falling, I know this is it.

Her Gravity Love

The ground's moving, breaking at the seams.
I can taste the decay, filling up into me.
She gives me a kiss, cradling my dreams.
She gives me a kiss, knowing I'm waiting.

The seas begin to drain and fade.
The dirt turns gray and blows away.
Our days have come and gone the same.
Still she gives me her gravity love.
Embracing my heart this way.

She takes my hand and dances with me.
She kisses the earth and breaks for me.
The ground begins to crumble and fade.
She smiles and wipes all those years away.

She holds me tight, taking away the tears.
She loves me nice, taking away my fears.
Embracing my soul and you're turning to coal.
I give her my hand, to take me away.
"I'll love her forever and always this way."
She gives forth her gravity love. So this world can crumble away....

Cutting Out the Sickness

For only you to see, now death has set me free.
And for only you to know, how the memory will unfold.

I'm cutting out the sickness, so I can think straight.
I'm cutting out the sickness, to end this mistake.

For only a child to see, now the darkness has set me free.
And for only his mother to know, how deep it is, beneath the snow.

I'm cutting out the sickness, so God can take me home.
I'm cutting out the sickness, so I can breathe the story un-told.
I'm cutting out the sickness, to answer all your games.
I'm cutting out the sickness, to end our yesterday.

For only you to see, now death has set me free.
And for only you to know, the end of our story un-told.

Burning Away My Eyes

It gets me through the day, the answers on her grave.
To why does a demon feel so sad?
It gets me through the feeling, of why I'm still alive in death.

I burn away my eyes because I've seen too much.
I'm burning away my eyes and breaking at each touch.
It was stuck but I knew how to take it away.
I ripped out my own spine and left it on her grave.

I burn away my eyes because I've seen the devil's face.
I'm burning away my eyes and leaving it in our grave.

Jesus knew the truth but wanted me to find it on my own.
I took a wrong step and fell down alone.

I burn away my eyes, to end these nights of pain.
I'm burning away my eyes, to get me through this day.

The Black Stone

About a mile away from home.
I came across a black stone.
I picked it up and held it close.

There seemed to be a strange glare.
It grew and grew the more I'd stare.
It had a chip on its edge.
It gleamed in the darkness, reflecting my death.

I know not why it seemed so warm.
And dripped blood from its core.
Though it was heavy, I knew it was mine.
I placed the black stone, back into my chest.
So I wouldn't feel so hollow in death.

It seemed real strange, that I would find it again.
As if it followed me home...
I felt solid inside, for another time.
My heart, as this black stone.

Childless

I can hear the crying, I can feel it dying.
I know you're lying but no one cares.

I have no child, only these miles.
Under my feet - the wear, but I know you don't care.

I can hear it whining, I know it's dying.
I know you were lying, straight to me.
I had a smile, now only denial and childless screams.

I have no heartbeat, only dead meat rotting away my soul.
I have no child, nor the means to know.
I have no love now, only a broken soul.

I know this darkness, because it's home.
I had once the shovel, to dig its hole.

I could hear it crying, I know it's dying.
And you left it there in the cold.

I know what happened but couldn't save it, now I'm all alone.
I can feel it crying, I know I'm dying "No child of my own."
I can hear you whisper and I'm no longer there.
I tried my hardest but I know no one cared.

The Last Laugh

Tell me now, who's laughing? Tell me now, what's happening?
Tell me now, who was there? Tell me now, did you care?
I tried to save you but lost instead. *I tried to save you but wound up dead.*
I tried to stop it but lost it all. I tried to save you but now I fall.
Tell me now, who's laughing? Tell me now, what's happening?
Tell me now, who was there? Tell me now, did you care?
I wanted to save you but broke my fingers.
I wanted to stop you but nothing could change it.
I knew the outcome but you wouldn't listen.
I tried my hardest, now dead in the kitchen.
I had to stop and think it over. I had to stop and remember my lines.
You had your chance then but ran out of time.
I've got the last laugh... and in the end "I was right."

Never Clean

My nose to the ground, swine of the earth.
I bathe in the filth of your lies.
Never clean.... No matter how much I try.

I swim in the depths of your sick games.
I hide in the center of your dark maze.
Crawling on the ground with my fingers in the dirt, eating at your filth.

Once as I've tried and then just died.
And scrub as I will, not never will it heal.
And I peel away the layers of shit.
Never clean, always sick.

My nose to the ground, just swine of your tormented nature.
Just a pile of filth you wish to wipe away.
Stained with blood and caked with hate.

Waist deep in your shit, logic lost and never sticks.
Always sick, swimming in your shit.
My fingers in the dirt, just a filthy swine of our earth.
Never clean, but I try. Never clean, just a dirty swine.

Hours of Dying

Not done till it's over. Not over till it's done.
I'll never stop what I have begun.
Not till the day falls. Not till I'm just one.
These hours of dying. It seems a little bleak.
These hours of crying. And tearing these sheets.

Not one more word, till this war is over.
Not one more thing, left for me to say.
And Oh you would be happy, if it were true.
Not over till it's done. "When the sky is no longer blue."

These hours of dying, they seem a little bleak.
These hours of dying, tearing away at me.
But it won't end till I'm finished. I'm not done quite yet.
Not till I obtain the darkness, into my chest.
Oh these hours of dying, wasting away my breath.

Acidic Torment

Dropped to the left side of my spine.
Torn in two, never shall it bloom.
Begin the count-down.
And take me away.

Swimming into the clouds.
Dragging into the hours of our grave.
These pills are singing.
Taking me away.

Shaking at its roots now.
And raining from the clouds.
Melting my soul and your head too.
I'm eating at these doorsteps.
And gravestones too.

Vibrating my heart.
And grinding my teeth on the stone.
Drowning in the acid.
And mushroom tones.

Eating at my eyelids.
So I can see what's next.
Tearing at my temples.
And digging into my chest.

This acidic torment.
Oh, what sweet bliss.
Of our souls becoming one.
And the taste of old death.
And demons on my breath.
Oh, this lovely torment.
Deep inside my chest.

Because I Cared

Remembering those days. Lost in my predictable faith.
Of when I held close my love. Now just a memory soon to be done.

I held you tight. I kept you safe from fright.
I did all I could. So you wouldn't feel pain.
I tried my hardest but lost you anyway.
Because I cared. I was lost in despair.
Because I cared. I was left alone to die.
Because I loved you, I now burn alive.

Because I cared, now burning away my eyes.
Because you loved me, now my soul dies.
But nothing could change it and never will.
So now I lay here alone, under this hill.

Remembering those days. Stuck in a rut, of this muddy grave.
So damn my predictable faith.
In a dream that never wins.
It was because I cared about you. I now burn for all my sins.

Kissing You Good-Bye

Placing my hands on her soft face.
Loving her eternally to the grave.
Knowing that she would stay at my side.
Holding her forever, kissing her good-night.

The days passed without my consent, I held her close, so love-bent.
To the years of knowing, that I'd love her till we die.
Holding her close and kissing her good-night.

Those days just passed me, with nothing I could do.
The years just passed me and brought forth my doom.
Her lustful eyes upon their graves. I held on my hardest.
Yet died anyway.

Placing my hands on her face.
Remembering her voice, remembering her grace.
Knowing that we were once alive...
I hold on forever and kiss her good-bye.

Acrimonious Deceit

A bitter taste when I'm done with you.
A sour face upon your doom.
Not happy unless it's yours.
Not one more chance.
For that pathetic whore.

Too many layers of lies upon your face.
Too many riddles and twisted games.
What a bitter taste in the back of my mouth.
Such a sour face when you were found out.

I spilt my heart out, only for you to laugh.
I cut even deeper, into my wrist.
For a giggle and whisper, yet nothing more.
Not one more chance.
For that filthy whore.

Too many lies to see the truth.
I've spent too much time, on the likes of you.
What a head-case *"you little waste."*
What a heartbreak, lost at the wake.

A bitter noise spewing from your head.
What a sickening lump inside your chest.
Not a word but you never shut up.
Not another word, *"just shut the hell up..!"*

What an acrimonious deceit.
And you thought you could get to me.
Tell your stories then get out of my way.
I'm done with your bitterness.
I won't play these games.

You're not happy till it's over.
Not happy till you have more.
And not one last chance.
For that worthless whore.

Egotistical Prick

Get off my case, get out of my face.
You think I care, you think you were there.
Not one more thought spent on this.
I've had enough, you egotistical prick.
Two faced sack of shit.
Stuck at the waist to your bitch.
Get out of my face, get off my case.
I've had enough, you twisted fuck.
You think I care, "*get out of my hair*!"
Two faced to the very end.
Stuck on yourself, lustful sins.
Take a walk into your world of shit.
You sick little prick.
I've had enough of this wasted thinking.
Funny-faced little weaklings.
Get your shit and piss off you little prick.
Take this blade, go fuck your bitch.
Get off my case, get out of my face.
You egotistical prick.
I've had enough of your lies and games.
Get out and waste my time no more.
Take this blade and go fuck your whore!
I've had enough of your shit. You egotistical little prick!

Shadowing My Tears

Hiding within my skeleton.
Hiding beneath what could have been.
Hiding behind all your sins. These tears building up far within.
Hiding behind your twisted faith. Hiding behind your shifted fate.
Hiding just under your forgotten face. Those tears building up far within.
Just a sideshow for you to mock. Just a shadow at the end of the dock.
Hiding behind your drowned fears, shadowing all my tears.
Wanting nothing more, than some life.
Needing nothing more, than less strives.
Knowing nothing more, than your lies. *Kill them all and crush the light.*
Hiding within my skeleton, hiding beneath what should have been.
Hiding behind all your sins and shadowing these tears all over again.

Rage #4

Right behind a bastard's books.
Giving forth your dirty looks.
Festering bodies of what I hold dear.
Still lusting each other in your darkest fears.

Biting down, till you drown in your own blood.
Light was a wish, then it flew away.
This monster knows all and stands on my grave.
Licking his lips, just picking its day.

Now shaking faster.
Just a lonely bastard, hoping you'll look away.
Fusing these nails to my brain.
Loving the taste of sweet innocent death.
And ripping my heart from my own chest.

Beating down this lonely bastard.
Watching closely as I shatter his brain.
Knowing how great it feels to lose your faith.
Now beating myself, hoping for hell...

Whipping these angels with a barbed wire.
Laughing while they bleed and die.
Ripping away your skin and face.
Watching you shake endlessly in pain.

Now I shatter my bones while loving a devil at night.
I'm crushing my hands, just to feel alive.
I'm loving my rage that brings me to life.
So I take this nail and shove it in place.
Laughing while I ram it into my face.
Knowing the answers to your lost faith.
But these dumb bastards just turn away.

Almost There

How many roads have I walked down?
How many words have I said aloud? How many more will it take?
To end this turmoil and dilute the pain?
I need some release to rest my soul.
I need to relax and empty my skull.
I need to lie down and just go to sleep...

I'm almost there... just a little more.
I'm almost there... the other side of the door.
I'm almost there... to end this pain.
I'm almost there... out of the rain.

How many roads does it take, to make me a man?
How many more scars, until you understand?
How many screams, do I let out at night?
How far am I, from making it right..?

I'm almost there... at the right state of fact.
I'm almost there... so I can relax.
I'm almost home... where I should be.
I'm almost there... so I can set it free.
I've spent years on these wars of pain.
I've had enough, so end this rain.
I've done my time and said it right, so I'm almost there...
"Out of the darkness... And into the light."

Let's See

Let's take one last look, before we go.
Let's take one last step, into the snow.
Let's breathe softly, to see the frost.
Let's dream real quietly, before all is lost.
Can God taste my reality, or is it just mine?
Please speak real softly, your needles into my brain.
Please place that bandage on, to cover the pain.
Can God forgive me, for living in shame?
Let's see, that one last thought on our minds.
Let's see, that one lingering thought on the dime.
Let's look further, to know how it ends.
Let's breathe no longer and let the dreams begin.

A Child in the Backroom

I was just a child in the back room.
Not knowing of my assured doom.
I was just a child, hoping to dream sweet.
I was just a child, now a forgotten beast.

All logic hammered into my head.
Pressure building until the end.
Snapping me in two, I was just a child, so confused.

Left in the darkness of my own sins.
I was just a child, once and again.
Left in the dark for me to cry.
Unknowing, of your certain lies.

All was a mind-twist for me to seep.
Then I bent the blade around at me and all logic pointed at my wrist.
I was just a child then, now a demon in the abyss.

I wept there for hours, in the darkness of my own life.
I stayed there for decades, with only my cries.
I was out of my skull-trust, now only dead.
A child in the back room, stuck in his own head.

Calm Down

Too far out for you to see. It's been too long but still it's sweet.
Laid out in the sun, burning away in dreams.
Too far out for us to know. It's been too long but still it shows.
Laid out in the sun, burning away like me.

As I crumble at each touch, breaking away into dust.
Those words I said seem to fade, all of my worries just go away.
As I seem to break down, you only laugh at my pains.
As I just melt down into my grave, all of my worries just go away.

Blood spilt down but no one sees, ashes rain down but only on me.
So who was left out, in the shadows and dread?
I just better calm down, before I am dead.

"Too far out for you to see." It's been a long time, since you spoke to me.
Now laid down in the sun, calming my every dream.

Can't Shake It

A slight vibrate, behind my throat.
A near earthquake, deep in my soul.
Every bone starts to ache, when I lay in the snow.
A close-call then but now it's whole.

Pushed in the dark, against the wall.
Pulled to the floor, silence over my words.
Tied down to the ground, taped shut.
And I begin to drown, in my own tears, of all my old fears.
I can't shake it, not even a bit. I can't stop it, it just won't quit.
They place their fingers into my chest.
They rip the hole open and I'm losing breath.
They hide in the darkness, I can't even see.
I can hear them whisper, as they begin to consume me.
They shove their hands in, to see what's inside.
They shove their knives in and eat me alive.
I don't want to open my eyes again. Not to see what they have done.
I'll never smile again. I just bleed, I can't see but I know, it's done.

A slight vibrate, behind my throat.
A near earthquake, deep in my soul.
My heart forever aches, when I'm alone.
It was a close-call then... But now I'm home.

You're So Cold

It was years ago, when I had a soul, now I have only my sins.
It was years ago, when I was alone, and held them close to me.
It was harder then, but once again, I know you hate me so.
Bring me an answer to this question.
Please give me, just one last second, to tell you how it ends.

I was once a devil, when the world called me so.
I was a lover then, now I stand alone, it's so cold, it's so cold.
It was years ago, when I had some hope, now I just need revenge.
It was years ago, when I stood alone and held close that whim.
It was harder then, but once again, I know you hate me so.
Bring me an answer to this question.
Please give me just another second - to tell you where it begins.
I was once a demon, when she called me so.
I was her lover then, now I die alone. *You're so cold, you're so cold.*

172

One Last Thought of Me

Ten toes on the edge of the cliff. Two eyes gazing into the pit.
One hand held over my heart. One last thought to tear me apart.
I could have told you, but I let you guess.
I could have saved you, but lost instead.
I should have saved you, but now we're dead.
I would have saved you, but you turned your head.
Nine lies to drive me over the edge. Eight little stitches over my wrist.
One last notion, to push me that far.
Zero emotions, lost behind these bars.
You could have told me, but you lied instead.
You could have showed me, but now we're dead.
You should have loved me, but you pushed away.
You should have killed me, now we're buried away.
Two eyes gazing into my heart. One hand, tearing me apart.
Ten more heartbeats, then I'm home.
One last thought of me then I'm alone.
We could have stopped it, but jumped instead.
We could have held it, but forever it's dead.
We should have held back, until the end.
We should have looked back, but never again.

Breathe Again

He told me to hold on, I stayed there for days.
He told me to move on, and forget this daze.
He told me to let go, and breathe again.
He told me to save you, but never again.
She told me to hold on, I stayed there for months.
She told me to move on, I stood at the front.
She told me to let go, and to breathe again.
She told me to save you, but never again.
They told me to hold back, and maybe try to see.
They told me to sit back, and once again breathe.
They tied you to the train-tracks. You just stayed there and screamed.
I told you to stop that, and quit playing your games.
I told you to look back, and maybe see me.
I told you to hold back, but you've never listened to me.
I told them the answers, but they always had to fight.
I told them to let go, but still they stay with strive.
I tried to tell you, but you couldn't hear.
So I just left you, to drown in your own fears.

As I Crumble

The angels ride forth into my eyes.
My thoughts begin to crumble.
My life begins to subside.
For all these nights of horror.
And tales of truth and love.
I want only to step away.
And to finally see above.

God holds me close to these words.
I spew from my face.
God holds me close, to my broken faith.
God holds me close.
As the devil whispers into my soul.
God holds me close.
And warms me when it's cold.

As the angels ride forth into my eyes.
I stand on the horizon and spread wide my arms.
I begin to crumble, into a pile of dust and leaves.
I blow away in the wind, and God comforts me.

Tell me a story, so I can go to sleep.
Please hold my hand when it's dark, and sing to me.
Please God, give me a chance to set it right.
Please my lord, forgive me for living in sin.
Oh God forgive me, for letting Satan in.

And the angels ride forth into my eyes.
My head begins to crumble.
My life begins to subside.
For all the Knights of honor.
And tales of truth and love.
I want only to step away.
And to finally live above.

The Darkest Place

All the beasts crawl out from under their stones.
As the demons wait for me to get home.
The darkest place in our world.
Is within my heart made of coal.

All the dreams begin to quake.
My eyes roll back, as my spine starts to shake.
And the world knows the answers.
But will never tell.
It's darkest in my heart, now burning in hell.
A shadow is only a sweet notion.
Left there for the damned to grasp.
It's darkest in my heart, with no compassions left.
It was harder for me to lose.
As the monsters await their food.

All the beasts crawl out from under their stones.
The ghosts are waiting for me to get home.
The darkest place in our world.
Is within my broken heart that you stole.

Surgery

The doctor ties me to the gurney.
The thoughts in my eyes are burning.
The walls are fading, broken glass and grime.
The floor and walls caked with rust and lime.
I can hear a woman screaming, but it starts to fade.
The doctor straps me down, and rolls me away.

The rooms are spinning, without me.
The floor is bleeding, a red blood sea.
The doctor has no face, only distorted flesh.
I hear the nurse whisper, as she starts cutting at me.
I can do nothing but bleed, I do nothing but weep.

The smell of death fills the room.
The doctors play with my guts, and hack at their roots.
The thought of dying is only a sweet dream.
This dread of living, as a pile of living meat;

Why is it that this nightmare feels so real?
They tear at my stomach, pulling out whatever I ate.
I hear the doctor laughing, behind his faded face.
I can taste the metal, at the bottom of my throat.
I can hear my heart break, as they chop out my soul.
What are they making me? Just a monster from hell.
What are they doing to me? Will I ever heal?

God has no power here, "*I've run out of luck.*"
The doctors shove their needles through my teeth.
I feel it grinding, as my brain cracks weak.
They shatter my bones to watch me cry.
"*I can only remember the moon.*"
"*As my soul begins to die...*"

Chapter 8

Awkward Existence

This Knot

I love the feel, when the smoke cradles inside.
I love the sensation of your tongue on my spine.
I love the thought of when we were alive.
I love this knot, tied deep inside.

What are we truly, to our Gods eyes?
What am I truly, for you to despise?
What was the meaning, for all the funeral-tears?
What am I truly, for you to fear?
A man standing on the curb.
An angel drinking from the pond.
A man waiting for his birth. "An angel singing its lonely songs."

I love the feel of the smoke pouring inside.
I love the lasting memory, of living a lie.
I love the thought, of when we were both one.
I love this knot, holding me until done.

Ending Soon

It's killing me, the torment behind this face.
It's killing me, your nonsense that you play.
It's killing me, this haze of my tragic doom.
It's killing me, the ending coming soon.

Our number falling from the desk.
The hours you count, inside your head.
Our answers rising above the rest.
The hours building inside your chest.
It's killing me, the poison dripping from your tongue.
It's killing me, all logic spewing from this gun.
It's killing me, this moon-trip I deserve.
It's killing me, the soon end of our earth.
Our child dying, before our eyes.
My hatred buried, deep inside.
Our child lost, before we knew.
The hours counting "*bringing doom.*"

It's killing me, the dreams I can't wipe away.
It's killing me, these stains on my grave.
It's killing me, the acid dripping into my tomb.
It's killing me, the ending coming soon.

Crowded Streets

Busy days and crowded streets.
Lonely walks, as angels weep.
Troubled minds and narrow lines.
Nervous words, as our memories die.

A hug and kiss before we leave.
To our pointless lies and crowded streets.
Lonely whispers and hollow drinks.
Troubled thoughts and tragic dreams.

An open wrist laid in the sun.
Our busy lives cooked over done.
Reason held without any fun.
The bastard laughs and loads his gun.

Mindless chatter, spewing from its head.
Pointless babble, and drunken breath.
Nauseous notions, pulling to its rights.
A nervous virgin, turning off the lights.

Tainted logic held in front.
Relentless potions, filling our lungs.
Fungus building under these sheets.
Such busy days and crowded streets.

A slap then hand-shake, and provoked earthquakes.
Drowning our children in these streams...
And the bastard laughs as he dreams.

Endless fire under our feet.
Burning daylight, haunting another's sleep.
Such diluted natures, printed on these sheets.
It's just busy days and crowded streets...

Take This

Take this with you when I'm gone.
Remember these facts and pointless songs.
Rant on as I may, to prove it my way. Only so I can sleep poorly at night.
Take another step, to the next spot of ink. Only to see where it may go.
Remember these lines, as I paint them for you.
Remember these times, of my shattered youth.
Take this with you when I'm gone.
To remind you of all those wrongs.
To admit my weakness, "that I can never quit."
To show-up the world and rise above their shit.
Take another step, to the next spot of ink.
Only to watch each love-song sink.
But remember these words that remind me of you.
Remember these rhymes, hidden behind each tooth.
So take me with you when I'm gone.
Remember all the things that I have said.
And rant on as I may, to prove it my way.
That even though you've killed me... "I'm not dead."

Loaded

Load me just the same. Take my head, out of the rain.
The insect smiles with its wings. She was laughing, just at me.
Take my hand... come follow me.
Then as the faded smoker strums the guitar with his tongue.
The owl stands screaming and you load my gun, Oh what fun...
Take my hand, so we can dance away.
Look through the glass till it has passed, so we can catch another disease.
Poison kisses, covering my breath.
And she wishes lust even beyond death.
Load me just the same, take my heart and thaw it in the rain.
So you can wash clean the shame.
And God smiles as I twinge in pain. Far-far pass the sane.
Forgive the thought that drove us to jump.
Forgive the words that pushed in and sunk.
Deep into the pit inside my lungs. Load me just the same, Oh what fun...
Heavy breath over her lips. That was the thought and this is the now.
Loaded with the things, that drive me through.
So we can dance upon another high noon.
For one to know but always to lose. For one to hold but never to choose.
Load it just the same... So our souls can dance away.

Those Things That Held Me

All brought forth upon angel-wings.
Not said the same but still it sings.
Mercy spoken on the tip of my eyes.
Those things that held me.
And brought forth good times.

Internally twisting as the winds begin to lift me.
A shiny pearl, held against me.
Kind words spoken, yet so little said.
All brought onward but not to mention a single thing I did.

Not another demented forest-beast.
The truth hidden behind a dragon's teeth.
For what was the answer to what she said..?
Brought forth upon angel-wings into my head.

Memory of the tiny gift I found under my bed.
The one lingering kiss, left on my breath.
All that held me so close to warmth.
For me to cherish forevermore.

The things that held me through the dark.
As all their hatred tore me apart.
The things that held me when I was alone.
As they pushed, shoved and threw their stones.

I still need those things that held me.
And got me through the bad...
"For I am a *Demon with Angel-Wings.*"
"Not said the same but still it sings."
And mercy spoken without any lies.
Of those things that held me.
And brought forth good times.

Armor Not Shattered

Go forth and live life full. Go onward and live as fools.
Be one with nature, just filthy swine.
Be one with your hatred and waste not my time.
Against my chest plate goes one's rage
Pushed to the sidelines for none to blame.
Head-loss of another hard swing.
Across my ribcage and now we bleed.

Bring on the next death-push, pulled down beneath your left foot.
See if you can see the sight of the sought crime.
With armor not shattered but choosing its time.
So go forth and live life full. Go onward and be just a fool.
Be one with nature and filthy lies.
Be one with your hatred and waste not my time.

Who Am I?

Gently against my bones goes the blade that scrapes away my soul.
For what was the reason I lost my heart?
Who am I? Just a man torn apart...

Why can't I find the answers behind your smiles?
Why must I weep here in my denial?
For a thought once faded now only a dream.
Who am I? Just a dead man waiting to be free...

If an oak held the feel all-along.
Then why have I been under this hill so long?
Giving my essence away at your demand.
Gripping tight this tainted ring from my hand.

Jerked and held to the nature of an awkward existence.
Dying for the love of a dead bride in the ground.
Who am I? Just a heartless clown...
Who am I? Just a poet bound to this fate I've found...

Who am I? Other than a sideshow freak...
Who am I? Besides a child grown too weak...
Who am I? For you to hate...
I stand faceless in the mirror but now I'm too late...

A Haunting Face

As the ink bleeds from my eyes, I feel my soul begin to subside.
To the curb with my predictable heart.
As my fears hold strong, while I'm torn apart...
So I walk across the frozen lake, left with the memories of that haunting face.
Such an unforgettable action in my eyes.
The sound of her scream, never fading away in dreams...
The world seems a lighter gray. I wish I could live this life to another day.
For all of my worries to simply fade. Just so I can forget that haunting face.
In the sink I burn away those years. A darker black ink draining as my tears.
As I break-down and hold close my fears.
Just so you can pass on, away from these love-songs...
Thin as the ice could be, still seems too damn deep.
And the ax never sinks, I only drown.
A haunting face, an unforgettable sound...
Side-torn to the next stage of death.
Love-torn and another demon finds its way into my chest.
So I breathe in, to accept this predictable hell.
Such a haunting face, my mind will just never wipe away...

All For Naught

Little did she know, how I took that hit.
Little did I know, in that life of shit.
Nothing could have worked, to release all the lime.
Nothing could have worked, I just lost every time.
Strength of every thought I held in my heart. All of those hits taking me down.
Into the earth where we should be. I fought forever to keep this truth.
Of all the years worn down onto my feet. Of all the flesh torn off of the meat.
I've killed them all, to keep the one. I lost it all, "*suicide never fun.*"
Little did she know, how I took that hit.
Little did I know, in that world of shit.
Nothing to stop it, she never saw my strive.
Nothing to stop it, to save me from my sacrifice.
I tried my hardest, only to lose my mind.
I fought the hardest, for only me to see.
I gave up my soul, to keep her free.
I lost it all and will never be released.
It was all for naught, I just want to rot.
It was all for naught, because I have always lost.
But in the end I was right. So I do have the last laugh.
"But naught the light..."

The Bleeding Pen

Shout to the north side of my sanity.
To see the sights of the forever unseen.
Fall down to the logic-break and set it aside for us to anticipate.

I have foreseen this lock of my skull-trust.
Left in the darkness of a sideways heart-fuck.
Now begin the countdown and place the knife there.
As the pen begins to bleed and I weep only air.
Tied to a light-post, darkness buried for the most.
To see the sight, I don't want to see.
To know how it ends and to just let it be.

Held tight, the bleeding pen. As then all the names appear before my eyes.
Logic found just the same, as with the demons behind my eyes.
Shout to the north side of my sanity.
And fight for those things that could never be.
Now falling deeper to the wayside.
I could try all I want but will never find.

The bleeding pen, spilling out my fate.
The bleeding pen, draining on my face.
A bleeding pen, knowing of my assured doom.
The bleeding pen, drawing closer me to you.

Dead in My Arms

Pulsating, a heartbeat at the end of the hall.
Regurgitating, and the blood begins to fall.
Anticipating, a better way for me to know.
Illuminating, the dead one beneath the snow.
I screamed my loudest, yet no one seemed to hear.
I died the loudest, with only a thought of fear.
I held on the longest, but only to fall.
I held her for hours, there covered in frost.
She wanted the bad guy, only to gain it after all.
She wanted the wrong guy, only for me to fall.
I needed a good drink, to get me through the day.
I need not to think, dead in my arms yesterday.
Pulsating, a heartbeat at the end of the hall.
Still waiting, as the rain begins to fall.
Anticipating, a better way for me to go.
Illuminating, "still dead in my arms" under the snow.

My Rotting Soul

A vibrate felt behind her teeth. All the while, I thought it would be neat.
Her frigid aftereffects felt under her sheets.
And the film behind my eyes growing sleek.
Opposite emotions found under my teeth.
All the while I thought I was free. To that notion of my dismay.
My rotting soul, just breaking away.
Ninety bottles against my head and the smell of death upon my breath.
Fester of the child I adored "just my rotting soul behind this door."
A quiver between her legs, a shiver felt deep in my grave.
And all the while, I thought I was right.
But I just rot with my soul, here buried beneath the ice...

Under The Frost

It's a memory that never fades. A time of all those loving days.
For me and her to hold hands and play.
To smile and know, it was ours to save.
Under the ice goes all those thoughts.
Deeper and deeper beneath the frost.
So how can I stop it from dying that way?
I wish I could turn it back and our love I would save.
Smiles forever frozen in time.
I wish I could just stop and rewind.
To those parties and that unforgettable kiss.
It's a part of me that I'll forever miss.
Laid so far away, frozen in time's abyss.

White to gray and red to black. All those thoughts just take me back.
A hug and smile on a cool spring day.
The smell of roses and a peppermint haze.
It's a memory that just never dies.
Stuck with me forever and under the frost of time.
To live this nightmare over and over and over again.
To remember those faces and spilt lives of sin.

Touch of the one fear now gone. Against her flesh and for way too long.
I've dealt with this far too long. How could I have saved us from all those wrongs?
Under the frost goes that kiss. Under the frost and frozen in time's abyss.
Under the darkness, I rock back and forth.
Trying to forget her but only remembering more...

Cotton Mouth

Before the dawn was right at fact. Before the swan was broken and ripped.
There was a place where I could go.
To live life in tranquility – to escape all I've known.
Before the demon stood in the light. Before the fruits of the forever were ripe.
There was a place where I could go,
To escape the torment – to melt the snow.
The words I can no longer find, bundles of cotton in my throat.
Nothing I could say, only choke back to the new-side of my broken faith.
Standing on the edge of all that was real.
Just waiting for you, under this hill.
To wash clean the wounds of our Mother-Earth.
Just hoping a sign from our dead-birth. Before the dawn comes again...
There was a place that I could hide. There was a day when all was fine.
But now far pass me, just faded in the book.
I have now nothing to say, so I sit back and look...
Before the dawn was right at fact.
Before the swan was frozen, broken and ripped.
There was a place where I could go.
To live life so tranquil – to escape all I've ever known.

Follow the Lizard

Biting down, on the roots of my nature, screaming at the top of our lungs.
Hiding under the sheets of silk, consuming death with every plunge.
Yellow paint-chips on the walls, black-light paintings dancing to our songs.
Sweat bleeding over a Devil's eyes. A numeric monster eating me alive.
Writhing star lights, burning through the blinds.
A God walking over the rivers of time.
Bleeding harder, as she bites my neck.
Consuming my nature, with every breath.
Follow the lizard, to see how this world ends.
Follow the lizard, to feel the pain begin.
Biting poison onto my wrist, under my tongue and another death-kiss.
Ages of old, fading onto my dreams.
Follow the lizard, to see the heaven's streams.
Beyond the knowing, of my child dead against the walls.
Follow the lizard, throughout the endless halls.
Pushing down, onto the roots my nature, screaming at the top or our lungs.
Follow the lizard into the house of the Gods.
Consuming death with every plunge.

Out of Control

My stomach, not feeling right. A bitter taste, besides the lime.
This horrid face, clinching to my dreams.
This bullet phase, not over till she screams...

Am I ready yet to take my throne? Am I ready yet to lose control?
Have I the malice now? To take you down?
Have I the malice now? To doom the clouds?

My head not feeling right, a bitter taste inside the ice.
This horrid fate, I've had to endure.
This murderous phase, heard behind the door.

My hands can't grip it. I'm falling over the edge!
My hands can't grip it. This cocktail plague!
The thunder screaming now, behind my eyes!
The thunder screaming now, yet it's no surprise...

Down the drain and all her pains are on me.
I can't forget this flame, because it's burning me.
I lost it all and seem to lose it again...
My whole world out of control, just like my head.

Diluted

Spiraling down my throat, swift shifting across my arms.
The diluted taste slamming into my head.
And not another word, until it is dead.
All the bugs crawling under the sheets.
Earthworms eating at this tormented beast.
A drape pulled down over my eyes.
This diluted heartache eating me alive.

Shattered nonsense taking me deeper into this hole.
The world quakes and I flake away into nothing but ash and mold.
As the peppermint spice drowns out all my thoughts.
Emotions raped and forgot yet not another word, until they all burn.

Sins building over time and time some more.
To the side of the never to be let inside again.
Diluting all my dreams of when we lived in bliss.
Not one last kiss, before I rip my skin away.
Diluting my thoughts of you, as I fester in my grave.

God Spoke!

Darkness in the darkest hour of my life.
It took me a while, to pull out your knife.
Shining blood-red across the land and we scream.
Blood draining onto the ground and it seeps.
Dry minded demons thinking they could win.
As God spoke gentle upon the wind to me.
My insides burned and my eyes began to bleed.

Dust drowning the cattle, but no shelter can we find.
God spoke to me... And said it would be fine.

The insects starting to cloud the skies.
Acid raindrops melting us alive!
And darkness only weeps for the truth.
All that was once shattered in youth.
But I want to be the one to take the pain away.
And God took my hand and cleaned off the blade.
But only my shame could reflect through the night.
Blood-red moons and purple star lights.

Darkness in the darkest hour of my life.
I wished to say one thing but I then lost the rights.
It took some time to wipe clean my skin.
And the demonic sins just built up on me.
Shaking inside and I could only weep.
The fire dripping from my eyes.
As the acid torment drained down my spine.
Death-Rain flooding all of the lands...

"The dusts drowning the cattle, but no shelter can we find."
"God spoke! He said it would all be fine."

A Zombie's Nature

Ages of lying under the scattered blades of grass.
Darkness forever flowing, letting nothing else pass.
Knowledge boiling between this decay and my soul.
Which way to navigate me out of this hole?
Pointless words spoken for no one to hear.
A child lying in the shadows, dripping with fear.
Her voice begins cracking, and only a cry.
Ages of this death trail for no one else to find.
Tearing open, the ground shakes apart for me to rise.
This limp body lifting above the fog and lime.
The little child weeping, awaiting a new sunrise...
Slamming against me, the echoes of memories passed.
The hope of a smile, above the scattered blades of grass.
Hunger of the sweet flesh, of all bastards must die.
Then feast upon the murder, when all else subsides.
The little child weeping, looking into my eyes.
With no drive to move her, she just waits to die.
Long hair decaying, falling off my skull. Brown eyes melted away with the old.
The child begins to whisper a medley...
Of all the pains she's endured, all must die now, all will burn...
Ages of sleeping, just waiting to rise again.
The fester of all my deepest thoughts and darkest sins.
Pointless heartache for this child to endure.
Tears begin to evaporate, Mother Earth giving birth.
A new dawn of all my natures, love, hate and death.
As now she stopped her whisper and demands her death.
How could I stop it from ending that way?
Darkness forever flowing, letting nothing else stay.
I gripped the child gently by her arm and wrist.
I leaned over and gave her a kiss.
On her cheek laid the truth of the world beyond her own.
So I lean back and rest against my headstone.
My heart is never going to beat again.
But all is set right for another child's revenge.
Dancing with my natures for no one else to see.
I begin to slumber and hope for another dream.
The child left there standing, with only a second thought.
Then she sees the sunrise and all her pains are lost.
Ages of lying under the scattered blades of grass.
Darkness forever flowing, letting nothing else pass.
Knowledge now boiling, inside the child's head.
She steps now onward knowing, that the pain will eventually pass...

A Lifetime

It's just as hard as one choice.
A step towards what you believe-in.
How hard would it be, to speak one thought?
How hard would it be, to take the blame?
How much torment, can one soul take?

It's only as hard as you make it out to be.
The blade's sinking into your breast.
As your tears rain-down over your breath.
How hard is it truly, to simply stand-up?
How hard would it be, to turn around and let it free?

Hours to days to months of the years in the decades we hold.
True to the thought of the ancients we admire so dear.
Breath after breath and life after death.
How hard is it, to say what you feel?
How hard would it be, to step away from the hill?
How hard is it, for one soul to control its life?

It's just as hard as one choice.
A step towards what you believe in.
Years growing above the roads and trees.
Ages gone and passed, just like you and me.
Death smiling as we return to the elements.
Water, fire, love and hope.

A lifetime of worries and pains.
It's just as hard as stepping away.
Sand to rock and human to dust.
Mountains moved aside for you and I.
How hard would it be, truly - truly?
How hard would it be? To make that change?
To control the world and our pains.
It's only as hard as one single step.
It's only as long as one human breath.
It would be only as hard, as what you make it out to be.
"It's only as hard as the choice, to give-up or to breathe..."

Dry Blood

Whore as I may be, by the eyes of justice and the free.
Held tight to the railroad-spike, sticking out of my heart.
Left in the town-square, to put fear into the hearts of all children.
Call me what you may and get out of my way you filth!
Leave me to my tools and waste not my time you fool.

Burn me if you wish and hate me if you will!
Spit on my wounds, as I bleed out your pills.
Drain me in the public-eye, to base fear for all to despise.
And drown what you hate, by the name that you gave...
Hit me harder till my brain spills out and onto the ground...

Hang me in the path of your enemies for an example.
Call me a demon and cut my wrist as your justice laughs.
Human-swine held high in the public-eye, of all your filthy lies.
Burn what you just don't understand, and never will.
Call me a monster and let the blood dry away in the sun.

Jagged to the core, of this wretched whore.
Nailed to a cross for all to see.
Dry blood caked to the corpse in the town-square.
Shaking dogs waiting for the dead-meat to fall.
Pathetic people throwing their stones...

My name is what you gave to me.
You stand so meek under the wing of your God.
Feeling that safety waits just under his roof.
Cut me if you will and watch the dry blood flake away.
As another innocent is put to death.
And in hell you are damned, for your manipulation of the Lord.
"And God weeps, as fragments of my dry blood shatter upon the floor."

Aside and Broken

Left in the middle of a mosh-pit.
"He was just a child at the age of six."
Now a man torn down to the floor and he screams.
The child not knowing the answers you seek.
Broken down and he wishes to be free.

Red-paint chipping away and the wall begins to break.
Black-light drawings covering his eyes.
Acid pouring into his mind and down his spine.
Mushrooms tweaking the stem of his brain.
The teenaged girl licking his cheek and face.

Faith melting away as he hits the brick.
His world begins to crumble and life feels like shit.
The man now broken as he's set aside.
Now he lives for only revenge and pride.

In the corner he cries as the lingering smoke begins to fade.
Life no-longer has its meanings.
All drinks and food no-longer have a taste.
Just bitterness of the actions that ring under his teeth.
Then he cocks the gun, ready for the day...
To him, there is no meaning to the things we say.

Sad and alone, the teenaged girl kisses his neck.
His eyes begin to blister and demons dance upon his breath.
She screams as he pulls the trigger and a flash!
His head bursts open and he just laughs...

Tickling the edge of his now shattered open skull.
Blood and brain growing cold.
He's dead and doesn't even care.
Left aside and broken with no air.
Would you care? "Why lie?!"

"I've been left aside and broken all my life..."

Torment-Tango

Leaning back, I put the cigarette out on my wrist.
Leaning back, I let out a heavy breath.
And the devil sleeps in my chest.
Said to the never once you thought I was right...
And give me back the rusted tool and turn out the lights.

Hope of a heart-lock to the true side of my skull-trust.
And she dances while I bleed at night.
She smiles while I scream in fright.
Hoping to set it to the right state of fact.
And never was I going to look back.

Zero emotion left in the bottle that I drink.
Shooting at my troubles and shooting at my dreams.
Loving this Torment-Tango you dearly insist.
And I scream as you lick my neck.
I try to run but you catch my wrist.

Throw me to the side-set story of sanity so lost.
Leave the money on the table and go.
We dance this Torment-Tango under the snow.
Kiss my God and watch me break in two.
Leaning back, waiting for you to choose.

Darkness now seems so sweet.
And you grab me tight and hold me close.
She was never there till it was cold...
I put another cigarette out on my eyes.
To feel something more than your despise...

Scream my love and three steps to the side.
Look at me with pride, that you are truly mine.
Cut my heart out and play it again.
Kissing the turn-back tale of sins.

Leaning back, I see all the grace fade away.
Zero emotion on the steps to my grave.
Compassions forgotten by the ones who cared.
So we dance this Torment-Tango deeper into our despair.

Laugh Myself to Sleep

She never took what I offered to her.
I laid down the path so we could end. "Happily ever after."
And those days of the memories seem to bring a chill.
Upon the notion that I'm still under this hill.
That day, she gave me a kiss to remember. "*And I do...*"
And I try to leave it all done, before I end up like you.

So I light this cigarette with my burning heart.
I close my eyes and begin to fall apart.
Before those pains had covered this man.
Before this nightmare controlled the land.
There was still hope and a sun to shine.
Now only pain...

She never took what I had to offer.
It seemed to be only fight after fight.
And hit after hit I took on the cheek.
So now I just lie down and laugh myself to sleep.
Because no one's here but me. "A dark room and cold sheets."

It all stood on the tip of a lie.
If only I said No instead of Yes.
If only I had tried a little harder than what I did.
Maybe I could be holding her still...
Maybe not under this hill and maybe I could smile...
But I just have these dreams and it seems she never cared.

I died and killed myself, over a love that will never last.
I cut the deepest and watched the blood drip.
Only so she could hate herself and feel sick.
And damn the fact that we were once in love...
Damn the fact, that I was the only one who tried.

So I smoke this down to my soul and begin to drift away.
It may not be home but just my grave, "yet I lean back still."
All alone, under this hill "where they put me away."
She never took what I had to offer her...
She just threw my heart and soul away.
It seemed to be only slit after slit.
I took it, hit after hit on the cheek.
So for now I'll just lie down here and laugh myself to sleep.

Half Empty

A dog waiting for its master to return.
Out in the freezing rain alone.
Never to be picked up and to die so cold and alone.

Hopeless in the gutter, the bastard takes another drink.
Coughing up his lungs and has no place to sleep.
The people point their fingers and laugh out loud.
The broken man does nothing but leave in shame.

A frustrated teen, mad at his parents.
Turns up the radio to drown out their voices.
And a truck collides with their car.
The mom and dad dead, and the teen left scarred.

A little girl walking down the street.
A strange man pulls her aside.
She cannot scream, after her mouth has been taped shut.
Raped in the dark and left there to bleed.
Broken and scarred, she can only weep - just weep.

There is no one who is going to shelter you from the truth.
You have only to be broken and dead in the end.
There are no shining gates, only the earthworms in the grave.
Why lie to try and make it better?
As all could just fall at once and maybe it should...
Then you could open your eyes and know the perverted truth.
That hatred and pain do overrule the all that is good...
The sick truth that we are frail and weak little children.
Why think there will be a happy ending?
The world turns on and on without you, so get over it.

Pointless, hopeless, helpless child wishing for sight.
We came in as just mindless babble and will leave the same.
Most, sooner than others and we'll just rot in our graves.
As the dog waits for its master.
And the bastard takes another drink...
There is nothing to say to the raped.
No comfort for the child left by himself in shame.
So why lie to yourselves and each other by saying it is all okay?
Just get with the program and out of the way.
There is no happy ending here, just a muddy grave...

Half Full

The wind blowing through the trees.
A summer rain falling upon her cheek.
The child held tight in her mother's arms.
True to the grace in their souls and hearts.
On the edge of a cliff stands a blind man holding open arms.
Wide to the truth and hopes that the sound of the morning will stay.
In his heart he knows that God stands there...
He kisses the lords grace and feels the soothing summer air.

A lonely soul walking upon a road of leaves.
Pointed towards his goals and beliefs.
Taking the beating so they won't have to feel the pain.
The man walks into the sunrise, with a grin on his face.
Along the horizon spreads the red-orange glow of the sun.
Across the land it flows into our souls and hearts.
Warming us and waking the day.
Growing upon the beauty of our earth.
Proving our lords grace.

True to the fact that there will be another day.
True to the fact that we just need some faith.
To hold us true to one another.
And keep strong what we strive to gain.
Reason and hope within our souls and beliefs.
True to the fact that we can survive.
It's just as simple as opening our minds.

Never give up what you fight for.
The knowledge of the ages gone and passed.
Keeping us true to those facts, that the Knight will return.
And behind the darkness the sun does burn.
Waiting to melt the clouds away and show us warmth.
Don't be discouraged when the rain begins to fall.
Dance upon the leaves and remember those words.
That true to what we know and hold.
A child or the grace of our own souls.
We can make it out of the darkness and find some hope.
You just need to believe in what you feel.
In your heart, beating through your soul.
The fact that you will only receive that which you have given.
"And to know that through the darkness, there will shine another day..."

Outside the Window

Leaning my head against the window.
Late in the day and cool in the frost.
I gaze deep into my reflection.
Watching the years grow upon my face.
I only wish to rest now... And to soon leave this place.

I can see them standing there in the halls.
Old friends, now gone away from all.
I can hear their voices now.
Upon all those days we knew...
But now they are gone and you are too.

Outside the window.
I watch the ages flow pass my eyes.
I can taste the frost upon the glass.
As I press my forehead harder. "Hoping they'll see."
I can hear their laughter but it's all just a dream...

Leaning my head back, I stare at the lights.
I can hear their chanting, as they call me out.
I wish I could play, one last time in the rain.
As she is also standing there waiting for me.
With a smile and rose in her palm.
Blowing me a kiss of true love and warmth.

Outside the window, they seem so happy without a care.
As they sing and dance with arms thrown in the air.
Voices ringing numb into my brain.
The beating memories that hold me to that.
A tear in my eyes and this load on my back.
I wish I could play, just one last time.
As they call me out with smiles so true...

Outside the window, stands my love and pride.
Looking outside the window and I begin to cry.
They all stand outside the window "I hope they find their way."
Outside the window, I stare beyond the frost and haze.
Outside the window, I gaze upon those old friends.
I stare outside the window, hoping we'll maybe meet again...

"Farewell and God-speed..."

Wax Doll

Standing tall, the voodoo love-machine.
Shaking her hips, in front of my face.
Gripping my tongue with her lips.
Driving me deeper into the acid trip...

Mixed with the blood of pure bliss.
And the Gods bless me and give a kiss.
As the voodoo love Goddess grips her hips.
And looks deep and hard into my soul.
Taking me down and through the cold...

She licks it nice and does it right.
So it just dissolves in her mouth.
And she smiles with death upon her breath.
And the obvious screams in the clouds.

Saturn rains down the lust we inhale.
I am just a wax doll melting on the shelf.
I am her prize that she gets at the end.
With a look of inward pleasure on her face.
And she snaps it right back into place...

Mother Earth in clear sight upon our lust-bout.
And all the demons scurry when she begins to shout.
Standing tall and writhing before the devil's eyes.
With love running down her legs and the stars in her eyes.

Turn up the drumbeat and take me now.
Step upon the face of the clouds.
And drink away the notions that we feared.
Ride me my love, just your wax voodoo-doll.
Between your soul and flesh.

Take me deeper into your temple.
That lovely place of worship.
And wash the death from your breath.
My voodoo love-monster gripping my tongue real tight.
Place me between your legs and let's start this right...

Awkward

I guess this is what happens.
When you live in a first-person state of mind.
Of all the things I once said.
Behind the words and under the bed.
It was quite awkward what was said.
And now we hold it till death.

So leave me on a dusty shelf.
To gather the years and begin to melt.
As the ink flakes off the pages.
After so many ages.
Of the awkward things I've said...

Run me longer through your hatred.
So no one will ever understand.
But not to be and never to see.
How this awkward child could grow.
In a life of grief and under the coal.

She burns me to light the furnace.
My cries fading in the ash.
The awkward truth that we hide.
Behind our words and pride.

This is the life I live and die.
These are the words beyond the lies.
To shine a better way.
But all I do is age and fade.

For all the things I've once said.
That dwelled in my heart and head.
Running onward through my blood.
Spilling onto the ground, it is ink...
What a one-sided point of view.
In my awkward existence, shadowing our grim truths.

Chapter 9

This Grin on My Face

No One's There

No one to hide me, no one to fry me.
No one to need me, no one to free me.
Someone just kill me, someone just kill me.
I need someone to embrace.
God I need a new fate, God I am a disgrace.

No one to love me, still they shove me.
No one to kiss me, no one will miss me.
Someone has hurt me, someone has burnt me.
I need to escape this fate.
God I need a better faith, God I need to accept my rage.

No one's there, to see me break-down.
No one's there, for this heartless clown.
No one's there to lend a hand.
No one cares for this heartless man.

No one to hide me, no one find me.
No one to feel me, no one to heal me.
Someone just kill me, someone just kill me.
I need someone to embrace.
God I need a new face, God I am a disgrace.

Leave me to be and set my lies free.
True to the fact that I'm still me.
Leave me to die, no one's there as I cry.
Love me to death and steal my last breath.
And you smile as I burn, smile as I burn.

No one to love me, no one to need me.
No one to help me, no one is there.
No one to kiss me, still no one has missed me.
I just fall away in despair, and no one's there...

Love the Blood

Love the blood, love the blood.
Till the end, till the end.
Love the blood, love the blood.
Love the blood of sin.

Still I fight, still I fight.
All damn night, all damn night.
Hear me weep, hear me weep.
As I sleep, as I sleep away all my sins...

Under dirt, under dirt.
Death till birth, death till birth.
Fire burns, fire burns, away this flesh of sin.

Love the blood, love the blood.
Till the end, till the end.
Love the blood, love the blood.
Love the blood of sin.

Rise Back

It's time to return to the spotlight. "It's time to return."
It's time to return to the spotlight. It's time they all know the hurt...

Foot to the stones upon the floor and it rings loud behind the door.
So kiss me... "My name is *Death*."
Move out of my way and out of my chest.

It's time now to rise back, into the limelight where I once stood.
It's time for me to rise back. Till this is all understood.

Just give me my life back and clear out the halls.
So I give you your knife back. "You sure did have the gall."
To push your love away and to watch him die.
Just give me my life back and end this fight.

It's time to return to the spotlight. "It's time to return."
It's time for me to rise back. Crawl out from under the earth.
It's time now for me to fight back. And to bring an end to all of this hurt.

Sideways Heart-Fuck

Lips against lips and tongues writhing hard.
On our knees and pushed in far.
It was a nightmare we shared before our last Christmas.
Or maybe it was just in my head.
As I tried to keep her, but lost everything instead.

**AND OVER THE NOTION OF YOU AND I!
I'VE DONE MY TIME, AND I TRIED!
BUT FAR TOO LONG, HAS THIS PAIN GONE ON!
I'VE TAKEN TOO MUCH, OF THESE LOVE SONGS!
DOOMED AND DAMNED FROM THE START!
LEFT HERE SO STUCK, AGAIN IN THIS...
"SIDEWAYS HEART-FUCK."**

So still I sit, in the dark corner of my mind.
Fighting these wars, time after time.
So now I wish there was a better way.
Yet still I love the love of going insane...
For dreams and hopes of her bloody grave.
I think she would be happy to know.
That her grave is still under the snow.
And all my sins lie beneath the frozen lake.
I think she would be happy to know.
I've done my time, "and I'm ready to go..."

**FURTHER AND FURTHER I FALL AWAY!
INTO THE SHADOWS, AND MEMORIES!
FOR ONLY YOU, TO KNOW WHAT I MEAN!
NOW I'M ASIDE AND BROKEN, JUST TOO WEAK!
WITH SLAUGHTER AND NONSENSE FAR INSIDE!
STUCK TO THE WALLS AND BURNED ALIVE!**

Unknown to the knowing of what we said.
We made sweet love but now we're dead.
And damn the question that she asked.
If only I could turn the clock back...
What a stupid question, on her lips.
I could have lied and not had been damned to live in shit.
If only I lied, then I would not have this.
I damn the question that damns me today.
I wish she never asked it, I just want it to go away;

DEEPER INTO THE DARKNESS, WHERE WE STAY!
AND DANCE UPON THE TORMENT IN OUR BRAINS!
FOR THE REASON SHE'S DEAD, I DARE NOT SAY!
ALL IT DID WAS DRIVE ME INSANE!
HER FILTHY ACTIONS AND MY TRUTH!
THAT SIDEWAYS HEART-FUCK, FROM MY YOUTH!

Dreams were set aside, and I could have lied.
When she asked if I had been with someone else.
I did not lie, I told the truth, and now she's dead.
"She was with her love at the time."
I had no reason to lie, but now I'm damned...
Because I cared and loved her so. Still her grave lies under the snow.
I dare not tell her that she's dead.
She seems so happy, with her broken-heart instead.

"And over the notion of you and I." "On I go, I tried and died."
"And forever that memory is stuck..."
"Eternally I'm left, with this Sideways Heart-Fuck."
"Damn you!"

Ages Unknown

Left there to wallow in myself, days of needles and burning nails.
Shoved under my skin, for as I scream there is no one here to navigate me.

Deeper into the darkness of my own games.
Still I sit here, drowning in shame.
For what was the reason, I'll not soon find.
Those ages unknown, hidden behind my eyes.
Nature unfolds and shows a neon-right.
For no lesson to learn, when we turn out the lights.
And die as we may and lay in our graves.
For the reasons unknown, and not soon shown.
Why these leaders must sacrifice me.
As left here to die, by myself I cry.
Days of the nonsense and burning nails.
Shoved under my skin, for as I scream there is no one here to motivate me.

Then deeper it sinks into the darkness of my games.
Still the curse and pain remains the same.
For what was the reason, I'll not soon find.
Those ages unknown, hidden behind my eyes.

Sinister Inferno

Digging into the rotten flesh, driving the hatred inside my chest.
Combing the waste aside, for all to soon see why.
As burning deeper-in, knowledge forming above their sins.

My dirty flesh, peeled back for the bone to show.
Ants and worms, crawling under my skin, eating at my filthy whims.
And they break off the limbs, to watch me scream to death.
They burn away my skin, until nothing's left.

Fire seeping behind the skies, then we burn and it's no surprise.
As swimming through the pool, burning our actions to their core.
And the notion of love soon dies, flowing red on the floor.

The eyes push me further into the back. I try to reach but still at a lack.
Nothing to comfort me, besides these pins.
Nothing to warm me, besides my sins.
Burning and burning within this sinister inferno.
Beyond all the answers, I do not know.

Her Faded Eyes

Smiles shining, white teeth gleaming.
Light shown, onto our laughs, jokes ringing, of ages passed.
Smiles shown, for all that's known.
Faces true, to the points we make.
All shining warm, but still feels fake.

I can taste the deception, from behind her lies.
I can feel the tingle, running up and down my spine.
And I can see the heart-break, behind her faded Eyes.

Miles shown, onto our memories gone.
Smiles shown, but they still feel wrong.
Laughing bold, solid as concrete - yet false.
Emotions true, ringing between me and you.
Years left in a picture, that I just can't burn.
Try as we may, but it still hurts.

I can taste the deception, from beneath her lies.
I can feel the sharp pain, in the middle of my spine.
And I can see the heart-break, behind her faded Eyes.

Arm's-Length

It could be the same thing all over again. I could just bleed over the stone and sins.
I could just cut and watch it flow. I could still love her but I let it go.
Relationships no longer mean a thing. The words were screamed but never stayed.
I could beat it harder but still it's dead.
I could reach a little longer but I walk away instead.
Try and try and losing all but the pain.
I've died and died only to watch us break away.
Not for now and mostly because of me.
I've had enough for one screwed-up dream.
Don't ask a stupid question, I'll give no reply.
Don't smile at me, not after I died... *Just so you can sleep happy at night.*
I could just pull the trigger, really tight and then flash goes the lights.
We could have worked it out, I could have held on forever.
You could have tried a little harder, but no longer shall this eat at me.
I've died enough for one lifetime and we stay at arm's-length.

Devil to Your Eyes

I drop to the tile. It sure has been a while.
I fall down and scrape my knee. I bleed in pain and you laugh at me.
The small one pushed aside, from your games.
I was the devil to your eyes, and you just cast me away.
Alone in a dark room, I nod my head and live confused.
I never did a thing "to hurt a Soul." I did nothing but was pushed out in the cold.
I wish to weep - I'm just so alone... "Slap me in the face, give me a sour taste."
You were my lover now - "what the hell??!"
We were once together, but you just pushed me to hell.

Spinning around in circles, paint falling onto my eyes.
Dizzy dreams drowning down the diluted detestation.
For forgiving forever the frosted frustration for death to I.
Breaking the bottom-bolt behind the buried breath.
Dead to the dawn of the dream dusting the dishonest.
Cold to its core - before I was the devil to your eyes...
Scream and bleed loud ringing under the ice.
Hold your breath and throw the dice. Call me a demon and rip out my eyes.
It sounds so sweet still sour stinging. Never to the nerve now frayed and bleeding.
Alone in this hole holding the handle hard.
Head hitting hot hatred to its core, and the blood drains onto the floor.
Still screaming sound sorrow shouting, "such a surprise!"
It was cold to its core - before I was the devil to your eyes.

Unspoken

Quivering bed-sheets, laid upon her dreams,
A slight vibrate heard through the night,
She grips her fist and bites her lip tight.
Wet frictions oozing over her dreams.
Grasped in her hands and writhing through the night.
Unspoken through the halls of our hopes.
She kisses soft the neck of mine, holding the stars in her eyes.
Unspoken lust under the sheets, a slight scream heard through the night.
She licks my ear and whispers to me.
Grasping onto the glory of her dreams.
Biting onto the roots of my nature, untold stories held under the sky.
Unspoken lust sessions of her long awaited night.
Squirming under the sheets, under the moon she begins to scream.
Wet between the place that I love so dear.
I bite down onto the glory of the Gods.
And watch my death brought so soon.
Quivering bed-sheets, laid upon her dreams.
A slight vibrate heard through the night.
This angel kisses her, soft upon the lips.
She begins to grip her fist, biting down tight.
Smooth friction above and over her hopes and dreams.
She holds it tight and never lets go of me...

Tuesday

Light the day for another strike. Against the wood, nailed out of sight.
Hold me warm when the sun burns out. *Kiss me sweet and let me shout...*
Another thought spewing from this head.
Anger building until it's dead. And Tuesday comes and goes again.
Burning out the day, and shadowing my whims.
Ignorant to the grave and then a little more.
So it begins to rain, red blood on the floor.
Freezing the actions in time and they stay.
Light a dark path, towards the end of this day.
Strike the match against my eyes, hold me close and turn out the lights.
Tuesday comes and goes once again. It rains red blood over all our sins.
Count the minutes before the thrust, watch the needle stop and turn to rust.
Begin the break-down of all that was real.
Just another Tuesday, under this hill.

Watching It Crumble

Tick, tick, tick and take it all away.
Tock, tock, tock, talk all you want in your grave.
Spin the orange-light and guide me away.
Drip the sugar down and melt this fate.

A winding cloud covering my hopes.
A man pushed aside, against the ropes.
Then his teeth hit the floor.
True-concrete bleeding from my wrist.
Leaving me here, never to be missed.

Strap me down so I can watch it fall.
It crumbles apart, breaking the walls.
Light not showing any reason to this.
Just pure nonsense and ignorant bliss.

Cut me if you will.
Take this blade and ram it into my lung.
Watch me cough and it's only blood.
Slimy sweat dripping from my hands.
A green mildew blanketing this man.

I just watch it all fall to pieces.
And laugh as they try to hide.
I live only to be there for what's in line.
I breathe only to pass my time.
I've done good deeds for the demon named "I."
I did my part, as now you die.
Push my head to the ground and I lick up the death.
Dirt so sweet of the destruction coming forth.
Now strap me in and lay me back.
I'm watching it all crumble and I just laugh.

An Ax Don't Lie

Jerk the handle back, falling deeper into her neck.
Smooth, straight to the bone.
Crunch to the bottom, then against the stone.

Starlight fading behind the moon.
Danger breaking upon this doom.
Numbed-down screaming through the clouds.
Her body falling deeper into the ground.

Bloody last thoughts that ring in head.
Tragic and nonstop, acidic death.
Another's depiction festering inside.
Dreams that won't fade and rip apart my mind.

True to the nature that we endure, an ax don't lie, nor reward.
An ax don't lie, only gives its worth.
This ax won't lie, the truth left stained.
This ax won't lie, as left beneath the frozen lake.

Burnt Flesh

Such an open space, no one's there. Just damp - cold air...
Darkness holds its new meaning.
As I sit there waiting for an ending.
Only shadows to call my friends, just lonely years of loss and sin.

I begin to cut it, to give me a new view.
I begin to eat it, to bring me closer to you.
I begin to break it, only to see how it ends.
I tear off my own flesh, and wash myself in the sins.

I can smell the burning of my skin.
As I sit here in my own personal hell.
I can taste the death on the wind "it brings forth an ominous feel."

Such wide open space, and I just sit here as such a disgrace.
As the memories build up, of nothing but pain.
I feel my flesh burn and my soul fades away.
Living life as this burnt flesh, a distorted man so alone.
Left here in this open space, holding darkness as my home.

Rage #5

It begins to shiver, tweaking over the chains,
It swallows its tongue, then shakes away.
It bites down on an open wound. It clinches the bone and meat too.
Tearing in, to know how it ends, eating the ashes to taste their sins.
Lusting the right-twist to the north-side of heart,
Holding it real tight and tearing it apart.
Echoes of the placid fire humming in my head
The anger builds-up and brings forth death.
Darkness called just the same. Then the demons laugh as it begins to rain.
Torn into the deepest part of it, ripping the hole wide to see what's inside.
I pull the guts out and play with them.
I lick the bloody part and enjoy this sin.
As the anger turns to rage, and the blood fills another page.
All the answers are still the same, you can't out run it nor brush it away.
There is no hope for the hopeless. There is no rest for the shattered-dead.
You can't cut it out, when it's in your head.
You can't stop this rage that quivers under your bed.

My Cannibal Lover

Shot to the darkest part of my dreams.
Held down to the shatter of all those screams.
Cold as ice, upon the walls and she laughs.
Biting down onto my wrist - "she loves that best."
Hunger of all those nights when we became one.
Rammed so far into the dark where it comes undone.
Then I begin to remember the stars and moon.
All the lights flicker and she giggles too.
Thrown down and I just can't move.
I'm held down as she begins to consume.
Nothing to change it but I never could.
She bites down harder and as never she should.
Wow was the answer to what I felt.
She looks me in the eyes and I'm so overwhelmed.
Will there be nothing left when she's done?
She begins to bite harder until it's all gone.
Once in the shadows we were one.
This night never seems to end, yet it does.
Will nothing be left to remind the world of me?
My cannibal lover just smiles as she eats away my dreams.

Chewing At My Rib

It's like a long nail going through my cheek.
Nothing could change this tormented beast.
It's like I'm shaking a million miles an hour.
Nothing could stop this unchangeable power.
Up-side goes the notion of the turmoil within.
Then down-shove of all those hopes and whims.
The dirt seems to have a better taste.
For some new reason I don't feel so enraged.
But then again that's just a lie that I tell myself.
To maybe sleep a little better in hell.
Nauseous pounding on the walls of my gut.
I can't take this anymore, "I'm shit out of luck."
I scratch as hard as I can, deeper and deeper.
Until there's no skin left, just bone and meat.
I start chewing at my rib, and it tastes so sweet.
To know how good it is, to destroy myself.
"And nothing can stop this tormented monster from hell."

Bloody Knuckle

How many times can I do this to myself?
How many times must I venture through hell?
Only to feel the same in the end.
I've had enough death for one life, "I'm done now."
"Take back your knife."
How much longer must it stay frozen in time?
How much longer must I just sit back and whine?
I think I should get my game straight.
And just watch the blood drip off my knuckle and onto the slate...
It must be fate, that's all I can think.
It must be my fault that I never awake from this dream.
And slam! Against the brick my fist cracks and the bones shift.
The answers are still all the same, and there is no logic for the insane.
So leave me to my tools and just go away.
And harder against the wall goes my rage.
Then I smile knowing that nothing will change.
I stand inside myself alone with only hate.
With bloody knuckles and a shattered fate.
But in the end, it's all the same.
And how many more times must I live this dream?

Tongue-in-Cheek

"This is just between you and me." As is the thing you already know.
That some old thoughts were left under the snow.
Forever to be left and forgotten.
Yet as you can see, nothing will take it away from me.
Oh those screams that still ring through the night.
Nothing will ever replace it, my eternal fright.
So only for you to know my friend, that there is a trail to all those sins.
It lies behind all the leaves and under these sheets.
But if anyone were to ask, just let them pass.
Tell them... "This is all just tongue-in-cheek."
As the moon knows the truth to the actions I made.
And all those steps towards her grave.
Under the dirt may still lie the answers you seek...
But it will be hard to find the answers. Between my tongue and cheek.

Ice-Baby

It's not up to me anymore. "As if it ever was..."
There is no horizon beyond these dreams.
There is no comfort at night for me.
So please hold my head back as I spew.
Just please leave all those thoughts inside of you.
There's no more meaning to what we do.
There is no more logic between me and you.
Hold me baby, before the night falls dead.
Hold me baby, love me like you said.
Hold me tighter, through the starlight we dance.
Hold me tighter and spill all the romance.
Love me baby, just the way you did.
Love me baby, and bite down on my neck.
Scream real loudly and soon gone away.
Scream no logic, and then the sky turns gray.
Shiver my Ice-Baby, through all the things we knew.
Quiver my Ice-baby, and hold me closer to you.
Open your eyes a little wider, to see what's next in line.
Reach in a little deeper, tear away what's inside.
Hold me baby, before the night's through.
Hold it baby, the little compassion between me and you.
Love me baby, just the way you did.
Quiver my Ice-baby, and leave behind the things we did.

214

Behind This Grin

No one knows how hard it's been, to hang here for days on end.
No one knows what it took from me.
No one knows what you did to me.

So I'm tied to the wall, and you throw knives at my skull.
I'm blind in the light but now I see.
I loved once an angel but now only scream.
So punch me in the throat, then laugh while I choke.
You giggle while I weep on the ground.
You smile while I bleed and drown.

So tie me to the train-tracks and watch as I'm torn in two.
Lie to me in this endless night wish. Then kiss me as you slit my wrist.
In the corner I wait for the end. In the darkness I seep all my sins.
Now in the right turn to the lost state of fact.
In the heartbreak, I dare not look back.

So you laugh while I bleed dry - you giggle as I scream and cry.
Now what lies behind you, I dare not say.
The answers to all your sins, "this grin on my face."

How dare the memory bring itself back to me?
But I only smile back as you try to strike me.
Now you see the truth behind this grin.
You could beat me all day but in the end... "I win."

Caught Up

I feel so caught up but I'm not understood.
I feel so locked up, "*escape*" I never could.
I've tried the hardest but only to die.
I've died the hardest but again I'm alive.
I've said a lot then but it just fades.
I've done my time now, throw me into my grave.
You hold the trigger and squeeze it real tight.
You hold all the answers but turned out the lights.
I feel so caught up, with all I once said.
I feel so locked up, in someone else's head.
I've tried my hardest but only to die.
I died the hardest but again I'm alive.

Jerk It Numb

Many years spent over this thought.
Too many tears spent over this shock.
Miles of so long it has been on my soul.
Grinding down my heart with the coal.
Blackened heartbeats pounding through the night.
A bloody ax and a monster out of sight.
It has been so long, since I could hold someone true.
I can't even kiss another, without being haunted by you.
So jerk it harder, the blade in my back.
I could reach all day, yet still this lack.
So jerk it numb this blade in my spine. Laugh at my pain that never subsides.
Days true to the once I've said I cared. Then I was lost deeper in despair.
For all that held once our love. Now only a memory that feels so numb.

Acid Rain-Dance

Place your hands over your eyes.
Sing it deep to your soul and mixed with the lime.
Drive it further through the darkness for someone else to see.
Ride it to the summit, locked in place and we dream.
Melt the handle to the floor.
Can you hear the memories, from behind the door?
Lick the rim of the truth now frayed and gone.
Consume it true and dance to our song.
Millions of stars rushing through your eyes.
This acid rain-dance brings forth a surprise.
So dream if you dare, of someone left in despair.
Then cower at the sight when you see...
Of all the wounds you've inflicted upon me.
It falls down beating till all is forgot.
We fall down screaming inside a wooden box.
Spice now flowing over your lips.
You sway your way to me, then give a kiss.
All of this, I soon won't miss. "Dear God I wish it away."
You place your hands over your eyes.
Afraid you'll see what's on the other side.
You shake and pulsate to the drum-beats.
The acid rain-dance melting your dreams.
Show me not the truth you hold, just give me a kiss before we grow old.
Gone and away as the dusts flow down.
As you dance to our song, and soon you will drown.

Rule of Nines

God, tell me when I can just let go...
God, can you please just take my soul?
God, have I done something wrong to you?
God, please take me away now, bring me to you...
The burn is no longer feeling nice.
My luck has run out, yet I throw the dice.
There is no reason to why I hurt.
Have my sins been forgiven? "I've got more to learn."
God once told me, that he loved me dear.
God once told me, not to live in fear.
God once killed me, only to see if I'd die.
God once loved me, but now I burn alive.
Deep in the pit of all my mistakes.
Insects and demons crawling through my brain.
Forgiveness forgotten, now only these pains.
Hatred overflowing with each sin that I make.
God, tell me when my flesh will grow back...
God, can I ever just not look back?
God, please take me away from this hell.
God, I just can't see, I'm so overwhelmed!
God once told me, that there was another way.
God once told me, but then it faded away.
God once cared for me, and I for him...
Now I burn to my bones, never forgiven for my sins.

666

Six hundred times, sixty places, and six more faces...
"Stuck in a life of shit!"
666 - The mark of the beast, 666 - the number of demons inside me.

Today marks the day, now all can be put aside.
Today marks the day when all my dreams will die...

How much longer can I take this strive?
How many more times must this poor soul die?
How much did it take for you, to kill my heart?
How much did it hurt for you, to tear me apart?

Six hundred times, sixty places, and six more faces...
"Stuck in a world of shit!"

No Longer

Teeth down on my tongue.
Ripping away all I've said.
Down biting, until it's done.
And all of you are dead.

No longer will I let this be.
No longer will I let you breathe.
No longer shall this pain rule all.
No more, it's time to fall.

Drive it closer to my wrist.
Sing me to sleep and give me a kiss.
Then shut out in the darkness of my own life.
No longer will I live in this strive.

I've been tempted once and again.
I was left out and waited with sin.
I don't want this, to ring anymore.
It's time to stop the screaming. From behind the door.

Teeth down on my tongue, ripping away all I once said.
Down biting, until it's done.
No longer will I live this life of death.

I Can't Let It Be

What is there for me to say? When all has already been taken away.
What is there for me to do? When everybody hates me, *even you.*

I just can't seem to get a grip, still I feel so, so sick.
Nothing comforts me since you left.
Please place my heart, back into my chest.
I can't seem to find a grip, the stone seems to know only pain.
I can't seem to get this out, my head so clouded, pouring acid-rain.
There was once that reason, but now we have only ourselves.
There was once that option, yet it brought only hell.

I can't let it be, I need to stop the press.
I can't let it be, I need to fill my chest.
I can't let it go, when I loved you once so dear.
I can't let this be, I need not to live in fear.

Just Another Shove-Down

Mirror, mirror, *snap*! Gone and all is broke.
Tainted logic and in the blood I soak.
Forgotten love-bouts and I seem to know.
This is just another shove-down.
And on my heart, I begin to choke.
It spreads across the floor, filling the open space.
It begins to flood the room, and we find no escape.
Torn down once again, to see how this world will end.
So soon upon the doom of all I fear, now I sway with this page.
Loving the true meaning of my rage.
Mirror, mirror, *snap*! Bind and all is lost.
There was once a reason, but now only frost.
Forgotten death-songs yet I seem to know.
This is just another shove-down and on these words, I begin to choke.

Coming Home

One foot in front of the other. If only it were as easy as that.
I wish there was a better way yet again I just take another step.

I once came across a picture of two.
Holding each other in love and warmth.
It did seem to hold the essence of love so true.
But the frame was broken, much like me and you.
It has been miles upon my soul, and so long I've tried to make amends.
It's just one foot in front of the other.
Upon the road of leaves once again.

I'm coming home, just to see your face.
I'm coming home, to feel right in place.
I'm coming home, to hold you once again.
I'm coming home, to wash away all my sins.

Step by step, and foot to the ground.
Can you feel the morning clouds? So close, clinching to your face.
I once crossed your path, it then threw me out of place.

I'm coming home, just to see you again.
I'm coming home, to wash away these sins.
I'm coming home, to feel alive.
I'm coming home, just to see the look in your eyes.

Chapter 10

Rebirthing

Hollow Collision

What more would you want than my pride?
What more do I have to set aside?
What more do you want from me?
Why must my wounds stay open and bleed?
And knowing that the world will never change.
I would love you just the same.
Nothing but our minds to collide, hiding only me.
What was the meaning to what we said?
Why is it that my heart still feels dead?
What was the reason to why you cried?
Why must our hollow worlds collide?
And knowing that these words will never change.
I would hold you just the same.
Nothing but our minds to collide, hiding only me.

To-Night

Days to night, and nights to day.
I sit here alone, to see what's coming.
And try as I may, to set the truth - aside for you and me.

Echoes singing, deeper into my ear.
The moon embracing, clouding all my fears.
I sit here waiting, alone in the clear.
Days forming the nights, and night holding me dear.

Diseased

Here we go again! Left to drown in our own sins.
Pumping the starlight back inside. Flaking away at the first signs of life.
Truth left in the cold. Beating just under the stone.
Now rub your tongue across my chest, bite me hard; "I like that best."

So whisper it softly, the needle inside.
Consume the answer, and all rests aside.
Just one last question, then turn out the lights.
Kiss me you demon, then reach inside.
Can't understand your logic, not anymore.
I can't understand this nonsense, just shut the door.
Spread your sickness further, inside my mind.
Take my heart away, then cast me aside.

Truth-Be-Told

As truth rolls over the edge of the blade.
All these actions still feel the same.
Not ever has this monster cared.
And never shall I know, more than this despair.

Truth-be-told, I only tried as hard as I could.
Truth-be-told, I've tried again but never should.
Truth-be-told, I loved so much, only to lose.
As the truth is told, that I tried again and my heart they took.

Pushed again, against a fence and over the edge.
I'm lost again, in their sinister world and inside my head.
I cut some more, to see the night and know what it's for.
As the truth be told, that I loved you once and again I lose.
As these tears hit the floor, nothing more could I give to you.

I've tried then died, only to watch you walk away.
I've tried and cried, only to be left deep in shame.
I've cut in deep, then watched it flow.
As the truth-be-told, "that I did love you."

Abandoned Again

How many more rants must I tell, to take me deeper into our hell?
How many more demons must die before these words can just rest aside?

Shout down, deeper into the things you feared.
Shoved down, darkness now growing queer.
Left alone, in the wonder of all those things.
Abandoned again, yet it's all the same.
Smashed against me, but what would you expect?
It burns within me, the devil getting no rest.
Then we scream for guidance, but now all is lost.
Alone in the forest, we hear the growing frost.

Blanketed above me, the fester of all my dreams.
Then it blisters inside me, and I hear the devil weep.
But all that happens, is just a rerun of my life.
All these feelings... I can never cast aside.

Relentless Nonsense

It has been too long, now I think it's time to go.
It has been so long, left there under the snow.
Beneath all the things, that I've ever known.
How is it? That I'm still left all alone...

Shut this darkness, and give me back my head!
Shut the window, and play the song again!
Cut me deeper, inside my heart!
Reach in again, then tear me apart...

It has gained no reason, but it rings still today.
It has no logic, now laid numb in my grave.
I have no way out, and again I want to scream!
Their relentless nonsense, it is still haunting me...
Just shut this darkness, and give me back my life.
Shut the window, then throw your dice.
Cut me deeper, down to my soul.
Reach in again, then leave me out in the cold.

Giving Up

Destruction upon the lips of grace. Sweet death was her taste.
Oh what a waste and now it drifts aside.
It tumbles away and into the gray.
That's where all my memories lie.

Vibrate me a new hope, behind your teeth.
Show me a new reason, then give me another week.
It no longer stands for truth and justice.
Only now are you seeing, what I've known all along.

As the sickness spreads over the lands.
It lies in darkness, the true death of this man.
Hold out your reasons, and give me some light.
Set not for any logic because "you're always right."

Destruction upon the lips of grace.
Now all our dreams die and just fade away.
It's in the nonsense that you wish to stay.
I've had enough for one lifetime.
Just throw me back, where all my memories lay.

All Over Again...

The skin begins to peel away.
The walls seem to breathe.
Nothing feeling sane.

What was it, that took you away?
Why is it, that you have to beat me this way?
Rough to the core and all slips away.
Now down to the bone and my eyes turn gray.

Left to the darkest part of my thoughts.
Left in the shadows, alone to rot.
Give me a razor, soon noon upon my grave...
All seems to be a little strange.
Nothing looks right, and still this sour taste.
Now throw my heart down, wipe it on the curb.
Just give me my life back and watch me burn.

Wake Up!

Get up! Get up! Shut the darkness, and leave me alone.
Get up! Get up! Lock the other, now all is thrown.

Get out! Get out! Why should I even care?
Get out! Get out! Just take away my air.

Knot to the lost state of fact. Locked down, bones begin to crack.
Zombie truth now holds it right. *Wake up my love, so we can end this fight.*

Get up! Get up! Now taste the rain as it falls - acid upon your dreams.
Get up! Get up! Laugh while you can, your wounds - never clean.

Get out! Get out! All my hopes now raped and dead.
Get out! Get out! I tried the hardest, only to lose again.

Locked now and always last.
Held down, beaten-raped and you just laughed.
It rings true to the Knight's honor and right.
Wake up my love! So we can end this fight.

Maybe It's a Dream

Anything other than this arrow in my heart.
I wish there was a reason, as to why you tear me apart.
Now I'm out of season, just growing old and decayed.
Maybe there's something on the other side, more than my fate.

So now it rings true to the fact that I'm only second best.
So now I hold the answer in, deep inside my chest.
But there is no motive as to why I'm hated so.
Maybe I'll find the reason, as I lie here alone.

Now I'm shot down in the hoping, of something more today.
Just pushed to the other side, of the wall inside my brain.
I'm only to die alone, that's my curse and fate.
I'm left here to scream alone, drowning in my rage.

But on the brighter side to this mourning, "I have only me."
On the brighter side of this horror...
Maybe - just maybe it's a dream.

Payment

It is as it always has been.
It is as it always will be.
Fight if you wish, but it's pointless to me.

Now take that handle and ram it inside.
Just shut it to the right state of darkness.
Go ahead and try to justify your lies...
"What's the meaning to what you say?"
I've taken enough for one lifetime.
So pay up, and get out of my way.

Now on the right turn of my surprise.
Then you read the words in my eyes.
So laugh if you wish, but it's all the same.
I loved you to death, now in my grave...
So pay it forward and then just shut up.
Give what you owe, and leave me stuck.
You've taken enough of my life for now.
"You could fight if you wish but it's pointless now."

A Broken Horizon

Eternally set to the left side of my heart.
Fated to wallow and tear me apart.
It's a nightmare, that just doesn't seem to fade.
It's a broken horizon, just like me.

Now nothing next to the never side of Nod.
Not to the never said, side-set sympathy.
Singing the songs about you and me.
Not meant to mean more than what you fear.
For forever feeling flushed, forgotten and dead.
Down deep into the dawn of this broken horizon.

Eternally set to the right side of my head.
Driven to only lose, my soul till death.
It's a notion, that just doesn't seem to fade.
It's a broken horizon, much like me.

Bitter-Sweet

Left beyond everything a man once dreamed.
Then he waits aside, hoping he'll be seen.
For the drive that once held him, now gone and frayed.
Left behind all his hopes, slowly they slip away.

When a single man holds all the answers.
What is he to do, other than seek a question.
It was once left between me and you.
But now he lives outside of compassion.

Then he sits back, hoping for a better day.
Only in his hands, lies the truth of this age.
Left beyond everything he once knew.
Then shoved out in the cold, left so confused.

Freezing raindrops, beating onto his soul.
Love was once his motive, now his heart beats cold.
So he waits a little longer, between hope and faith.
He owned the world once but slowly, it all slipped away.

Enough

Running the razor across my lips.
Smiling as I give *Death* a kiss.
Now burning some pencils, inhaling the old.
I smile and giggle, as this story unfolds.

Laid down two by three. I fought my hardest but you never see.
I needed a hand then, to help me up.
But you walked away, so that's my luck.

I've had enough of this, one-way fight.
I could scream here for hours, but still out of sight.
You've never once, tried to see it my way.
I fought and died, "it's all the same."

I'm done with this, pointless bout.
I scream and cry, bleed and shout!
Enough of this heartbreak, taking me down.
I won't fight for someone, who doesn't want out.

Enough of this torment, inside my aching soul.
Pain is all love has given me, just a hollow soul.
So now, I'm the bad guy once again.
"So I guess it's my fate, for you to walk away again."

Love-Bout

It all seems the same. I hope it means something in the end.
It all fades away. I hope someone will remember these sins.

Dropped deeper into my wrist.
She held me tight, and gave one last kiss.
Soon to flow over my head and then it's forgotten, when I am dead.

So backwards, this life I live.
My friends are my enemies... My enemies are my friends...
But in the end, love is all I hate.
So now I drown it all, deeper into my shame.
So who are you, just a reader with some time?
Who am I? Just a poet, waiting to die.
But you think I planned this, and thought it through.
My whole life was just a pointless love-bout, fought between me and you.

Satan's – (Asshole)

The hardest part, is taking the next step.
It was a twisted nature, felt inside my chest.
But hope was hopeless, and never seemed to work.
Fate found me hiding, deep under the earth.

So I'm the loudest one in hell.
It's good to know, I'm heard above all your yells.
So time's hammer still beats me hard.
But it is no bother, when you have no heart.

Left deep under, all the dreams I once dreamt.
Buried under the leaves and behind the nonsense.
So there it is steaming, and gripping my lungs.
I can feel it peeling, away at my soul until done.

Hollow wishes, but I'm the one who's heard.
It stands gripped and vulgar, inside me so absurd.
I'm the biggest reason, for you to hate.
I'm the worthy demon, scraping at your shame.

So pray if it helps you, but I'm the biggest asshole around.
Lock the door if I scare you, and you dream so loud.
But the hardest part, is taking the next step.
So, *I'm Satan's greatest "asshole" in hell.*
"Stealing your last breath."

Nailed to The Wall

They raised me up, on their mantel and praised to me by the night.
Then they pulled me down for sacrifice.
With nails shoved through my eyes.

Nine inched blades, shoved inside.
She was never happy, though I've tried.
Cut the world in two, keep it between me and you.
Above all that meant something once, now dead.
I cut it for hours, still not dead. A nine inch blade, shoved inside.
She was never happy, though I tried.

They raised me up, on their mantel and praised to me by the night.
Then they pushed me to the wall and held real tight.
I loved them all once, but now these nails shoved through my eyes.

230

Raped With a Knife

Whistling above my bed.
The nightmares groping inside my head.
Hour-less head-twists felt inside.
I loved you dear, but now I cry.

As has it been told.
True to the whim of what I know.
Held against my will, torn down as they peel.
I scream and cry, but I'm held down tight.

So take my innocence and wipe it away.
Take my dreams and turn them gray.
Love my torment and laugh as I weep.
You enjoy my suffering, and I ball up so weak.
Now light the candle and wax my wrist.
Rub my eyes with the blade, begin to consume my hate.
It boils over and begins to blister.
They raped my youth away, with only a whisper.

So tie me to the ground, and spit on my wounds.
Grind me down, and erase my tomb.
You raped me with a knife, inside my heart.
I loved you to death, so you tore me apart.

Enemies Gone

All by my hands, left to scream.
If I was your hero, then why do you hate me?
Sure I've let you win, but you're not happy now.
I can see it upon your sins, oh your lonely frown.
So if I was your lover, now dead and lost.
I once loved you, but you must've forgot.

It dances upon that jest, then it flakes aside.
I beat it there for hours, till blood dripped from my eyes.
As all by my own, then set down for you to cradle.
We lusted there for hours, sweet upon that fable.
Now the rust seems, as my only companion.
All my enemies gone, lost with my compassion.

Selfish

Smooth against my lips, she pushes another kiss.
Felt so warm-alive, – oh her soft-blue eyes.
Slowly stealing away my mind.

She places her hand on my heart.
She fills in the pieces – each and every part.
But still it seems absurd, as I wait here until I'm heard.
Yet no one ever seems to care.
Her selfish actions, pushed me to despair.

Falling gently over my breath.
She licks my ear and kisses my neck.
As we laid there on the floor.
Her selfish actions, were all that was heard.

Rock & A Hard Place

Standing tall, as it begins to vibrate.
Seeping through the walls, felt only as my heart breaks.
Pushed against the door, for feelings never heard.
Love once set aside, but now her memory dies.
As I begin to grasp the dirt, my hollow cries are all that's heard.

Shoved deeper to the wayside, all my hopes begin to die.
Left alone as only one, the stone crumbles away until done.
So here I'm stuck, between fate and youth.
All my loves forgotten, "*Even you.*"

But nothing takes it further, other than my pain.
Life and love, truth and hate.
So here I'm stuck... "Between this rock and hard place."

Now all the actions begin to shift.
Thorns and whispers over my wrist.
Lifeless feeling, of only my pride.
Timeless peeling, away my eyes.

Felt true now, as ever it could.
Here left between, your blood and soot.
Driven deeper into my grave.
I feel so stuck, between this rock and a hard place.

Screaming Shadows

Snakes now hold it, but God doesn't care.
The logic found it, yet it never stayed.
Now rub my spine harder, with that nail.
Place the mushroom behind my eyes, and sing me to hell.

1,000 miles left on my soul, mixed-up with the coals.
Love me longer, until the days fade clear.
Spit your poison down and watch the demons crawl out of my ears.

Shave it closer to my spine, laugh it deep in your wine.
Shadows screaming, far inside my head.
A night-less dreaming, in someone else's head.
So hold it closer, but never look.
Fade the screaming shadows, then close the book.

Inhale

It lingers in the air, stale and stiff.
It brings on despair, both cool and crisp.
As I lean back in my chair, gazing at my wrist.
All the actions once forgotten, when the record skipped.

Darkness throughout my home.
In this cold I wait... all alone.
Burning some pencils.
As I cut heaven and hell into my wrist.

It lingers in the air, bringing back despair.
It reminds me of a time, when once you cared.
I inhale the memories, the smell of burning lead.
It makes me feel warmer, now that you're dead.

I inhale the smoke, of an age once mine.
I inhale the memories, before they subside.
It feels so stagnant, so cold and weary.
It fills the room, the ashes of our burning memories.

Brick-Kissed

Shot through my cheek, now you watch it bleed.
Metal against my bones, heart beating all alone.
Then you cup it tight, taping up my eyes.
Grounded to the sea, and never was I free.

Grab that brick and beat me hard.
Rub my lips, to feel the scars.
Now wind the clock, and load the gun.
Kiss me with a brick, passion over-done.

Light the walk-way, tell me it's alright.
I feel the gravel pumping, though my veins at night.
Give me a sweet hug, hold my hand as I weep.
Kiss me with a brick, and laugh as I bleed.

Soon an ending as once I said.
Brick-kissed, right against my head.
Lovely little stitches, over my fingers and tongue.
Then you kiss me with a brick, passion's over-done.

An Hour-less Clock

An hour-less clock, ticking in my head.
An hour-less thought, dancing on my breath.
A hopeless nature, felt deep inside.
As I watch each second, be pulled from my eyes.
"An hour-less clock, taking me down."
An hour-less thought, as I begin to drown.
A hopeless nature, of nothing left but time.
As all of these needles, start beating me alive.

Heavy sands, falling over my eyes.
Demons and angels, whispering in my mind.
Timeless frustration, snapping it in place.
An hour-less clock, reflecting my fate.
"Endless wonder, as I wander away."
Timeless nonsense, shaping my faith.
An hour-less clock, ticking in my head.
An hour-less clock - tick, tick, taking my breath.

Kiss Me Grace

It keeps me down, to your love.
It held me tight, and kept me above.
Jerk it louder, till I scream.
Bite me deeper, and watch it bleed.

Shut it further, and smile sweet.
Light the candle, under my feet.
Just love me forever.
"Come dance with me."

Kiss me Grace, before I awake.
Kiss me Grace, before I end this fate.
Love me forever, until the song fades.
Dance with me forever *"just kiss me Grace."*

So Familiar

I've made peace with my enemies.
But now my friends want me dead.
So I cut out my tongue.
For not another word said.

And oh that face, I won't soon forget.
So I end this memory on a smile.
"Just as it should have been."

It seems so familiar, this ring in my hand.
It seems so familiar, the scars on our wrists.
As far as I could throw it, deep in my soul.
As much as I feared it, now my heart pumping cold.

I've made peace with my enemies.
But now the world wants me dead.
So I rip out my tongue.
For not another word said...

Bite the Trigger

Ram, gone-said-did.
Lost, snap-twist-split.
Shot, down-left-out.
Damn, it begins to shout.

Shake my hand, and lie to my face.
The earth begins to melt, just like my faith.
Round - it falls in, each and every hole.
Burning away, just like our souls.

Bite the trigger, to taste my fate.
Bite the trigger, with a smile on your face.
Bite the trigger, to stop the voices at night.
Lick the barrel and drip the sulfur in your eyes

Dead-Energy

A dark-mass in the middle of the room.
Over the coffee-table it looms.
I try to gaze in but see only doom.
The vibration of my soul, shifting out of place.
The sense of ghosts, licking my brain.
The atoms bending, shattering under my nails.
The dead-energy pounding, groping me in hell.

Under the ice, it begins to twitch.
A dark-mass, making me feel sick.
All the tears flow, over my hands.
The dead-energy grows, and death fills the land.
Like a puzzle breaking, I begin to flake away.
Like God weeping, it begins to rain.
Each atom losing, now they make me cry.
The dead-energy growing, right behind my eyes.

I'm Back!

Take a good look, can you see my scars?
Take a good book, and place it under the jars.
Do you know, who I am?
Does this grin, remind you of him?
Who was I, other than your friend?
Who was I? The lonely one left in sin.

Take my hand, guide me to the lake.
Take my heart, and my soul that you raped.
Doesn't this seem, a little strange sometimes?
Doesn't it seem odd, that I'm still alive?

I'm still waiting, always and a day.
I'm still burning, left in the gray.
It seems a little louder, now that I'm here.
It does seem a little clouded, incased in fear.

"I'm back." The asshole that you hate.
"I'm back." I hope I'm not too late.
"I'm back." The demon once a man.
"I'm back." To rule this world again.

Take a good look, can you see my scars?
Take a good book, and place it beneath the jars.

"I'm back." The asshole that you hate.
"I'm back." I hope I'm not too late.
"I'm back." The demon once a man.
"I'm back." To destroy this world again.

Chapter 11

Crisis Corpse

Meant To Be

Wave it deep in your smiles. I can see it flutter, passing up the mile.
Take it further into the next stage. As all that was meant to be just fades away.
"Doing lines, living rhymes. Telling your son a story."
Beware the demon, that hides behind the page.
Beware the man, that will never change.
As all that was meant to be. It takes us further into our dreams.
As all that was meant to be. It all faded, but you'll never see.
Shave it closer, and hold me dear. I'd tell you a story but it'd take years.
Rub the bore away and clean your tears.
As all that was meant to be, now only fears.
We were once meant to be but I hold now, only my tears.
"Doing lines, living rhymes. Telling your son a story."
It was meant to be, the miles of fears.
It was meant to be, my falling into despair.
It was meant to be, all that I have endured.
I'd tell you a story, but you'd get bored.

Beyond the Blue Sky

From red to black, left alone in the book.
A song of the memory passed, flowing over the laughs.
Swaying as one, held both tight and calm.
A notion never passed, it flows further into the back and there it goes.
Now it begins to fly, emotions overflow and the clouds drip from my eyes.
Beyond the blue sky, where once our dreams would fly.
Beyond the blue sky, where now my hopes hide.
As slothful as the moment passed, as thoughtful as the child's laugh.
When once we held back. It was soft - but now it cracks.
Beyond the blue sky, a hug and kiss held real tight.
Beyond the blue sky, a flower of warmth held inside.
Beyond the last tear, dripping off my lip.
Behind the past years, running together like my fears.
From red to black, emotions thrown and then they crack.
From start to end, overflowing at the rim.
From stars to moon, held once but now they loom.
And there it goes, now it begins to fly.
Emotions shocked, like the stars in your eyes.
Beyond the blue sky, where once our love thrived.
Beyond the blue sky, "where now will I hide?"
Behind the past years, and all the frozen tears.
Further behind the moon - it was soft but now its ashes loom.

Stagnate Wonder

Across the rusted dock.
Hollow words rippling through my eyes.
Stood at the edge of the dock.
It stands still, and my soul it mocks.

Hold my hand as we walk down the hall.
You are my bride, together we're whole.
Now can you smell it? "The taste in the air."
Now can you feel it? "As it whispers through our hair."

The thought seems stagnate, so very null.
The echo of a hummingbird, ringing in my skull.
Nothing to fill it, and rub lime on the rim.
Nothing could steal it, this remaining stagnate whim.

So I begin to ponder, wondering how I got here.
So I begin to question, each quiver that I hear.
It feels so numb, the bottom of my feet.
I feel so stagnate, though my heart still bleeds.

A question never answered, standing still in the rain.
A motive never questioned, still I hold the blame.
Nothing really changes, or goes away with time.
It all just rearranges, and becomes a void inside.

So hold my hand, as we stroll down the street.
You were my bride, but now you just sleep.
Now can you taste it? "The truth in the air."
So can you feel it? "As it swims through your hair."

It feels so stagnate, the thought of how I got here.
It feels so voided, nothing seems clear.
I feel so gummed up, I just can't think straight.
It's such a stagnate wonder, as I gaze into the frozen lake.

Lip Scars

They never knew what to tell me.
They did nothing to make me feel fine.
All their smiles glaring on their faces, *"Blood & Grime."*

It must've been a wrong step. That's why I'm falling aside.
It must've been a bad slip.
But then they rub them, the scars on my lips.

I knew the answers, but still there was nothing to say.
I don't know what really happened anymore.
But still I hear the screaming, from behind the door.
"Nothing seems right, just a bitter sight."

All that mattered, still looks shattered.
So she seems to lock the gates.
While I'm sleeping, I can hear them weeping.
So then they rub them, the scars on my lips.

It felt so rough, our last kiss.
It seemed so stuck, pouring over their skin.
They never did, seem to know what to say.
They did nothing to make me feel fine.
It must've been, all just a bad slip.
So then you kiss them, the scars on my lips.

Over the Hill

Is there a reason, as to why onward you still read?
Can we find a motive, or are we too weak?
There was once a rhyme... but now a song.
There was once a rhyme... but you won't sing along.

So recite me a riddle, as together we dream.
So sing me the chorus, and now it rings.
Dance by the starlight... come on, take my hand.
We don't need a reason for this...
"They'll never understand."

Love Sick

So to let it all just fade.
Her face no longer means a thing.
If brushed against, in the halls.
Would I even notice her at all?

Then it reminds me, that I don't remember.
Then it sings to me, of our last September.
It's been awhile, but I can't recall.
Her hopes and dreams, mean nothing at all.

So I'm a monster, "now you understand."
So I'm a demon, laid under the sands.
Just take this note, and burn it away.
I once felt Love-sick, but then you faded away...

Demon Skin

Each one, brings me closer to the end.
Each thought, floating upon a whim.
Every second, bringing me closer to doom.
This demon skin, keeping me away from you.

Left between angels and friends.
It was told as a guideline, but it shifts again.
My inner torment, felt as my only pride.
Every vision, that was pulled from my own two eyes.

Down upon the only nature.
Soon all my dreams will burn away.
I'm only a pointless nonsense.
"Writing my life away..."

So I guess it scares you, now that I'm awake.
So I think I've hurt you, again it breaks.
But nothing washes, this sin is mine to wear.
It's this demon skin, that covers all my affairs.

Each one, brings me closer to the end.
Each thought, floating upon a whim.
Every second, taking me right next to doom.
It is this demon skin, that stands between me and you.

Felt Darkness

Slowly it rolled down my throat.
It kind of tickled, but then I choked.
It steamed over, and out of my eyes.
It felt so darkened and oh, to my surprise.
There never was a way out of here.
I only wanted back those wasted years.
But it felt so darkened, and beyond my grasp.
It seemed so hazed, reality never lasts.
I'm only waiting here, for my fate to be complete.
I needed not to fear but still it felt so near. *"So how was I the one in charge?"*
Why did I lose it all, and then just fall apart?
So slowly it rolled down my throat.
I could hear it whisper, beyond all the notes.
It seemed to be, some kind of dream.
I felt only darkness, as my soul began to scream.

Ants In My Mouth

My eyes can't reach it, not the top limb.
My soul can't forfeit, "No, not again!" And I can't seem to shake it.
It's still on my path. So I could have just took it, and never looked back.
But remember who we're talking about, I'm the man, now a poet waiting to see.
You never understood a word I said. "And that meant a lot to me."
So we go our separate ways, never caring about the end.
So you just walked away, and never took a second glance.
Now I can feel them, thousands of ants in my mouth.
Now I can taste them, as they crawl in and out.
They are here for their obligations, on the path home.
So they eat my heart away, and shit out my soul.
You seem a little shaky, not on your game today.
Does it disturb you, to watch them eat me away?
Thousands of ants, biting at my gums.
I can feel them in my mouth, as they swim in my blood.
But they are here for only my decay.
They have no remorse, *"much like you on that day."*
So they march onward, into my mouth and throat.
I can taste them all, as I swallow down the smoke.
My eyes can't reach it, not the top limb.
My soul can't wake-up, "not ever again."
I can't seem to shake it, it's still on my path.
I can feel them all biting, just under my wrist.

Crisis

You sit me back in the chair.
You reach inside, taking my despair.
A hollow hole in the middle of my chest.
You tore inside, now nothing's left.

So break the moon away and take my life.
You should have asked me, but now I'm blind.
So there's no more hope now, "I'm all alone."
There was once a heartbeat, now an empty hole.

I try to fight back, but I just flake away.
I try to bite back, but you locked the cage.
There's no more room now, the ground's growing cold.
There's no more man now, just an empty soul.

What a mess-up, I thought I could have helped.
What was the lesson? "*I know only hell.*"
It's such a crisis, nothing's alright.
It's such a lock-up, I see no light.

So you sit me back in the chair.
You tear inside, taking all my air.
A hollow hole in the middle of my chest.
You tore inside, now nothing's left.

Under the Sheets

So you need not the reason why.
You only want me to die.
You feel not, my pain and grief.
You only laugh, as my whole world bleeds.
So it begins to decay, mold growing thick.
I can feel it all steaming, now I'm in a rut.
There is no more reason, only pain and blood.
It starts to whisper, under the sheets it hides.
It starts to whimper, it sees no light.
So I'm waiting, for the flood to take me away.
Under the sheets hides the answers.
"Within this pen hides my fate."

Stained Forever

A red moon, drifting over-head.
A muffled scream, numb ringing in my bed.
A pointless head-shot, felt as my break.
A rusty ax, frozen beneath the lake.
Over all my hopes, now they're nothing I need.
It stands above all my thoughts, and still it bleeds.
I hammer away, beating me to the floor.
I can still hear her screaming, from beyond that door.
So it spills, and I'm covered in the shame.
It was all I ever wanted, but it's not the same.
I needed once, the drive to be pass it all.
Yet now I'm stained forever, shivering-cold and lost.
Because I needed a reason, to guide me to the day.
My hands are never clean, it just won't wipe away.
All those love-notes, they haunt my heart and mind.
I'm stained forever in this shame - forever covered in this lie.

Blood Soaked

So I stand there, with frost stuck to my face.
So I just wait there, for a better turn of fate.
So there it goes now, still I'm in this rut.
So here we go now, forever soaked in blood.
As it drips off my hands, there is nothing to say.
As it flows down, on my face and down the drain.
It smells so bitter, yet it tastes so damn sweet.
I'm soaked in their blood, from my head to my feet.
So I just stand there, waiting for another day.
So I just wait there, for another taste of rage.
So there I am now, standing on that stone.
So here we are now, yet I'm still alone...
So beat it down now, harder with that spike.
So beat me down now, so you can dream at night.
As it drips off my fingertips, the smell now driving you sick.
As it flows down, my arms and chest.
You weep now, because you know nothing's left.
So I just stand here, covered in frost and blood.
Soaked to the bone, and dry in my lungs.
So I just wait here, for another twist of fate.
As here we go now, and still I love this rage.

Bite My Lip

Her mother stood there, with a smirk on her face.
She asked how I was doing, nothing really changed.
Her sister stood there waving, saying hello.
She never did question me, everyone seemed to just let it go.

But murder is murder, and hers was a treat.
No one really asked why "damn that's neat."
So as I stood there, with a smile on my face.
I just bit my lip, because there was nothing to say.

So I bite my lip, as everyone seems to know.
So I just bite my lip, because she's still under-snow.
Now all has faded gone, yet it all seems right.
Her mother asked how I was doing. "I'm just fine."

As now her corpse begins to rot.
No one cares, why she's lost.
When you dig a hole, that deep to hell.
When you kill your love, whom was so overwhelmed.
Does the world give a damn about that girl?
"The one who is gone and destroyed."
I just bite my lip, as she falls deeper into that void.

The Zombie's Requiem

Hands held, for the moment soon passed.
Thoughts remembered, but they won't last.
The sound of the wind howling through the scattered blades of grass.
It's on that feeling, that I might find rest.

So on goes another push to the side.
I can still hear it ringing, echoing deep inside.
A hummingbird hoping, for just another day.
It feels so calm, the cool fall rain.
She tries to escape it, but there's no way out.
She tried to break it, but then bottomed-out.
There is no remorse here today. There is only this zombie and his fate.

We all push it to the side. We've all watched it, then laughed inside.
So here I am, laid on the leaves of that choice.
So here I wait, for the angel's sweet voice;

Now sing me my last-rights, and put me to rest.
Tell them the story, and try your best.
There is no happy ending, only truth and fate.
I asked for forgiveness, but found no escape.

Rotted flesh still falls from my bones.
So here I wait, forever and always alone.
But the wind kisses it, and the moon holds my soul.
Calm upon all the dreams now dead.
I can feel it, the echoing in my head.

Tall but soon just ash. I lay upon the leaves, awake but still dead.
Under all the years, they came to me with tears.
I've saved so many, and damned just me.
This is my curse, for the sins in which I believed.

Now she's seeking, but there's now way out!
She's beating and bleeding, she screams and shouts!
I've wept my tears and held her tight
She wants just another day, she just wants out...

I've waited the longest, only to be damned in the end.
I'm still just a monster. Wishing an end, *wishing revenge...*
A decaying beast, which rises and seeks human flesh.
I'm not really a role-model, just a demon doing his best.

So, it's not what you wanted to hear.
I've done my time, in the dark and over the years.
I've seen their worries, and tasted their tears.
She wanted out, so I lent her a hand.
She asked for escape, from this rotted man...
All the angels spread their wings.
Very few can hear it, but they began to sing.
It hummed so clear and felt so calm.
The Zombie's requiem, the rain in the fall.
She needed a way out. I took her to the door.
She needed to scream and shout, to release all the hurt.
I held her close and guided her way.
She spread her wings... Then she just flew away.

Taped Up

I'm a loser, "baby."
I'm a dreamer, "that's right."
I'm a tragic-nonsense, "rubbed-in with the lime."

I've been waiting, "all day."
I've been thinking, "all night."
I've been left in this hole, "buried alive."

Tape me up, and take me down.
I push and scream, bleed and shout!
So take me down, and tape me shut.
I weep numb sound, "I'm shit out of luck!"

Left in the dark, shivering so cold.
Left in the back, weeping all alone.
Now tape me down and tape me tight.
You close my mouth, and shut my eyes.

I'm a loser, "baby."
I'm a dreamer, "that's right."
I'm a tragic-nonsense, "wasting your time."

I've been hoping, "all day."
I've been drinking, "all night."
You left me in this hole, "buried out of sight."

So tape me up, and take me down.
I push and scream, fight and shout!
So take my heartbreak, and tape it tight.
Take my soul then, bury it under the ice.

Hit the Brakes!

All would seem as just another day.
A wide-open range of emotions upon the lines.
It would seem as only a passing thought.
A notion felt time after time.
Yet soon it comes and it all begins to break.
It slams against me, so now I'm awake!

Wow! That seems like a bit much to take.
It begins to burn through, so hit the brakes!
"You would think that," but I know it's you...
You never looked back, you just tightened the noose.

So all is at the same junction, a passing lock!
All still seems hazed, broken and shocked.
So the tires begin to melt away, metal bent and pulled.
You tried to make your point, now bleeding in this pool.

So we tried to make it through, but all still seems dire.
We came off the trail, and now on fire.
You think you're happy, and were right all along.
Hit the brakes! So I can die alone...

It smashes against me, beating my skull.
It slams against me, now burning with the coals.
It shoves the metal through me, my face now bleeds.
All along I thought we were fine, "you were never happy."

Hit the brakes! The tunnel of lights is coming near.
Hit the brakes! I don't want to die in fear.
Hit the brakes! So you can just leave me alone.
I hit the brakes... And beat my head on this stone.

Old No. 7

It kind of makes me feel at home. It really does warm my soul.
I never did lie to you. I loved you dear but now alone.
So I take this dance and ride out the night.
So I take this blade out from my spine. Take my hand and kiss my cheek.
I dance and twirl, till my legs grow weak.
It warms my body and cleans my face.
It takes my heart back, but never replaced.
So I love that drumbeat, felt inside.
I love that moment, when we were alive.
So sing my soul away, and I bite the bullet hard.
I dance my nights away, and pump out my heart.
I free my worries a bit, so maybe I could forget.
But in the end, I still feel my sins...
Old No. *7*, was it maybe just a dream?
A pocket full of rice, a mind never free.
Old No. *7*, was I ever even alive?
I think I can remember, only the amber-spice.
It kind of makes me feel at home. I never did like being alone.
So I dance this night-into-the-dirt...
I loved you dear... but you went first.

Scraping the Bones

Can you feel that chill? Can you take that feel?
Could I ever try? "Why won't I just die..?" "God save me!"
Pulled tight, can you hear its scraping-loud ring?
A hammer held firm, a blade licked sweet.
And all those angels scream, left alone in the dark.
Under my bed, "*left in my head*" alone and never free.
It scrapes the bone, and I feel it tearing away.
It's rough and jagged, rusted and decays in me.
It scrapes the bone and takes me home, right where I didn't want to be.
So can you feel it, could you steal it?
Please God, "What the hell is happening to me!!?"
So can you wake it, could you take it? Free this demon that's starving in me...
It bites at my wrist, trying to get out.
I makes me feel sick, so I bleed and shout!
Nervous and flushed, it begins to scrape at my mind.
So I rip open my flesh, sit back - and look inside...
Mom, dad, God - can you hear my cries?
I need an arm around me, quick!!! "I think I'm gonna die."

The Knight's Honor

Forward marching into a time of remorse and grief.
I head onward into a sunset, hoping I'll be free.
As upon all the thoughts and orange leaves in the wind.
I march still, hoping I'll get ahead.

So the angels take my heart and fly away.
The demons lick my soul, so now I am stained.
Are there any more dragons, left for me to slay?
Or am I only to lie down, and await my fate?

So at the blades side, and the echoes in mind.
To a time of all those smiles and glee.
I could just fall down, and watch my life escape me.
Yet at the dawn of all my strives.
It is by this honor I live, and in these worries I die.

Still hoping an ending, to this journey of mine.
But I slip forward, and deeper inside.
Her face seems distant, almost just a dream.
Her lips still haunt me, it's her love that I seek.

So it's this honor, that drives me closer to you.
It is this honor, that keeps this knight awake.
I hope I can find you, before it's too late.

As forward marching, through the fields of wheat.
As I fight more monsters, and find no sleep.
Rest was only a thought, so far-gone and away.
It is this honor, that keeps me going.
So I will never forget her face.

True to the pledge of my soul in her hands.
For all of my children, and for all of this land.
I shall keep true to my honor, "not dead till it's over."
Because it is true love that flows between me and you.
My fate must wait, because this journey is not complete.
As onward I march, upon this road of leaves.

At the Wayside

Soon a moment passed, gone in the haze.
Soon the morning gone, just another day.
Felt as only time, yet nothing ever changed.
I sat there for years, now gone and I decay.
Pushed to the last step, I need just one more.
Stuck to that torment, forever I'm a bore.
So now at that moment, when it all makes sense.
I find myself wasted, drowning in their shit.
At the wayside, where all my dreams die.
At the wayside, I drift and flow right by.
So blow me a kiss, and salt all my wounds.
I sat there for hours, each one bringing doom.
So this is the answer, "you've wanted a reason why."
So this is the ending, but I never said good-bye...
Now here in this torment, gone and I'm away.
Here at the wayside, I just drift insane.
Soon all my dreams, just turn to mold.
Soon all my fights, go on untold.
I'm pushed to the sideline, where no one can see.
Here at the wayside, decaying like my dreams.

I've Been Around

Inhaling, a clove on the tip of my tongue.
It numbs my memories, yet they stay strong.
It's been some time now, but I think I can go...
It's been some time now, "this stale lingering smoke."
When and where did it all start?
Maybe it was at the school, maybe at the park.
Maybe I could dig deep and unlock some things.
It's been some time, and so very far away.
So it slides down my throat, amber-spiced and sweet.
So it cools my soul, yet makes me feel, oh so weak.
So what is it you're looking for today..? Just take it all, and go away...
I've been around, and seen my share of sights.
I've been around, and seen my share of fright.
Timeless torture, upon my skull and brain.
It's been years, yet it's still the same.
So I bite the top lip and watch it bleed.
I drink the last sip, and begin to scream.
As the acid-cloud rains the pain on me.
I just inhale again, and begin to weep;

I've been around and seen enough.
Death was only a thought, yet still you're gone.
I've been around, I've had enough!
I've taken the time, but still I cough.
When was I not the one who cared the most?
When was I the bastard? "Now a lonely ghost."
You act like you give a damn, don't even play.
I've tasted enough sin. I've lived enough shame.
I've been around, and still I'm here.
I've been around, yet still in fear.
I've seen the ending, but missed the start.
I would reach out for you, yet you fall apart...

Judgment For the Damned

No one can heal this gaping wound. No one can fix this shattered skull.
There is no more hope, no hope at all. It seems so very unkind.
It does seem to take some time. But in the end, it might seem right.
But for now, we turn out the lights.
So whip me with the thorns, till I bleed ice.
So beat me hard, and rip out my eyes.
This is the payment, for all my lies.
So true it does, seeming to be only a pit.
Judgment of all my sins, forgiveness never sticks.
So honest it was, but will never be again.
It's judgment now, for all that I did.
Ripping and raping the angel's heart.
I stole it away, and tore it apart. Endless amounts of friends, I just drove away.
Endless times, I just laughed insane.
Now this is the chorus. *It's judgment for the damned.*
You could never forgive me, "but I understand."
No one cares about how I suffer.
No one will ever clean my wounds.
I've stolen and beat the life out of friends.
I've taken away the light and broke their limbs.
I'm just a demon, a bastard with no faith.
So I burn in this hell, for each sin that I've made.
So whip me with the barbed-wire. Leave my wounds open to bleed.
It kind of seems unkind at times. But this judgment is mine to keep.

A Needle Beneath My Eyes

Locked in place, and on the tracks.
It shakes and quakes, yet never turns back.
It seems so rotted, the flesh under my teeth.
It tastes so salted, and seems so sweet.
Now all my muscles begin to twitch.
It feels so strange. It's making me sick...
So tie me to the streetlight, and leave me be.
Watch me pulsate, cracking my teeth. Felt so smooth and very leveled.
Placed under my eyes, now I'm growing disabled.
But can I not find myself a grip?
This needle beneath my eyes, it's making me sick!
As all the sour chunks of old flesh come up.
I try to swallow them down, yet I choke.
It tastes so rotten, yet it seems so dear.
It's scraping at my mind, and right behind my ears.
It goes in real smoothly, it breaks no edge.
You push it in slowly, and watch me as I flinch.
It drives me crazy, to think it's something new.
It's just a needle beneath my eyes. Like the nails under every tooth.

Rage #6

I grab the scissors, and cut out both of my eyes.
I swallow the razor, in such a surprise.
It tickles my tongue, and cuts at my heart.
It felt real warm, but it tears me apart.
I place another razor, just beneath my chest.
I push real hard, till I'm out of breath. *I tear inside pulling on all my guts.*
I rip them out and tie them to my neck and the post.
I kick off real slowly, until I begin to choke.
Reaching into the gaping hole. I pull a thread out from my spine.
It's covered in acid, rust and lime. As so why is it still making me freak?!
It pulls on this demon, and I begin to tweak!
So cut me bloody and ram that blade inside.
Fill my body with hate, lust and rhymes.
I'd take a moment, but I just sit here and cut.
To take out my anger, over that filthy slut!
I grab the saw-blade and start cutting at my teeth.
Then the burning nails, I pull out from me.
You can never stop this monster "I'm on a roll."
So I rip out my eyes and place in the coals...

Take My Hand

Hope was just a word before I met you.
Life was but a dream, but now I see...
Maybe on another level, it could thrive.
Maybe if you cared, maybe if you tried.

So take my hand, as to the heavens we fly.
Take my hand, for by this kiss we take.
Hold me tight, before it's too late.

Faith was only a two-sided thought.
Now I keep true, and wipe clean the frost.
For what was the meaning, only love I say.
Just take my hand, so we can fly away...

What Have I Become?!

Can you picture it, the flashing lights?
Can you picture it, cold and numbed sights?
Red and dimmed, blacklights swinging overhead.
A lingering smoke, a child under his bed.
Locked to the right-side and out of the way.
Left in the darkness, to live with only shame.
What have I become? And where will I go?
What have I done? Still so, "so cold."

I was once a man, honorable and clear.
Now I am a monster, cowering in fear.
For what may lie beyond that door.
The thoughts of truth, still nailed to the floor.

So can you picture it, the room so out of place?
Can you picture it, the child's distorted face?
As he waits, for a better dawn to arise.
What have I become? "Who the hell am I..?!"

Alone As I Weep

Falling to the deepest part of all my fears.
It's been some time, maybe even years...
As so many tears, left to drift through time.
It was so many tears, dripping in my mind.
So take your time and give me a heart.
Stab my thoughts, just tear them apart.
Echo the one thing, to so many smiles.
Take me further, to the end of the mile.

So I grip me tighter, my arms now bleed.
Alone in the closet, alone as I weep.
I'm tired of fighting, I'm tired of this face.
I've spent enough time, yet I'm still out of place.
So turn the clock back, to end the struggle.
Grip my neck, and my screams are muffled.
Alone in the back room, alone as I weep.
No one truly cares. No one cares about me...

Shot Through My Heart

Gaze in deep, to the end of the hall.
Can you see my face, can you see at all?
There is something in my hands but never will you take it from me.
There is something in my heart and you just raped it from me...
Shot in the dark, through my emotions-gone.
Left there to bleed, and sing this song.
To the memory of trust now only dust. So gaze in deep before it's gone.
Can you see? Can you see me at all? There is something in my hands.
Something you wanted all along.
I hold it in my hands, at the end of this hall.
Where no one can see me, as no one cares. But never shall you take it from me.
As never you cared. While gazing in deep, be careful of what you find.
There are more than just monsters.
On the other side of the line. Gripped in my hands, in my soul and mind.
I hold it in my heart, yet you tore it apart. You just raped it from me.
Shot in the dark, left there to weep.
Shot through my heart, yet you'll never see.
Of all the memories, just fading to dust.
Gone with the emotions, gone with my trust.
Swinging at the end of the hall... From my heart - bleeds only dust.

Christ Can't See

Damn this day, and every one before it.
Damn this haze, and my every passing moment.
Hopeless waiting, just a childish thought.
Pointless gazing, at all the scattered stars.

He's not waiting, for you and me.
He has given up, and so have we.
Christ can't see, you've blinded his heart.
Christ can't see you, you've tore him apart.
Pointless hypocrites, selling their lies.
Hopeless bastards, drowning in wine.
So take your time, just throw your stones at me.
Do what you wish, "Christ can't see..."

You've raped his hopes - you've destroyed his dreams.
"Damn these wars," and all your political screams.
He's not waiting, he no longer cares.
He's not helping, our endless despair.
Christ can't see, you've taken his drive.
Christ can't help you, now that he's blind.
Hypocritical nonsense, selling out those books.
Endless shelves of a story now dead.
Hopeless struggle, when the answers of peace are right here.
Do what you wish. Burn, stab and throw your stones at me.
It no longer matters, "Christ can't see..."

Chapter 12

Kill Me Already!

I Loved Her

With her there, by my side.
I tried to live but still I died.
With her there, by my side.
I tried to live but still I cried.
With her there, by my side.
I tried to see but still I'm blind.

Life was once only a notion brushed aside.
Now we have only these lies.
So true to the emotions, *I once cared so dear.*
Now what can I do, to wipe clean these tears?

With her there, by my side.
I tried to breathe but could not see.
With her there, by my side.
I tried to be "Oh God why!"
With no one here, by my side.
I tried to live but now I die...
"Oh God I loved her..."

Nightmare

Can no one ever just take my thoughts away?
Just freeze my heart and let it break.
I would love it so, if you could just let me go.
And smile as I flake away.

Please don't try to wake me... The night is still on my side.
Please just hate me and let me cry.
For all my thoughts that are still inside.
This is only a nightmare, that grows with time.
"Can no one ever just take my life?"
Kill my thoughts and turn off the lights.
I would love it so, if you would just let me go.
And laugh as I crumble away.

Please don't try to wake me... Let me stay in this eternal fright.
Please just hate me, stab me as I cry.
For all is still a shattered emotion.
Echoing forever through my mind.
This life is a nightmare *"yet awake I die..."*

Once More

There was a little whisper, in her ear.
There was a little question, through the years.
Yet darkness was, and forever will be.
Set with the lime, and over the rhyme.
Left to fester inside of me.

What was the meaning then?
My answers are growing weak.
What was my purpose then?
Now my hopes are falling sleek.

Into the dreams of once I owned the world.
Now I fry and question why...
I damn this heart that's inside of me.
Forever now and always to be.

Once more, I feel the chill run up my spine.
Once more, I nail it shut, and bury the pine.
To box-clear the numb thoughts of us.
Once more, it breaks into dust.

Yours

Given further into the shadows and grime.
Shields and blades, clashing through the night.
For it is this honor that keeps me afoot.
It is this armor, forever covered in soot.

I set-way, so many years ago.
When will I return, "I'll not soon know."
Faith may set itself aside at times.
But still I hold you in my heart.

As it's spilled out onto the ground.
And the beasts lick away the truth.
When once we loved, so clearly in our youths.

Please don't question my actions and ways.
Please don't worry, for I am on my way...
As given another step upon the leaves.
Dead or alive, "I am yours to keep."

Mine

Tied to both of my wrists.
She leaned over, and gave a kiss.
Now it rings like a tumor inside my head.
Soon the answers will be mine.
Soon I'll bring it all to an end.

So they begin to lift.
And down-shove of all my whims.
And it tickles, as they break my limbs.
For now it's growing and coming soon.
Through the dawn and upon a noon.

Locked to the joints of all my being.
Then they snap, and I start screaming.
But not to worry, nor give a damn.
Soon the answers will rest in my hands.
As you are mine, laid under the sand...

Lost

Who? What! Where? Why?!
How many times, must this soul die?
To prove the fact, that I'm still dead.
Gone and away, in someone else's head.

Festered dreams of a man in the mirror.
He asked a question, it ended in fear.
But who's to know and answer this?
Who was there, to sew up my wrist..?

Under the fog, wandering through the night.
Timeless torment, tangled tight to terror.
Right ringing rough round and through.
Blackened bleeding boiled blisters steaming.
Seeming sorrows swallowed inside.
Lost in this world, forever lost in those eyes.

Look Into Me

Through it all...
Nothing even matters anymore.
Just my fingers smashed in the door.
"Come to think of it."
Nothing else matters at all.
Just my brain, splattered against the wall.

Now a hollow skull.
Look inside and reach in deep.
Can you feel my soul, as it tries to leave?

So what's left of me?
Other than this sack of flesh and rage.
Please my friend, "look into me." Tell me what you see...

Through all the mounds of paper and ink.
What am I, just a child too weak...
So flesh doesn't really matter any more.
Just my tongue, smashed in the door.
"And come to think of it."
This really doesn't matter at all.
So my brain, splattered against the wall...

The Calling

Smooth as it strolls through my ears.
It tickles my spine and feasts on my fears.
It makes its way through, and finds its goal.
It echoes for hours, and rings in my soul.
I can feel it haunting, my every step and thought.
I can feel it howling, rough through the halls.
I know it's waiting, and licking its lips.
I know it's out there, patient it sits.
That is the calling, "*for all my sins I must pay.*"
I can hear it ringing, feeding on my fears.
And now they drip, purple acid tears.
As now I drown, in the crimes of those past years.
Sleek, it makes its way through my dreams.
It provokes my anger and brings on the steam.
So now I'm hungry, and I must feast...
I heard the calling, "*now this man is a beast...*"

Am I Alone?

It starts so cold, he's all alone. Nobody holds him tight.
The records play, it starts to rain. The tears from his eyes.
A silent whisper, ringing through the age.
A lonely soul, hoping to be saved. Am I alone, or is someone there?
Was I alone, or did you care?
Am I alone, or just asleep? *"If that's so*, then please wake me..."

It starts so cold, he sits alone. Nobody at his side.
The records play, and still it rains. Forever through the night.
"Just a second hoping." Of maybe something more.
Still I wonder, what lies beyond that open door.
Am I alone, or are you here? Was I alone, when I drowned in fear?
Am I alone, or is this a dream? *"If that's so, then please just wake me..."*

Funny

Throw the stone, and now we skip. Further into the hallow.
We dance deeper into the sticks. Singing away the hours of our youths.
It takes months of a daze. To make sense of this noose.
So I bite the lead and watch it bleed. I sip the blood and drink the ink.
It takes me closer to the truth. It brings me back to my youth.

Set the stone and now we play. We skip and dance into the haze.
For hours at a time, endlessly blinded rage.
Salt the wounds and watch us cry. Squeeze the handle and don't ask why.
For Knights and nights of shooting stars. Dreams and hopes taking us far.
So never question or look back twice.
As we skip and play, as we throw the dice.
Now truth unfolds and you start to scream.
Over all of the evils, they've pushed onto me.
Yet you question, and you really want to know why.
"Now that's just funny..."

Abort!

I can't seem to focus right, there's just no way to set-it in-line.
There must be some sort of reason to this.
My life of pain, feels so cold and sick.
There's just no place I can go, to be in peace and call it my own.
There's just no place I can hide.
To escape my troubles and end this strive.
It's time to end this, and draw the credits near.
It's time to pull down the curtain, and filter my fears.
I'm about done now and still so stressed.
I should just give up now... "I did my best."
I can't seem to stop it, nor could I ever be in peace.
Just stop and shut it, to calm-down the beast.
So soon as it seems to fade.
We need to stop this, and just watch it break.
There's just no place I can go now, there is no place I can call my own.
All these scars remain here, frozen and alone.
"There's just no way to abort this!"
I only wish to hide, deep under the stone.

Loveless Face

Go ahead and laugh. It's all the same...
Go ahead and laugh. I know I'm not sane...
There is no point, nor a logic to be made.
There is no warmth, "still freezing rain."
Judge me if you must, but it's alright.
Kill me already! Let's end this night..!
There was once yet can never be again.
An angel to hold, and wipe clean my sins.
There is now and always shall be.
A demon in the mirror. "A monster behind me."
So shuffle my hands and shake my soul. *Just take me deeper into the cold.*
As now you see, "*never a love for me.*" Only this hollow hole.
So go ahead and laugh. Just break my heart and throw me back.
Just go ahead and laugh. Take my thoughts and watch them crack.
There is no meaning to these rants I make. *Still I proceed onward in rage.*
So now you see, this loveless face, now you see, this unworthy disgrace.
I'm not a man anymore, just a bastard, beating the door.
I'm not a child anymore, just a ghost now, wanting more...
I've been damned enough now, so just let me go.
This loveless face has nothing to say. So now I just, fade away...

Forever Forgotten

It once took me, for a midnight stroll.
It once held me, when all went cold.
There was an angel, I loved so dear.
But now I can only remember, those past years.
It was upon that notion, that I took a walk.
It was upon that heartache, when I fell out of luck.
Now on this side-trail, towards what I feared.
I can only wipe away, each of my frozen tears.
Now dropped deeper into my respectful domain.
Beyond the realm of shadows, and into pain.
I march again, into the hoping of something more.
Only to find, that blood soaked door.
"Forever & Always."
That was the dream in which I held for you.
Yet through it all, it still rings true.
As is the nightmare, that I lost all my loves.
Yet again I'm awake, and still they're gone.
Dead and un-remembered, the judgment of my soul.
For some odd reason, I feel very cold.
Awake and wide aware, of the morning haze.
The path leading me, into that daze.
It took me once, for a bright-night stroll.
It took me once, out of the cold.
There was a place, I kept for you and me.
But it's forever forgotten, *"as are we..."*

At the Shore

Warm as it brushes against my feet. It tastes so cool, it seems so neat.
How endlessly I could gaze up at the stars.
It's soothing, now that it has come this far.
As it washes against my face and hair. I feel so at peace, I find no care.
There seems to be, no motive, nor drive.
I somehow feel calm, and somewhat alive.
As it begins to bury, cooling down my dreams.
I feel so tranquil, somehow at peace.
There's not much, for me to look back to.
Somehow, it all just faded away...
There's not much left of me now.
But forever I'll stay... *"Awake and at the shore."*
Calm as the water runs through my hair.
Though I repetitively try to look back, *"I truly don't care..."*

269

Rage #7

For a moment it clatters.
But now it splatters, and spreads across the floor.
It seeps within, and beyond that whore.
Forever more, on the notion now dead.
So I rip out my eardrum, now numb and un-said.

Biting deeper into my memories of that day.
Now I can only dream, but still it stays.
And on that moment, I begin to slit my eyes.
To spill out the sights, of those years in the dirt.
Far beyond any reason, and deep under our earth.

Dust filling my lungs, and smoke rolling behind my eyes.
I can only beat my skull, until the thoughts subside.
Now your legs are sweeter, and so very fine.
For what other reason would I need, than this?
Standing in a pool of blood, waste deep in their shit.

So nothing could nor should ever stop this raving beast.
I have no more of a drive, other than to feast.
Shallow yet over my head, it rings forever and always un-said.
Upon all my tears and lonely drops of blood.
I have now only to wait here. Six feet under this mud.

See the Untrue.

There's nothing left to change it, there's no way I could wake it.
It seems she always faked it, Oh God, how I hate this...
Blind was only a word when we met.
Sight was only a nerve when you left.
Answers were, the only drive I could find.
Still she lays raped and broken. "Justice forever blind."

Hating each moment to the next, forsaken and never to find rest.
A pointless mind, seeking the truth *but it skips away deeper into my youth.*
There's nothing left to change it, I was broken, but still you raped it.
I see now, she always faked it, Oh God, how I hate this...

Gray

Clouded judgment, pulsating behind the walls.
The corpse is shaking, far at the end of the hall.
Mother wakes me, but I can't seem to breathe.
The shadow is waiting, far inside of me.
Levitating, rising above the fog.
Mindless chanting, bringing back the frost.
A hungry monster, licking at my soul.
I stand pale and wasted, growing so cold.
I drank the embers, to taste the new.
I ate the ashes, to bring me closer to you.
There's no more reason, only a gray abyss.
I have no heart, just an open stitch.
So wave it further, beyond the notes.
Kiss me soft, but then you choke.
Mother wakes me, but I could never rise again.
I have no soul left, just a gray abyss.

One At a Time...

Unknown, yet at the very same time.
In circles of salt, dust and grime. I left only to see if I could.
I loved you once, "*I knew I never should.*"
Of all the things I held so dear to my heart.
Only for them to decay and tear me apart.
So unknown, and buried under the lime.
I held you close, but now only slime.
I took it all, just one at a time.
I loved them all, but now it subsides.
I took it all, just one at a time.
It seeped in deep, such a filthy rhyme.
Over and under all my fears, locked away like all my tears.
I have now only a few things to say.
"I loved them all, but they just walked away."
Unknown, yet at the very same time.
In loops of filters and un-shown times.
I took it all, just one at a time.
Endless needles of fire, breaking through my eyes.
Unknown, and forever misunderstood.
Of all the ink hidden beneath the soot.
It took me onward, so very far over the edge.
I took it all, one at a time "*now I'm all that's left.*"

Tune My Heart

It seems I'm always left in the back. *I've tried to reach yet forever at a lack.*
My mind knows how it goes yet my heart, can only break apart.
It seems as if I'm always second best. *I've tried so hard, now I wish to rest.*
There never truly was, an angel on my side.
I know that now but still we died.
Can no one ever, pull all the pieces together?
Could anyone just take my life and set it straight?
Is there no one alive... To see through my eyes.
And know of all my pains and mistakes..?
Just grip my soul and tune my heart.
Take my pages and tear them apart.
Because nothing truly matters, "it all just scatters."
All my hopes and dreams just melt away.
Tune my heart and take me there. Kiss my lips and tell me you care.
As no one is here and alone I bleed. *Tune my heart, so I can be set free...*

In My Throat

Full pace with my breaking soul. Down in the gutter, alone in this hole.
Mindless as the seconds flutter by, like a headless child, asking why..?
Smooth as the monsters dance down my spine.
Charming as they look at me, "and you rot alive."
In deep of a depressing nature of only rage.
Have I anything more than that to say..?
So in pace with my throbbing heart, please just laugh as they tear it apart.
Now upon the dooms of all my hopeless wants.
I have only to vomit the ashes from my lungs.
So forever I shall take the word of the damned.
Mirror-less friends of a time now shook.
It once truly mattered, but now a moldy book.
For only to replace the notions you took.
So fully overwhelmed with all that you once said.
The lies just poured and poured off your jagged breath.
So homely of a thought, "you on top of him."
How stupid of a thought, of believing you again.
So ready and unwilling for another day.
Just slap my cheek and rip off my face.
Roll the demons down, in my throat.
Fill me with your lies, just laugh as I choke.

The Winter Comes

Every night is just further from the day.
Every day, just takes it further away.
It slides across, and hurries out.
We hold each other close, "alone and without."
So take me further, bring me closer to the edge.
Take me onward, so I can stand on that ledge.
As I read the snowflakes, before they melt.
As now I can only wait, "alone and overwhelmed."
A changing wind, the feel of a turning age.
A broken whim, still covered in shame.
It's coming closer, with every breath.
It's almost over, "just give it a sec."
The winter comes, bringing on my tomb.
The shadows draw, forever they loom.
An hour waiting, just freezing alone and gone.
The winter comes "it won't be long."
Every night is just further from the day.
Every day, just takes it further away.
It falls within, yet never out.
We hold each other close, "alone and without."

A Darker Scream

Shaking head-twists, of a lonely dream.
Broken fingers, and the child still screams.
Alone in the corner, as he bites back his nails.
Weeping now colder, his soul overwhelmed.
A senseless logic, within my skull. A pointless target, beyond this hole.
Mindless shattered, to the bone. "Come on baby, take me home."
I hoped an outcome, now this endless pit.
I wanted some logic, but you gave only shit!
Enough of this heart-lock, within my grips.
I feel it getting darker, as I rip out this stitch.
Pointless numbers, as the world grows queer.
Mindless babble, ringing through my ears.
Have I a reason, or should I just die?
The screams are growing darker, "*and so am I.*"
A senseless logic, within my sins.
A darker scream, howling through the wind.
A monster stirring, within my soul.
Mindless shattered to the bone... "*Come on baby, take me home.*"

Comfort My Soul

Hold me close, before nothing's left.
Hug me dear, say I was the best.
Just give me a smile, and leave it that way.
Kiss me again, "don't take it away."

Rub the roses over my chest.
Sing the poems, that you loved best.
Was I a hero, or only a fiction-tale?
Comfort my soul, before I go to hell.

So take my riddles, and dance towards the lake.
Sing my songs, and make no mistake.
Because I was a dreamer, whom never found sleep.
I was a love-note, you just wouldn't keep.

Comfort my soul, and take me beyond that day.
Kiss my lips, and leave it that way.
Tell me I was your world then, before I close my eyes.
Comfort my soul, before this poet dies...

Take it! Take it!

Scream a number between one and twelve.
Sing a lyric that rhymes with hell.
Take a moment before they're all gone.
Take it! Take it! End this damn song...

I burned my eyelids, to see the flames.
I drank the poison, to take the blame.
I hate this monster, behind the books.
He gives only nightmares, as he waits and looks.

Lick my top lip, and bite my neck.
Give no reason, just ride me to death.
Take a number that ends in a six.
Take it! Take it! Just end this shit..!

Vomit the right state, over their heads.
Drink of their acids, and take them to bed.
Hold me down south, and grip my soul.
Take it! Take it! *"Just leave me alone..."*

My Burning Eyes

There seems to be, no way to escape.
I tried to jump, but landed in shame.
I drown in tears, of my own despise.
The dust just grows, it's burning my eyes.

It seems funny to me, that you don't remember.
Yet I could never forget, our last November.
Just take my heart back, and melt it away.
I can see nothing now, only shame.

My head is twisting, right out of place.
My heart is shifting, never replaced.
Broken and decayed, rotting like my soul.
My eyes are burning, "ashes and coals."
Embers flowing, through my blood and mind.
My soul is tired, we wish only to die.
So give me release, and take me away.
Through it all, "I have nothing to say."

Un-Shattered Grip

Count the numbers, as they fall.
I don't really think, you cared at all...
God is waiting, for the clock to strike.
Up at my attention, and down goes the light.
Breaking at my intentions, just before you laughed.
Groping in my wisdom, drowning in the back.
Frozen in the middle, standing firm and grim.
Forever immobile, forever an un-shattered grip.

Not-said side-sought, breaking beneath the light.
Have I any remorse, have I any tears to cry?
Just take my hand now, guide me through the mist.
I can't seem to forfeit, not beyond this un-shattered grip.
So count the bullets as they roll over my tongue.
You won't be happy, not until it's done.
So just hum the last words, and God won't care.
"I won't let go of this un-shattered grip."
That brings on *your* despair.

As I Fall

Dirty faces, as they pass me by.
As I fall into the pit, un-knowing of why...
So many masks, held over the truth.
I pass them by, as I forget about you...
As I fall, there is nothing left but shame.
As I weep, still in the freezing rain.
Alone with the knife-point, into my neck and heart.
As I fall, their faces just tear me apart.
Filthy dreams, of a Demon with Angel-Wings.
Again in this rut, as my whole world bleeds.
As I fall, there is nothing to say, as I fall, it all just flows away.
Un-remembered thoughts, of a time I cared.
It was a holiday, that brought only despair.
As I gave my thanks, of a soul once mine.
For as now I fall, I don't know why...

This Hollow Drink

I lean my head back, on the thought of that fable.
I watch as my eyes - melt onto the table.
Over the spice, and into my glass.
As I watch it steam over, "I can only laugh."
Twist me some lime, and get out of my face.
Write me a love-note, and show me some grace.
As-has been told once, over the stones.
I seep it deep, straight to the bones.
Simmering snowflakes, clinching to the ax.
Listen real close, "can you hear it laugh..?"
So take my hand now, pour me a hollow drink.
I can't make it on my own, I feel "so – so weak."
The spine-melt seems, so sweet sometimes.
Crack my teeth, and rub them with lime.
Salt and soot, stinging me to the core.
Pour me a drink... then lock the door..!
I lean my head back, on the thought of your lies.
It seems so clear now, "I wonder why..?"
Has there been a conclusion, or just another small step?
Have I anything to say, with my last breath..?
Twist me the lime, and rub it in with the dirt.
Come to think of it - that might hurt...
Just a bit, in the endless abyss called my heart.
"I damn this hollow drink, that tears me apart..."

GoodNight – GoodBye

A light mist, but still I reach out my hand.
I try to grip, and hold you close again.
Maybe to end a notion, or answer a question of mine.
I reach out towards you my-love, before we're out of time.

A motive taking me, onward into the dark.
Pass all of the light-posts, and into the park.
It seemed so familiar, when you called my name.
But now I can only weep, alone and in shame.

There's nothing more - to say than goodnight.
There's nothing left to do, just kiss you goodbye.
There's nothing left to say, so I'll turn out the lights.
There's nothing more to say, so "Good night – Goodbye."

A step into the memory, where once I loved you dear.
Now I can only struggle, and fight away the tears.
When darkness brings me heartache, I can only sit back.
I'll never find love again, nor will I look back.

So I sway in the wonder, of the bright-night, dark-day.
I'm just trying to push it over, and end another page.
So kiss me with your smiles, and wave your hand, side to side.
The mist is growing colder, so "Goodnight – Goodbye..."

My love, it's drawing closer. Each breath is towards the last.
Hurry and turn it over, try to hide it your best.
So on I reach, in this haze of a youth forever torn.
As I tried to reach... you just smiled and turned.

There's nothing more for me - to say than goodnight.
There's nothing left to do, just kiss you goodbye.
There's nothing left to say, so I'll turn out the lights.
There's nothing more my-love, so "Goodnight – Goodbye."

End Me..!

Somebody, take my hand and break my nails!
Somebody, draw the line and bring on hell!
Somebody, take my eyes – out of my head!
Somebody, end me now – off with my head..!

Somewhere, I left the answers behind the book.
Somewhere, over the edge and beyond the brook.
Somewhere, you'll find my soul and where it hides.
Somewhere, they took it away and burnt my eyes.

End me now! Take my life and drain it out...
End me now! Kill my heart, just rip it out...
End me now! How many more times must I say...?
End me now! Throw me back, into my grave...

I learned my lesson, but had no questions.
I took the blade, and scraped out my eyes.
I know this face, was never mine.
Please just end me! Take away this lie.

Somebody, that was the dream of maybe so.
Somewhere, six-feet deep, under the snow.
Someone, please take that blade and ram it inside.
End me now! Then turn off the lights.

Chapter *13*

Beneath a Frozen Lake.

Leave a Message...

"Please leave a message after the tone..."

There was once a time, when her love was all I craved.
There was once a time, when I stood firm and brave.
There was once a time, when I reached out my hand.
"Yet I was never saved."

So take this as a last request. Think it through and do your best.
Nail tight the rim and salt the worms around.
I've fought enough over your lies.
"And still my heart's un-found."

I may not have the time, but still I'll try.
That seems to be more than you could say "right..?"
So just leave your mask there and don't try to play me.
There was once a time I loved you but now it's fading.

I don't really think it will matter soon.
Or maybe you'll someday open your eyes.
Hopefully I'll get the chance, before this is through.
To finally say goodbye.

So listen close to these things I say.
Someday you'll get them right.
The truth in the end about you and me.
Is that I ....
....
....
....

"Message erased..."

Shifted-Faded

There's no scream now, that I haven't seeped.
There is no blood now, that I didn't drink.
There is no hope now, you had better run.
There's no escape now, locked – ready – done...
It crawls across, the tile caked in rust and ash.
It shuffles quick, along the wall and towards the back.
It's darker now, more than I had ever dreamed.
There's no point now, so why should you scream..?
Six feet tall, as it climbs up the wall.
Red and black, a demon with no face.
Long hair mauled, broken and its body limp.
It slides against the top, above as it whispers.
A needle into my ear... deafly sleek as it enters.
Blood oozing from its throat, an open hole, yet it never chokes.
No words to describe it, nor a thought to bear.
There's no point to be made, it just shuffles with no care.
There must be a motive, or am I going to hell?
It asks not of me, a one single thing.
It just lingers, limp with its shifted face.
What am I to say, in awe of the demon before my eyes?
What am I to say, as it slowly eats at my lies?
Please God, take it away! I'm not ready just yet to go.
I have a little more to say, before it takes me down into the dirt.
Right before it shifts and fades. I would like to get my say.
So hurry and wake me! Before I'm taken away.

Old Friend

Hello old friend, how have you been?
"Please try to get some sleep tonight."
I know you've felt it, and took the blame.
"Please just try to rest, alright..."
Grasped firm in the eyes, of the nothing you didn't know.
Laid warm and calm, far under the snow.
As the children skip towards the end.
The sidewalk red - leaves of a gentle wind.
So, can nothing change the facts I've made?
As you sway in your chair, watching the stars.
"Please just let it go this time..."
Hello old friend, how have you been?
I can see that you're just barely alive.
So take it real slow and just let it go...
" We cannot bring her back this time."

Sideways Intake

It seemed to be, right in tune with my scream.
It seemed to be, that I would never be free.
I tried to climb, but again I fell.
I tried to love, but so overwhelmed.

In the darkness, I try to reach.
In the shadows, I can hear the beast.
Though I love this wonder, I have nothing else.
All though I loved her, I'm still in hell.

Clouding my judgment, I have no way to breathe.
Clouding my logic, there's no reason in me.
I've fought the monster, but still I died.
I fought those nightmares, yet still I cry.

As I wipe the tears off of my face.
"Oh the mourning touch, that was never replaced."
I can't seem to reach it, I'm blind to all you see.
I've tried to grasp it, but still too weak.

In darkness growing, flowing over my wrist.
I inhale the lingering spirits, that peel away my stitch.
An open heart, melting in the sun.
A broken thought, but now I'm just one.

I lay shattered and weeping.
My tears spread across the floor.
I reach out and push in, the needles from off the floor.
Because there is no more reason.
Only this nail through my mind.
I lay sideways as I intake, the demons into my eyes.

As I Rummage

Groping inside my skull, I can feel it digging a hole.
Will ever I find a motive for you? As I search, I can't break through.
I reach inside, but find only lies. A coating called earth and fate.
There is nothing now, that will replace.
I can't get out, there is no escape.
Hammer my tongue to the ground, and I twitch.
Grope me in my lungs, now I feel so sick...
But there's nothing I can utter, other than my strives.
I won't live this torment, nor will I survive.
As I rummage, there is nothing left to save.
As I wander, out of the hallow and into her dreams.
As I scream, there is nothing left but pride.
It gropes me in my heart, slowly eating me alive.
I reach out hoping, maybe I'll get a hand.
I reach out knowing, never again - never again.
My skull is bursting, the center of my brain is coal.
I can't escape this torment, so fill this gaping hole.
As I rummage, through all the memories of your lies.
I can only shutter, never knowing why.
So hammer my tongue into the dirt, then watch me weep.
As I rummage through the ashes, I can't even find me...

My Taken Dream

It seems to be, that love was just never enough.
It seems to be, that "I" was just never enough.
Her thirst was so great, that I could just never quench.
I kissed her with love, yet she never flinched.

She took my dream, and just threw it away.
She took my heart, deep into her grave.
Now an open wound, but there's nothing inside.
Such a sad ending, yet I'm still alive.
She took my dreams, far under the sea.
I have nothing left, "I can't even weep."

It seems to be, that love was just never enough.
It seems to me, that "I" was just never enough.
She took my dreams and heart away.
Now with this open wound, "I lie awake."

Get Me Through

When I was blind, she gave me sight.
When I was dying, she gave me life.
A chance to get through, and find another day.
"A chance to get through, and finally awake."
She took my hand, when I needed help.
With only a smile, she pulled me from hell.
A chance to get through, and live another day.
A chance to get through, and leave behind my shames.
When I was broken, she found that missing piece.
When I needed help, she gave me release.
She got me through, so many strives.
With only a smile, and her angel-like eyes.
It gets me through, knowing that she cared.
It helps me through, knowing that she's there.
With a hand to lend, for those whom need.
"A chance to awaken, and finally be free..."
When I was dead, she brought me back.
When I was frozen, she helped me relax.
You got me through, so many things.
It gets me through. "Now that I can do the same."

Deeper Within

Sick as I dance in this circle, for hours a day.
Dumb as the wonder lingers, upon that stain.
How far could I go, before I hit the ground?
How deep have I gone, "will I ever be found?"
Call my name, in the darkness I wander.
Love me now and hold me forever.
I dance in the shadows, so maybe I'll fall.
I call for that angel, but find only frost.
It sinks in deeper, my tongue into the ground.
I dance here forever, "*hoping I'll be found.*"
So as the moment just passes, I can only hold my breath.
It fades so quickly, it's gone now and I can't rest.
I kiss the granite, hoping God will see.
I hold that moment, and keep it between you and me.
As it sinks in deeper, my soul can only scream.
Sick as I wonder. "*If I'll ever be free?*"
Found deeper within, my tongue and cries.
Shoved deeper within, my heart and eyes.
Dumb as I remember, these scars on my lips.
"How far must I fall, before I hit?"

Last Wish

A timeless dream upon a falling leaf.
Endless as I wait for another drive to seek.
Pointless as I walk into the waking night.
How far have I gone, "away from the light?"

I hoped once, that you would be at my side.
I hoped once, that you would keep me alive.
So now the troubles are fading, and only snow I see.
A small want of a child, a dream upon a falling leaf.

My last wish, was for you to be mine.
My last wish was to keep us alive.
So now it's pointless, or maybe just a dream.
What can I do now? I only wanted you to be happy.

An endless story, of my youth forever dim.
I had a wish once, but now it's fading grim.
My only hope, was for you to hold me close.
"My last wish now, is for you to free this ghost."

Separate My Skin

Separate me from my skin and leave me exposed.
As all the elements blanket me, dust, ash, and mold.
Of all the fears I once held inside.
There is nothing now, that will set them aside.
For I am, what you think me to be.
A demon from hell, an angel with blood-red wings.
Take away my hopes and lies, slit my tongue and pull out my eyes.
For I am not worthy enough, to live in grace.
"*What a load of shit.*" Just throw me back into my grave.
Take away my flesh and dreams.
Drown my children, leave them below the sea.
Pull out my spine and rub it with lime.
Salt my open heart "just laugh as you tear it apart."
Sink the blade into my chest, reach inside and take my breath.
Nothing now, can take away this nightmare.
So separate me from my skin, leave me exposed to the air.
As all the insects eat at my soul. *I feel nothing now, "I'm too damn cold."*
Take my life and piss it away. Leave my body, out in the rain.
For there is nothing now, that I don't know.
So separate me from my skin, and leave me exposed.

As Satan Weeps

I don't really care, but still it gets to me.
As the golden idol falls before my feet.
I can do nothing but laugh, as the angel cries.
You may call me heartless, *just a filthy swine.*
Maybe I was just a little rough.
But in the end, this heart won't rust.
As Satan weeps, and my emotions flush.
I just light the candles, and she begins to blush.
Kiss me sweet-heart before God sees.
Take my hand, come follow me.
As Satan weeps over the death of my soul.
"I just don't care - I'm too damn cold."
Nothing makes sense now, nor ever it did.
Nothing matters now, so come on and sin.
The devil is waiting, for us to just pass him by.
He can do nothing now, I just threw him aside.
There is nothing more, for the monster to eat.
He had his fill, so now we slay the beast.
Light the walkway, towards the back.
"As Satan weeps, I just point and laugh..."

At The Edge of Night

True to the point of the ages thrown and gone.
Standing on the edge of all those broken love-songs.
Have I anything more to state than my rage?
Please answer these questions, before I pass and fade.
So true to the emotion that flows through my veins.
As I wait alone for the hour-hand to strike and let me free.
Across the field and under the hill we hide the bane.
So take me further into the misery of my shattered dreams.
As waiting alone for the rain to just tear me away.
I stand at the edge of night, hoping a better form of release.
So take my last words and drive yourself away.
Watch as the last grain of sand falls and I slowly fade away.
Was ever there a reason to the strives of my life?
Take my hand before the dawn destroys our dreams.
I could wait here forever, so alone the child weeps.
So true, the facts of the vows we've made.
I stand at the edge of night, wondering if I was ever free.
Please just answer my questions, before we fade and leave.

Across the Pavement

My back lain against the dirt and jagged stones.
I stare up at the blood-red moon, as it holds my despair.
I begin to wonder, if she ever cared; "*did I ever care?*"
My hands nailed to the ground, as I sing away my life.
I lay here dreaming, as blood pours from my eyes.
It took me some time, but I think I'm okay.
It took me some time, to get out of the rain.
So frozen and lonely as all my hopes die.
Did she ever care, "*did I even try?*"

My lips broken over the stones of my shattered youth.
Taken and I hide the answers under my tooth.
So they take my faith and run my tongue across the pavement.
They watch as my blood spells out the *spell* of the end.
They run my face across the pavement, and bathe in my sins.
There is nothing I have now that I didn't deserve.
All my pain and grief, leading me away from my beliefs.
As nothing was meant to mean more than what I said.
I would love her still, but now she's dead.
So they run my face across the pavement, and rip out my eyes.
They smash my head between a rock and hard place.
They laugh as my whole world grows disgraced.
They run my body across the pavement "to rip away what I did."
They run my faith across the pavement, and drown in my sins.

2Faced

I can taste it, as the heat rises off her breast.
I can feel the demon stirring, trying to escape my chest.
Can you see the screams, as her dreams are torn away?
Will you ever care, about her pathetic ways?

As nothing means more than my endless push.
Still I shove my way through, trying to get a better view.
Nothing now has a reason, nor did it ever in the start.
I have only to lie down now, and gaze up at the stars.

Oh, her actions that drove me so close to the edge.
I can only smile now, because I got the last laugh in the end.
She made me feel, like I was some kind of great man.
So now as a demon, "I just don't understand;"

So broken and *2faced,* I damn her filthy lies.
So untrue and very fake, she had no reason why.
Fight as much as I ever could, only to lose so misunderstood.
She was my love once, now just a faded thought.
She was so fake and *2faced,* her heart forever locked.

I can taste it, as the heat rises off her breast.
I could see them, the lies forming from off her breath.
Can you give justice, to the lies that she told.
She was just so *2faced,* "and now I'm forever cold."

Dyed-In-The-Wool

Awake-yet-dead, I try to lift my head.
Down-yet-broke, in the angel's tears I choke.
Of-all-now-gray, I wish that I could stay.

As I pull myself through the halls.
I find a rusted box from behind a wall.
Though I want it to open, forever shut it stays.
I beat and beat it, against my skull and brain.

Scratching at the back of my neck, I pull and find a bloody thread.
I place it into the lock, shake it and nothing said.
As never to move, it stays forever incased in wonder.
I put my ear against it, now I hear the thunder.
I'm not going, nor-ever-have-I...
I'm-not-lying, I didn't blink my eyes...
I'm-not-crying, it's just dust anyway...
I've always been like this, and forever-damned I'll stay.

Awake-yet-dead, I'm wandering lost.
"In someone else's head."
Down-yet-broke, on the sour meat I choke.
Of-all-now-gray, I truly wish I could stay...
Scratching at the back of my neck.
I pull and find a bloody thread.
I whisper to the box, and nothing more said.
Forever rusted and damned, much like my soul.
I unravel with the thread, and like the box I stay cold.

At the Dawn

Wrecked and abandoned, as all the days pass me by.
Alone in the back alley, cold with no tears to cry.
"Was there ever, an arm around me?" Can you help get me through the night?
Take me away from this reality and fate.
Bring me to the other side, and show me grace.
Take me further, upon your wings of pure. Please get me out and shut the door.
Alone and broken, with no shelter of my own.
They call it a house, but I wanted a home.
Was there ever, someone out there who cared?
Please just wake me, take me away from here...
At the dawn is where I'll wait, standing on-top the hill - welcoming the day.
At the dawn is where I'll be. Come take my hand, come set me free...
It's at the darkest part, when you'll find the strength.
It's in the deepest pit, where I hide my shame.
It's at the dawn where I wait for my love. When at the dawn she'll take me above.
Hold my hand and guide me through. Take my heart and clean my soul too.
Please get me out, of this dim story called fate.
It is at the dawn, for you I'll wait.

Infuriation

It means nothing, now that the numbers are gone.
It held the handle, it turned the water into blood.
We mean nothing now, but once we were alive.
It means nothing now, so stop wasting my time...
I've had enough, so take that bullet and push it through.
I've had enough, so stop the press and get me out.
I want to stop, and pull the needle out of my brain.
You need to stop getting to me – "quit fuelling my pain."
Give me some sort of better view, and take me there.
Guide me to a better truth, then take away my air.
Because there is nothing now, that means more than this.
There is nothing you can say, so give me my last kiss.
It gets to me, the beating of my soul and brain.
"Why do I laugh as the children scream in pain..?"
It gets to me, as the monsters consume my soul.
It gets in deep, it's making me cold.
You made me feel, like I could be a better man.
Then you took it away. You left me under the sand.
As I drown, I can only remember the smile on your face.
It really does get to me "and that's why I tore it away..."

"Fuck On a Pancake..?"

Slap me silly, and take me to the next stage.
Love me dearly, then shred me up and throw me away.
Call me your hero, then curse my name.
There's no way to win at this, "your sick twisted game."
Though I try to hold it, somehow it burns my tongue.
Then the acid falls in, soon it'll all be gone.
For I am the answer, lying at the bottom of the trash.
I am the reason, forever denied and out-cast...
Suck me clearly, then you never look back.
Fuck me silly, but then I just laugh...
Cut me open, take out what's inside.
Rip them out slowly, then cook both my eyes.
There's no meaning, as on I babble and blurt out this shit.
Rub me gently, calm me down - then suck my dick!
Oh did I offend you "*I truly hope I did...*"
Beat me down, "suck-a-fuck," and bury me under your shit!
There's no winning, to this game you play.
Though I tried, I truly don't give a damn today.
For no reason to your logic, nor a motive to your dismay.
"Well, fuck on a pancake..?!?! I guess were both insane."

Counting Down

Sing it as you slip through the halls pass the point.
Leave it behind the glass and give me no better muse.
I have nothing to say today, so I stand here confused.
There they go, falling down the hill.
The golden-sands reminding me, that I'll never heal.
Can you hear the screaming, as the clock burns alive?
Will there be an ending, to this pointless strive?
I'm counting down, to the last hour till noon.
I'm counting down, thinking about me and you.
If there was ever a reason, I think this was it.
For me to die, and for you to laugh about it.
When will it pass me, and take me through the haze?
Will there ever be a *happily ever after*?
"No, because you just raped it away..."
So sing it as you slip through the cracks in my head.
Leave it behind, our story forever unsaid.
I have nothing to say today, I'm just counting down.
Until the last point is made, until it's all beyond the clouds.

Where is God Now?

Beneath a tall oak, lying down - gazing up.
I rest my head against a stone, as I look up.
I begin wondering if there will ever be.
A better way, to set myself free.

So where will we all go, when the lights burn out?
Where will we all go, when there's no way out?
What will they say, when the bell rings numb?
Where are all the stars, where is our beautiful sun?

Does it really matter, what goes on after the credits roll?
Does anyone care, what lies beneath the coals?
So where is your justice, when the innocent are damned?
Where is your God? "Will he give a damn...?"

What was the point, to this endless war?
What was the reason, screaming behind that door?
How can we just sit here, thinking it's alright?
It's time we stood up. "Now turn out the lights."

Where is God now? Does he truly care?
Lie if you wish, but you're just wasting air.
Where is God now? Did he set aside a place for you and me?
I'm sorry that I'm laughing "but it's not that easy."

Such hypocrites ruling the lives of this nation.
To a faceless idol, they place their dedications.
But in the end, it won't truly matter.
Where is your God now? *"Do you think it really matters?"*

Beneath a tall oak, lying down against a stone.
I gaze up at the stars, but do not feel alone.
You're wasting your lives still.
Over a question that's already been answered.
Where is God now? *"Does it really even matter..?"*

The Maggot Feast

Where once your hero stood, "now this demon sleeps."
Beneath the golden sands, and into your dreams he creeps.
As tossing and turning in the middle of the night.
You scream and cry, *"he doesn't know why."*
Though the morning, brought more than just light.
You may never know, but still it stands firm and right.

I can begin to taste it, over the hill and pass the street.
I can begin to smell it, I lick my lips and grind my teeth.
I am ready and willing, bring forth the maggot feast.
I'm ready now, to set my rage free.

It took me miles, over the years of wondering who I am.
It took me ages to clean off the sand.
Now I can taste it, the sour rotted meat.
As it cooks in the sun, blistering hot on the street.

I tear at its carcass, biting down onto the meat.
I stand in rejoice, of the fresh maggot feast.
Though it took me ages, to understand why...
I care not anymore, as I eat both its eyes.

I hope this does not offend you.
Making you think twice about my drives.
Making you toss and turn, all through the night.
But now it is set right, the fact of my horrific revolt.
Put true to the notions you bring day-to-day.
I am truly grateful, now that I'm awake.

Where once your hero stood, now this demon stands.
Behind all your regrets, beneath the fallen sands.
Though you may never understand, or even care.
I am grateful for this maggot feast – as it fuels your despair.

Gallery of Bodies

As I make my way through the crowd.
Thumbing my way through the clouds.
I can hear a whisper echoing through the space.
I can hear it calling, grim and somewhat out of place.

Making my way through the halls.
Turning the knob, from inside the room I hear their calls.
Rhyming their needle's-points, into my left eye.
I stare up at their glory, stunned and surprised.

They all tell a story, of both anger and grace.
I gaze up with wonder, however did they befall?
Standing firm and noble, I dare not touch a single frame.
The artwork amazing, I can't seem to look away.

So lifelike and seeming to reflect my soul.
I begin to feel a chill, up my spine running cold.
Though I never knew that art could be this dear.
I look up in wonder, and a small bit of fear.

When did they come to be, whom fashioned their essence?
How did they come to be, the artwork reflecting me...
But I can only stare up at the glory of this gallery.
"Stood both grim and true."
At one end stands this artist, within the frame stands you.

I pay my honor to each masterpiece.
As I walk through the gallery of those who passed.
They remind me of who I was, and what lies ahead.
I pay my honor to the artwork, stood in the world's clear view.
As we're incased in this gallery of bodies.
"Preserved both humble and true."

Adrenaline

I can feel it quiver in my legs as I remain calm.
I can feel it run up my spine, driving me to react.
I know now, that it all meant something in the end.
I can feel your words pushing me, onward into sin.
Taking the last step into the damnation of my soul.
Breathing the last breath, it feels somewhat cold.
I can't hold your hand forever, as now you're gone-away.
I can't hold on forever, now you slip into your grave.

Rushing the demons further into the darkness of my heart.
I can feel the angel's song, tearing me apart.
Rage seems to be, my only love today.
But once I held the world true, but now you're in your grave.

Never blame, what you never understood.
Never push me, move on and hope an end.
Don't you understand, "this demon painted as human?"
You will never understand... Just hurry up and run!!!

I can feel the eyes glaring, as I rush further into the dark.
I know you loved me once, yet now torn apart.
It made a difference, to all you see before your eyes.
Your words pushed and pushed, your needles into my spine.

Now the hatred is looming, seeping into my dreams.
I can't wipe your face away, now I can only scream!
You thought you were right from the start.
"But I loved you dear."
Your words pushed me too far, "*now you fall away in fear.*"

Cocktail Plague

Lifting above the lingering clouds of smoke.
Dropped to the bottom of the amber glass...
My lost nerves flinching, taking the emotions away from hell.
Cold-remaining, as all my hopes forget themselves.

God spoke the reason, to our midnight wondering.
Now my soul can do nothing but search for peace.
Nothing to replace the girl that held my heart - alive.
I can dream nothing now, "I wish she'd open her eyes."

Now it's pouring into the bottom of my lungs.
Driving deep the emotions that never meant a thing.
God gave me a hand, but now I'm insane.
As the murder reminds me of only my pride.
This story is getting darker, so I think I'll close my eyes.

Steaming above the lips of my corpse.
The smoke draining from my soul, onto the floor.
Ink just spewing, from both my eyes.
God took my dreams away, but won't let me die.

As drowning myself in the plagues of the forgotten.
Serving the flesh to a world which never gave a damn.
It seems quite pointless, "they'll never understand."
But it meant something, when my heart was alive.
Now the memory haunts me, forever behind my eyes.

God gave me an outlet, but it causes only pain.
The world damned me when I was a child.
Now a man, artistically insane.
So I drown myself in this cocktail plague, of their voices.
As the paint covers only my soul and brain.
The smoke will never subside, only grow with time.
"There is no escape from my sins and mistakes."
The destructions matches nothing, other than my pride.
This story is getting darker, "so I think I'll close my eyes."

This Knight's Blade

True to the forces of all my being.
Left behind for that fact of this knight's last days.
I have spent all my heart on these thoughts.
Still they drive me onward, and through the haze.

Troubled minds, of all that means more to me and you.
What must I say, to take me to the end of all these pains?
Why must I hurt, from behind my spine and under my teeth?
I drag myself further, through the cold and blistering heat.

How many more demons are left to taste my soul?
How many years have I been wandering through the cold?
And why is it that God never seems to let me fade?
I have nothing to protect me. I have only this knight's blade.

So true it was and always shall be.
I'm coming home my love, so you can set me free.
Soon to let go and obtain the goals which I seek.
I have nothing to get me through, nothing to save me.
It was honor and so much that I never knew.
I'm coming home, to rest my soul with to you.

Troubled thoughts that still haunt my lonely mind.
This road it growing longer...
"These thoughts are losing their mind."
How much must I battle, before I can just break away?
How much blood have I lost this year?
How many nightmares have kept me awake?

It is through and under all these motives.
That brings me closer to the edge of myself.
It is above and beyond.
The thought of heaven and the doors of hell.

I can't escape my demons, only battle with them day to day.
There is nothing to protect me, only this knight's blade.
As I hold it's handle, firm and true to my heart.
It gets me through all of the worries.
Taking me closer to what it is I seek.
I'm coming home to you my love.
"Maybe then I could sleep."

Melt the Snow

Calling forth to the faces of your Gods.
I was left there standing frozen in awe.
Broken in the bottom of my faithless wants.
Flat in the un-thinking of our child now-gone.

She grows without me needing to be there.
She smiles through all the anger and despair.
I would take her far away from those fears.
But I can do nothing now. I can do nothing from here...

Break the chains and thaw the ax.
Melt the horror and take those words back.
Send me a hammer to undo these locks.
Melt the snow, "get me out of this box..!"

Midday hoping for another chance of fate.
Dead-dawn in the knowing, that it was my mistake.
I can't make you answer, nor care for my flaws.
I killed and died once for you, "yet you never cared at all..."

Melt the snow, to get me out of the eternal.
Let me go and drain me down the funnel.
I've had too much, of this damnation.
Now my child grows, alone in frustration.

Forgive me for not staying at your side.
Forgive me for not getting to say goodbye.
Someone kill me or get me out.
Call forth your Gods, to break the ice and free me now!

I've spent too long trying to gain what I already had.
Now here I stand alone, forever frozen in sin.
Murder was the only way to save the soul I loved.
Now I'm damned for not thinking ahead.
Someone melt the snow, to free this aching soul.

I am sorry my child for not getting to say I loved you.
I am sorry my love, there was no other way to save you.
Just melt the snow, so I can find the missing pieces.
Thaw the memory, so I can rest and fade with dreams.
Melt the snow and let me go, so I can rest with my child...

Distorted Reaction

Against my face as her hand drives my eyes behind.
Slapping my cheek to state some sort of inform.
Oh how I wish there were a reason to what she said.
Against my cheek, now my eyes – blood-red.
Taking-out the frustrations of the demon's life gone-wrong.
I did nothing to drive us to that point.
Against my lips as her hand drives my emotions behind.
Slapping my face in the hoping of some sort of reaction.

Now the needles fall into my flesh and break on-through.
As the pills roll over my brain and drive into my tomb.
Salt is holding but won't keep me fresh forever.
Did you like the way you took me so far over the edge?
As you hoped a stating, now gone and still waiting for an end.
My eyes are still blind, and I could never get you out.
You could run if you want, but it won't help you now.

Lost to the last state of so little not done.
She wanted a reaction, now blood filling her lungs.
As hacking at the roots of the reason she's wanting a reform.
This demon will never stop till all are dead, *and nothing more.*
But in the end, I was right from the start.
You wanted a reaction, now your body torn apart.

Lifeless hopes of something I never thought was right.
Pointless strive as the reason drifts above and below the end.
My thoughts no-longer have their motives.
My body no-longer has its skin.
Just this distorted reaction, that she so demanded.
Why in God's name did she treat me that way?
Against my lips, she gave that kiss, that drove us into our graves.

South of Hell

So many steps towards what it is I need.
Taking me further with every dream.
How many years has it been?
How many more till I'm free?

Bloodshed was once my only muse.
I loved her to death, now gone-confused.
It takes me further with every moment.
As I lay awake, drinking the smoke.
And break under the torment.

I'm going home now, so will you follow?
I'm taking the last step towards what it is I need.
God told me it would cost me my soul.
I should have listened the first time. "*Don't you think..?*"

Fused to the remainder of all that was once my soul.
God told me to free my mind, and just let it go.
So ignorant to the purpose for all my strive.
"I'm going home now, to find rest tonight."

Further than what most call forever.
Longer than what you would call a life.
Left down-far below.
Where no one else will survive.

Down-broken, to once a man now decayed.
Left-shot and open, so you can laugh all day.
Still I'm a demon, buried-down south of hell.
Forever I'm just a man, moving onward towards what I've held.

So many tears fallen, over the grave into the dirt.
So many words spoken, left alone to burn.
Now I'm stepping on-forth, towards what it is I seek.
Here-now, south of hell.
Now only one more chance is all I need...

When I Return

Take this note and remember who I am.
Take this kiss and hold it forever through the night.
Love me endless and on just a little more.
Remember my name, before we close the door.

When will you just leave it be and love me true?
Please just hold me, before you leave too.
I never took it, or gave more than they asked.
Please just kiss me, and never look back...

When I return, will you remember my face?
When I return, will I still know grace?
When I return, I hope you'll be there.
When I return, from all the lies and despair.

Take this note and keep it always close.
Take my heart, rub it clean and wait for me.
Love me forever-now and always till gray.
Remember these words, and take them to your grave.

When I return, I hope to see your smile.
When I return, I hope you'll know who I am.
I've been gone some time now, and still a little more.
I've taken and done my dues, now awake today.
When I return, "I hope to see your face."

Rage #8

Paste me above and below all the lumps of flesh.
Take your questions and fuck them till you're out of breath.
Love my sickness, and drive it to the bottom of your lungs.
Eat at my man-hood, taste the glory of God's forsaken son.
Now knife-the-point to the last state of so little and still...
Place it between the flesh, as the child screams for help!
Nothing to grasp as you tear the two points apart.
There is no escape from what you're doing.
Still you rape him and laugh all the same...
Slurping the sour chunks of old rotted meat.
Drown it in liquor and sing the devils song till you bleed.
As the hole in my chest beats only pride and fate.
Take my arms and I pull her from the grave;

Now you might want to avert your eyes...
As I fuck the love that never seemed to give a damn.
Funny little demons dancing upon my teeth and brain.
Now I can only smile as all my dreams are raped away.
So shove your hand in and pull out my spine.
Suck it clear and ride it hard, so good till I'm satisfied.
You'll never find the nails from behind my eyes.
Glory of the angel dead and eaten in her place of grace.
She did scream yet the world turned its head.
The mirror can't lie, only give its points forever in a rut.
You lick up my blood and eat at my guts, steaming sweet...
Laugh if you will, but we'll never heal. Only scab and break!
Here on the top of all my wants forever true to the grim.
Fate lost its chance, now I dance with the devils wife.
Fucking her till the day breaks and light subsides...
Oh how you wish that I would just die and leave.
But you'll never stop what was never yours...
I will never give-up, this pain and torture.
Now I pull that last remaining thread.
I unravel each thought that I've said.
Till noon gives me a reason to fuck you no more.
On and till I'm now a mad-man lusting the grave.
I laugh still over the spilled ashes of yesterday.
Vomit the only reason till blood fills this broken glass.
Give me another pill and watch me rip off my own head.
You got in the way too many damn times.
Now this monster is your responsibility, till the day you die.
Give into temptation and rape this child again.
Give me another knife to swallow, and shit it into your eye.
Give me my full rage and purpose.
Demonic dreams, drowning-down death's dirty deeds.
God given glory going-gone till Satan weeps.
Forever frozen frigid and far behind disbelief.
Ram the rusted nail behind my tongue.
Till death is all we fuck each other with.
Dry bleeding, open hole gaping, No soul!
And we forget about our children, left under the sea.
Leave me alone to my tools - give me no reason to let you breathe.
Never to ask for forgiveness, damn you all today!
Till your dead and I had my fill.
Roll me under and take away my bones and flesh.
Rape me till I feel only regret, spite, hatred and so much fear. "I can't say."
Leave me in this pit of acid and rage...
Give me my last rights to eat your soul.
Beneath this frozen lake... Forever cold.

The Thing Inside

Walking through the door, no welcome home...
Walking through the hall, no light or warmth...
I try to say hello, yet no one seems to hear...
I could scream at the top of my lungs, but no one cares...

It's stirring louder, making its way through the cracks.
It's tearing at the walls of my skull, breaking the last bolt.
I can't just stop it this time! You had better run away...
I can't just save you this time, run! Run! Get away!!!

This monster is waking, making its way through my mind.
This demon is hungry, soon you'll be out of time.
There is no more path left, only ash and nothing more.
You had better run now, quick – lock the door.

Walking through the door, no welcome home...
I make my way through the halls, no light or warmth...
I try to speak one word, but no one seems to hear...
I could scream at the top of my lungs, but no one cares...

It's getting restless, starting to tear me apart.
Soon I'll be torn wide open, so you can see, "I had no heart."
It's waiting for the right moment, to make its move.
I can't stop it this time, it's bringing on your doom...
This thing inside, it's getting the best of me.
The thing inside, that I wish I could just let free.

The monster is waking, hungry and ready.
I've held on too long now, I can't save you this time.
Quick! Lock the door, before I'm torn in two.
I loved you dear, so great and true.
But this thing inside, breaking my mind apart...
I can't stop it now, it's too late for me.
I truly did love you, but now I'm fading...

Haunted Midnight

Spoken to the twilight, when dreams can't seem to find me.
Darkness overshadows, covering over my needs.
Grace stood there waiting, her heart aching inside.
As I spoke with the moon, and danced in the starlight.
Lifting above and through my emotions. "All my shattered whims."
An old feeling returning, soft upon the wind.
Cradled in my hollow soul, ringing through the age.
Darkened and somewhat – another form of faith.
Her lips still haunt me, restless I scream...
Those years have passed me, "maybe just a dream."
Hope stood there waiting, her soul aching inside.
As I fused with the moon, and drank of the starlight.
Haunted by *Midnight*, "wishing for day."
Scarred over my broken mind, never to fix.
Cradled in my hollow thoughts... "That one last kiss."
Darkened and overshadowed, remaining behind my tears.
Standing firm with the twilight, of my past years.

"*Unravel...*"

Dark... Red-black walls – blistering-heat rising.
Faded drapes... A purple-ash growing over it all.
There I stand, no hope or faith as I fall.
In this broken room, mold holding together the pieces.
In this grim hole, what once they called a home.
Here I stand, alone and once known as human.
Now only a memory, soon to fade.
Hollow... locked-jaw – blind as I reach for a reason.
Take your compassions and nail tight the rim.
As I stand here in this collapsed hell, waiting for fate.
The heat is still rising, steaming, choking, blinding my view.
I stand here and always alone, eating the sands of my youth.
I begin to scratch my body all over, tearing away my skin.
I scratch at my eyes, the roof of my mouth, and again...
I know there is a reason, as to why I feel this pain.
I notice something new, something not in place...
One little thread, from under my fingernail.
So what am I to do with this new logic-bust?
I begin to pull on it, and my body feels flushed.
I tremble and shiver, my spine colder than ice.
I pull on that thread, and spill all my thoughts un-said;

I pull and pull and my arm begins to unwind.
I pull and pull and my body feels, not so fine.
I'm beginning to unravel, and dust spills from inside.
I begin to unravel, soon gone and only a single thread.
I begin to unravel, each thought that I've once said.
Unspoken to these grim walls of my domain.
Though I unravel, these old pains remain the same.
Faces and thoughts, voices and numbing dreams.
A chill running up my spine, as I come apart at the seams.
So I was just one of God's little play things, *"so he could get his kicks."*
In this darkness, it seems right, as I fall to the ground.
Red-black, grim-notes, faded-loves, still I choke...
Upon and under all that was once my faith.
Faceless in this mirror, which was once a man's grace.
Left there alone and unwelcome, breaking-down into tears.
I pull out that thread, and unraveled those years.
It seems a little strange at times, but I remember once again.
That I was always this knotted and flushed. "It's truly nothing new to me."
Now only a thread remains, bloody on the floor.
Dust, ash, mold, and death un-spoken today.
I've unraveled this shell of a man, now my body gone.
There is nothing left for you to break.
So now I can just laugh, as this whole world slips away....

It Crawls

There it goes... Can you see it pushing through?
There it goes... Eating at my soul and spine.
There it goes... Soon we'll be out of time.
It makes its way through my heart and brain.
It leaves behind only torment and pain.
It pushes and bites at the roof of my skull.
It shoves its way through, making me cold.
It crawls inside, and looks from behind my eyes.
It crawls within, and files my dreams in dirt.
It beats me good. Soon I'll pull a bullet through.
It eats me-up, now that I can't save you...
There it goes... Can you stop it before it wins?
I can't give-up now. I'm too close to the end.
Never will it stop it's feasting, my soul so worn-down.
It crawls inside, it eats my mind.
"Now this bullet shoved through-and-out ..."

The Zombie's Reckoning

Cool in the midnight haze, a mist lingers over our dreams.
As here I lay awake in my own prison called eternity.
Lying respectful in the cradle of not my choice, but yours.
I lay here aware of all which dwells outside my bed.
Still the roots crawl and whisper, in and through my head.

Light, not meaning anything more to me, than to you.
Midnight cries of the owl knowing that this is the end or so...
He calls to the gates of heaven and hell, weeping-out his soul.
He drops to the ground, un-aware of the end to his legend.
Now his children will stay awake.
"Waiting for father to come home."

As now I rise again, pushing my arms through the muddy-dirt and ash.
Stumbling my way out of the case in-which held me so calm.
Now I hunger once-more, bring on the flesh of those I seek.
Bring on the slaughter of all whom stand in my way.
This shall be the end to their lives, and a feast of souls un-saved.
Now I break those chains and stumble my way out of this lot.
It's time now to settle the score, and finish what I began.

And here I am, already at the house of those who damned me.
I stand outside, just biding my time.
The door weak and now I break the knob - they stand in shock..!
Who would have thought?
That their demons would return so soon.
It's time now to end what began so many years ago.
This feast is all I need and deserve.
This Zombie has awaited this moment from death-point on...
Now we shall settle what needs to be done.
An eye for an eye - blood for blood...

Now screaming and fighting, trying to hurt this corpse.
There's nothing they can do now, nothing at all...
And this Zombie smiles, because revenge has come today.
This reckoning soon satisfied, so forever I can sleep.

Then they tear-apart like sheep, so easy to break them down.
Bloody screams, but nothing can save them now.
I remember, "*Maybe*" that I loved them dear.
Now I begin to feast, tearing away those years;

Breaking their hopes and taking their souls.
Yet I seem to notice that there's nothing to obtain.
They weep on the ground, more hollow than me.
And it brings on a smile that I soon won't forget.
That I need not damn what already lives in shit.

Weak as they scream for their mothers to take them away.
To save them from this monster which stands before their eyes.
Broken wastes of flesh, yet one by one they fall away.
Eating the bullets through and out the back of their heads.
Here I stand and laugh as they all fade away.
For today holds true the reckoning of this hollow soul.
But I couldn't kill what was already damned.

They have tried to stop me and end my life.
Yet I am much more than just words and pathetic flesh.
This zombie remains, and they still die in pain.
Fearful as they empty out their own heads.
Spilt across the ground, and it seeps.
Revenge was once my motive, but still it's funny to me.

How many years did I spend loving them all?
Now here I walk dead and forever faded decay.
Rotted skin hanging off the bone, yet still.
Though I may rest my head under this hill.
Forever those who did this will burn in hell...

True to the points of all that meant something back then.
I am now and forever a wondering soul for the weak.
Although they did this, I still got the last laugh in the end.
I think we can call it even now, I reckon that it's just fair.
I lay my head down again today.
"Knowing that I was right all along."
It took the reality of their own mistakes to do them in.

"Now here I go, *until this zombie awakens once again...*"

Wait For It...

Give me a second, just let me take a breath.
Give me a hammer, so I can finally rest.
Please give me a last thought, don't forget me now.
Please remember my name, because I have nothing else...

Take my hand, guide me to the gates...
Take my hand, hold me because I need you now...
Take me again, to that last place we held dear...
Take my dreams, wash them clean of fear...

End my suffer and let me find some rest.
End my torment, don't let it get the best of me.
Just let me go now, so maybe I can awake.
Please answer my questions, before it's too late..!

Wait for it... Then let me fade into your heart.
Wait for it... Right before we're torn apart.
Wait for the last strike of the clock.
As it rings numb in the back of our minds.
Wait for the last grain of sand to fall.
"Then kiss me good-bye."

Thaw My Heart

When that day fell upon you, and you set in-motion these events.
God took a step back, so he could fully grasp this.

Point – reason – trust – honor – faith.
"Did ever these words mean a thing to you?"
Love was all I ever needed, "*just that and you.*"
But in the end, I'm still haunted by your face.
In dreams I just can't forget, nor ever replace.

Please take my aching mind and let it rest.
Thaw my heart and watch it spill.
Ink flowing over the stone and under the hill.

You can't just heal this shattered wound.
Please just hold me tight and let me melt.
Because in the end, I know this true.
I'll have only these notes, and so shall you;

Please take my aching mind and let it rest.
Thaw my heart and away in smoke I fade.
Beyond all the sweet words we spoke.
Under all what once held us in faith...

Far through and around what you think.
Truth – hate – love – pain – suffer – night – grace.
"Did ever these words not affect you?"
Please, someone out there...
Thaw my heart, "don't let me break."

One.

Throw me the line, and give me some hope.
Hold on real tight, snap and I choke.
Left in the bottom of the remains called *Just.*
Left in an endless tug, ever on the pull to what I don't trust.
I feel you lick the back of my ear, jagged and I cough.

Now under six-feet of stone, dirt and ash.
Dust beginning to fill my lungs, as I swing endless through the years.
Hours building upon, now soaking in red-tears.
Alone yet never by myself, hollow I scream!
I can't seem to find a place to call my own.
From this insanity I'll never be free.
Clouded and never to mend what was always grim.
I stand alone as just "one" a hollow man of sin.

So throw me the line and tie it to the post.
Hold on real tight, and sing to me as I choke.
Because I can't seem to escape this.
Nowhere in this world can I go to be free.

I stand alone as just "one." Nothing ever to be...
Set in the rhyme of so little not free.
So give me the longest needle, so I can swallow it down.
Blanketed in the decay, of once I was alive.
Now a soul standing broken yet firm.

I am now just one.
That - *and nothing-more...*

Friends Forever...

Here you are, where I thought you would be.
I've been around and just a little more today.
Faith – fate and remember that you were once a part of me.
But years have gone, smooth with the wind.
It all just fades, upon that road of leaves...

Taken behind and so far where I could never see.
You threw me up onto that cross, and left me to bleed.
Can you remember a day, when I would have died for you?
Can you list a moment, when I wasn't thinking about you?

So here you are, where I thought you would be.
I've spent some time; "years, months and weeks..."
Trying to find a reason as to why you just left me there to die.
I pondered over the thought until blood poured from my eyes.

For there are no more tears I can weep over those souls.
I can't die anymore, I'm just too damn cold.
So that's what I've gained from you, "*and I am thankful...*"
I would have killed if you had asked it of me.
But in the end you just walked away, and me alone...

So here you are, where I knew you would be.
See, we were once a force to reckon with.
But I had to learn how to make my way through on my own.
So I guess I owe you that, and just a bit more.
You taught me so many lessons, but the last one was grim...

So now I live on as a shell of a man, broken and never to fix.
Yet I think I like it this way, because it is real.
I loved you all to death, now gone and under the hill...
Because I was a dreamer, and did what I had to do.
So maybe I could bring you along, "*oh what a dream.*"
But I'm awake now, "life was not as it seemed."

So here I am, waiting for you to answer this question of mine.
I loved you so much... "Why did you leave me to die..?"
So in the end, all my dreams came at a great price.
"*Friends forever... Right..?*"

Revenge

Truly unknown to the steps I'd take.
Unaware of the path I had made.
Far-broken and left outside in the cold.
Winter, now-frozen "it cost me my soul..."
I've spent so many years, trying to figure out who I am.
I spent so many years, trying to gain my revenge.
It cost so much, and took me far.
It cost me my love, *and friends torn apart...*

I had to lose all I ever loved, to gain what was truly mine.
I had to lose all I ever loved. To hold justice true - and clear my mind.

Truly unknown to the steps I'd take.
Further into the twilight, and far beyond the grave.
Because I loved you, that is why I hurt now everyday.
I thought that I could save you *"that was my mistake..."*
But in the end, I am truly grateful, now that this is done.
I am glad that you're here now, right before the sum...
Handed out and taken when you would least expect.
I know now what it means to be a man.
So here I swallow down all the bitterness of yesterday.
So maybe I can pass it through and forgive my rage...

Truly, I am happy, now that you're here.
Because I've awaited this moment, for so many years.
As now I wipe clean my tears, and shove them over.
Soon to rest... this beaten soldier.

So come with me, and open your eyes.
Let's take our last step, into the forever of our dreams.
Quiet upon the clouds of grace, and in revenge held sweet.
Now upon the faces of all whom I loved.
The leaders of the world and so many more.
True-now and always through the gray.
Behind open doors, and beneath the frozen lake...
All my hopes and dreams have come true.
I have gained my revenge, *"even though I lost you..."*

So remember these words, as you turn your head away.
Remember these wars, "you just can't wash the stain away."
Take your last step, into the awesome of our dreams.
Now I can rest, for revenge has set me free...

Extras:

Following the conclusion of Wars of the Mind Vol. 1: (Upon the Road of Leaves) This second chapter in the series has followed the writer further into his darkest and most horrific thoughts and pushed his limits far beyond anything that he had ever dreamed possible. Now years since he had begun his quest into the deepest pits of mankind's fears and dreams. Jonathan W. Haubert had forced himself to the brink of true madness. Based upon the shames, regrets, fears, hatred and angers of a teen into adulthood.

Volume 2: (Beneath a Frozen Lake) follows immediately after Volume 1: (Upon the Road of Leaves) continuing in the storyline of the writer's heartbreaks and frustrations of losing both family and close friends. This journey delves further into the ongoing madness, shames, and fears of Jonathan W. Haubert's poetically demented mind. Again Jonathan W. Haubert takes both himself and his readers further into the carnage and torments required for a sole individual to transpire from depression and to acquire true mental stability and happiness.

So I welcome you to this second chapter in the ongoing Wars of the Mind series, to again journey further than insanity, further than pain, and further than death. This step is only the second in many more to come, a step closer to the outcome that we all wish for in life. So once again I welcome you into a world where we are our own heroes and villains, a world where justice can only be acquired when we are willing to earn it. So I welcome you to the second battle of the Wars of our Minds.

Jonathan W. Haubert Would like to thank:

Once again I would like to thank you the readers for joining me.
For taking this second journey into the Wars of the Mind.
And to everyone that picks up this book and holds it true to their heart.
"I thank you all..."

And Jesus rolled over on the couch.
He looked into my eyes and said...
"Turn up the music."

Coming Soon:

Wars of the Mind
Vol. 3: (*Behind Open Doors*)